AF792169

Series Editors

W. Hansmann
W. Purgathofer
F. Sillion

N. Correia
T. Chambel
G. Davenport (eds.)

Multimedia '99

Proceedings of the Eurographics Workshop
in Milano, Italy,
September 7–8, 1999

Eurographics

SpringerWienNewYork

Dr. Nuno Correia
New University of Lisbon,
Caparica, Portugal

Dr. Teresa Chambel
University of Lisbon,
Lisbon, Portugal

Dr. Glorianna Davenport
MIT Media Laboratory,
Cambridge, MA, USA

This work is subject to copyright.
All rights are reserved, whether the whole or part of the material is concerned, specifically those of translation, reprinting, re-use of illustrations, broadcasting, reproduction by photocopying machines or similar means, and storage in data banks.

© 2000 Springer-Verlag/Wien

Typesetting: Camera-ready by authors

Graphic design: Ecke Bonk

Printed on acid-free and chlorine-free bleached paper

SPIN: 10749648

With 85 Figures

ISSN 0946-2767

ISBN-13:978-3-211-83437-4 e-ISBN-13:978-3-7091-6771-7
DOI:10.1007/978-3-7091-6771-7

Preface

This book presents the results of EG Multimedia'99, the Fifth Eurographics Workshop on Multimedia, held in Milan, Italy, on the 7th and 8th of September, 1999. The workshop title was Media Convergence: Models, Technologies and Applications, and it covered technological areas of media production, processing and delivery. The program consisted of a keynote address, twenty one technical papers, and two demonstrations. Technical papers were organized in the following seven sessions: Content Analysis and Processing, Content Based Retrieval and Security, Distributed Multimedia Systems, Object Models and Multimedia, Authoring Paradigms and Media Integration, Hypermedia and Web, Education and Entertainment. The first demonstration presented a hypermedia system for representing contemporary architecture, integrating several media, and the other one explored the intersection of science and art in a multimedia perfomance, involving music, dance, and images. The keynote address provided provocative insights about the relations between improvisation, creativity and expression with new media.

All submissions were reviewed by the Program Committee and their recomendations used for selection. The Program Committee members were the following:

Betty Collis, Univ. of Twente, The Netherlands
Bodo Urban, FhG-IGD, Germany
David De Roure, Univ. of Southampton, UK
David Duce, Rutherford Appleton Lab, UK
Edward Fox, Virginia Tech, USA
Farshid Arman, Informix Software, USA
Gunnar Liestøl, University of Oslo, Norway
Hong Jiang Zhang, Microsoft, USA
Joaquim Jorge, IST/INESC, Portugal
John F. Buford, GTE Labs, USA
Jônatas Manzolli, UNICAMP, Brazil
Lynda Hardman, CWI, The Netherlands
Marc Davis, amova.com, USA
M. Rui Gomes, IST/INESC, Portugal
Michael Bove, MIT Media Lab, USA
Nuno Guimarães, FC/UL, Portugal
Peter Scott, Open University, UK
Philipp Hoschka, W3C, France
Pietro Marchisio, CSELT, Italy
Rainer Lienhart, Intel Corp., USA
Ryohei Nakatsu, ATR, Japan
Scott Watson, Disney, USA
Wolfgang Herzner,
Research Centre Seibersdorf, Austria

We would like to thank all the authors and speakers for their contributions and the Program Committee Members for their support and cooperation. Thanks go also to Prof. Giorgio Valle, Prof. Daniele Marini, Alessia Spada, and the student volunteers, Luana Cifola and Filippo Lottici, for their help with the local organization. For financial support, we thank FCT (Fundação para a Ciência e Tecnologia), Portugal.

Nuno Correia, New University of Lisbon, Portugal
Teresa Chambel, University of Lisbon, Portugal
Workshop Chairs

Glorianna Davenport, MIT Media Lab, USA
Program Chair

September 1999

Table of Contents

Keynote Address

Distributed Multimedia Systems

Object Models and Multimedia

Authoring Paradigms and Media Integration

Hypermedia and Web

Education and Entertainment

Demos

Shaping Creative Research in New Media (Keynote Address)

Glorianna Davenport
MIT Media Lab
gid@media.mit.edu

Abstract

Improvisation - the drive to make something out of something else - is fundamental to the human experience. All traditional objects of expression - writing, filmmaking, musical expression, theater, and even human conversation - present some trace of the process through which it came into exist. The very vitality of the expression is intimately connected with its passage; inspiration touched by structure, transformed and realized in a palpable entity. This trace reveals the human bricolleur who struggles or plays, attempts control until resigned, accepts the fragile state and relinquishes the entity out to the world. This talk presents research case studies to explore improvisation and bricollage as forces which can help grow context while driving researchers to unexpected but powerful new explorations.

Replay Detection in Sports Video Sequences

Lifang Gu, Don Bone, and Graham Reynolds

CSIRO Mathematical and Information Sciences
GPO Box 664, Canberra, ACT 2601, Australia
Email: {Lifang.Gu, Don.Bone, Graham.Reynolds}@cmis.csiro.au

Abstract. In many sports, the majority of highlights are confined to relatively short durations of intense action. In some sense these segments capture the essence of a game and summarize the moments of important action. Automatic detection of these highlights could provide an important browsing mechanism in a video library of sports games. In this paper, we present efficient algorithms, operating in the MPEG domain, for detecting two kinds of replay from sports video sequences. These replays often correspond to highlights in a game and can be used as indices of a sports video. The first algorithm detects exact replays while the second algorithm detects slow motion replays. Both algorithms operate directly on MPEG-1/MPEG-2 video data and thus they are very efficient because the expensive decoding operation is unnecessary. Experimental results on several video sequences show that the proposed algorithms are effective in detecting replays in most sports video sequences.

1 Introduction

In a sports video library, one may find thousands of hours of recordings, representing many hundreds of individual games. Fortunately, in any given game, not every minute commands the same interest. A majority of the excitement is contained in a small fraction of the coverage of the game. These highlights are the essence of the game and present a succinct summary of the significant actions and events. For many viewers of sports video these highlights are all they are really interested in seeing. Detection of these highlights is therefore of interest in itself, but might also serve as an important indexing mechanism for searching for more substantial sections of material from large archives.

To detect sports highlights in a video it is essential to analyse the video content. It is also vital that the detection be automated as much as possible so that the tedious intensive manual viewing process can be avoided. The increasing emphasis on automatic content analysis of sports video is reflected by recent research papers on the subject. The parsing of soccer games to determine the field positions has been reported by Gong et al [2] and the visual tracking of American football under certain assumptions has been explored by Intille and Bobick [4]. Extraction and presentation of soccer highlights have been presented by Yow et al [8], while Taki et al [7] have developed a motion analysis system for quantitatively evaluating teamwork in soccer games.

In this paper, we present techniques for detecting replays in sports video, which are often the highlights of a game. Section 2 briefly reviews the extraction of the block DC component image sequence from an MPEG-1/MPEG-2 stream and some characteristics of typical replays. The technique for detecting exact replays is then presented in Section 3. Section 4 discusses the detection of a special slow motion replay. Experimental results are then given in Section 5. The conclusions are finally presented in Section 6.

2 Background

2.1 MPEG Standard and Extraction of the DC Image Sequence

Since most videos are stored in compressed format, due to limited storage space and transmission bandwidth, it is advantageous to perform processing directly in the compressed domain to obviate the need for computationally expensive decompression.

We deal here with MPEG-1/MPEG-2 compressed video. MPEG-1 and MPEG-2 are two international standards for video and audio compression [5]. Both use a suite of techniques to reduce both spatial and temporal redundancies in a video. Since the 8×8 block is a basic unit in an MPEG stream, it is also the smallest unit on which our algorithms work. Specifically, the DC value of each 8×8 luminance block is used to represent the block and a DC image is thus formed from all the luminance blocks in a frame to represent the frame.

For an I-frame, the DC values of luminance blocks are directly available from the MPEG-1/MPEG-2 compressed data. For P- and B-frames, not every macroblock is intra-coded and therefore DC values of some of the blocks are not directly available. Fortunately, we can approximately reconstruct the DC value of each luminance block in these frames by using the method suggested by Meng et al [6]. Finally for each MPEG-1/MPEG-2 video sequence, a corresponding DC image sequence with a reduced spatial resolution can be reconstructed with minimal decoding.

2.2 Characteristics of Replays

In most sports videos, exciting events are often replayed. These exciting shots normally correspond to highlights in a game, e.g., actions near the goal posts in a soccer game or moments when the batsman hits a 'six' in a cricket game. There are several types of replay which include:

- replay from the same camera ('exact' replay)
- replay from another camera
- slow motion replay from the same camera
- slow motion replay from another camera

Exact replay is achieved by simply replaying the shots previously recorded by the same camera. Note however that, when a video is digitised and encoded into the MPEG-1/MPEG-2 format, an exact replay will not be exactly the same as the original shots in terms of actual signal as the replay might be encoded in a different frame pattern. Replay from another camera presents the same scene captured by a camera from a different angle.

Slow motion replay from the same camera can be achieved by repeating or by interpolating frames in the original sequence at a frame rate and playing the modified sequence at the normal frame rate. The number of repeated or interpolated frames depends on the desired speed of slow motion. A slow motion replay sequence can also be obtained by playing a sequence captured by an expensive high speed camera at the normal frame rate. Slow motion replay from another camera is similarly generated except that the sequence is captured by a camera from a different angle.

To detect replay from a different camera angle, it is necessary to recognize the same scene from two image sequences captured by cameras with different camera angles. This normally involves some high level understanding of the scene and is difficult to achieve using current techniques available from the field of computer vision. In this paper, we are interested in the somewhat easier problems of detecting exact replay and one special form of slow motion replay.

3 Exact Replay Detection in MPEG Video Sequences

Before performing the detection of exact replay, a video sequence is first segmented into shots by using one of the algorithms suggested in [1,3]. Most of these algorithms detect shot boundaries by thresholding some frame difference measure. A shot is a sequence of images taken by a camera with continuous motion. The problem of detecting exact replay thus becomes one of finding two shots which contain spatially and temporally matching segments.

Suppose that there are S shots in a video. The total number of shot pairs needed to be compared will be $\Sigma_{i=1}^{S}(S-i) = S \times (S-1)/2$. If the two shots to be compared are L_1 and L_2 frames long, the total number of frame pairs to be compared is $L_1 \times L_2$. If F features are used to represent each frame, the number of operations will be roughly $F \times L_1 \times L_2 \times S \times (S-1)/2$. This number rapidly becomes too large even for short video sequences.

In order to reduce the number of operations, a two stage approach is taken. If two shots are very different, i.e. they do not contain any similar frames, their feature vectors will not intersect in the feature space and there is no need at all to perform detailed frame comparison within them. We use the mean and standard deviation of the grey level values in each frame as its features, and calculate them for each frame in the shot and then their ranges for each shot. If the mean and standard deviation ranges of the two shots, which are two rectangles in the feature space, do not intersect, they will not be compared further. Only when the range rectangles of the two shots intersect will they be compared at the second stage in more detail. This will reduce the number of shots to be compared significantly. This is illustrated in Figure 1. Instead of comparing all possible feature point pairs, only the feature bounding boxes of each shot are checked and compared. This process can be seen as fast pre-screening for similar shots, which need to be compared further. This principle can be applied to general pattern matching problem to speed up the matching process as long as suitable features are selected.

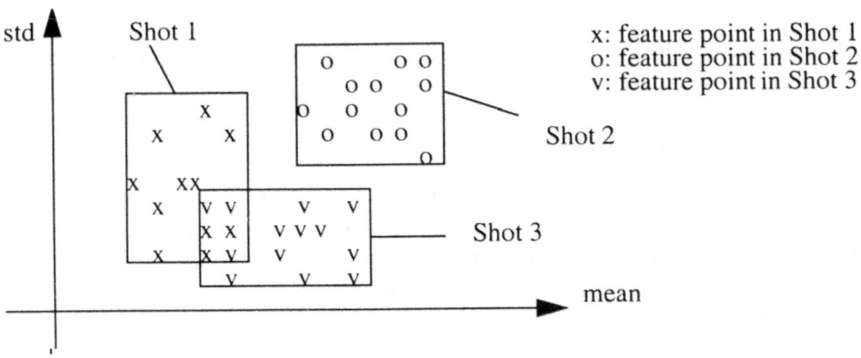

Figure 1. Illustration of the process used for quickly finding shots which potentially contain common content

The ideal feature vector for each frame should have a minimal number of elements and yet should capture the character of the spatial distribution of an image to some extent. We choose a six element feature vector $\vec{f} = [\bar{g}, \sigma, g_1, g_2, g_3, g_4]^t$ to represent each frame. The first two elements are the mean and standard deviation of the frame grey level values respectively. As mentioned above, they are used at the first stage for finding similar shots. The third to sixth elements are the mean grey level values of the four quadrants of the frame and are used for comparing two shots at the second stage. This feature vector is calculated from each DC image and can in fact be computed off-line for each video sequence to increase efficiency. In the following, we discuss how to compare two similar shots efficiently at the second stage.

Since most shot boundary detection algorithms cannot detect gradual transitions, which connect two shots smoothly by fading one shot out and fading another shot in gradually and are often used for inserting replays, the problem of detecting exact replay becomes one of finding two exact segments from two similar shots detected from the first stage. We believe that the temporal pattern is more important than the spatial pattern of the individual frame in detecting exact replay. Even if two frames in the two shots match, no exact replay can be detected if the temporal patterns following these two frames do not match. Since the length of a replay is unknown beforehand and can vary within a large range depending on particular scenes, we first find two matching segments with a given length, which has to be decided carefully. If this length is too short, too many matching segments might be detected. If it is too long, some short replays may be missed. Based on the assumption that a replay shorter than three seconds will be too short for most viewers to watch comfortably, a length of 25 frames, which is one second, is chosen. This means that there will be at least two to three consecutive matching segments for a proper replay. Therefore, the first shot is divided into segments of 25 frames and a match for each of these segments will then be searched in the second shot. The search is performed with a shift of one frame. As a result, the total number of segment comparisons will be roughly $(L_1/25) \times L_2$.

When two 25 frame segments are compared, the sum of their frame feature vector distances is used as their difference measure and calculated as following:

$$S_{diff} = \sum_{s=1}^{25} \left|\vec{f}_{1s} - \vec{f}_{2s}\right| \qquad (1)$$

Each element of a feature vector is normalised according to the following equation before the above distance calculation:

$$g_{in} = (g_i - \bar{g})/\sigma \qquad i = 1, 2, 3, 4 \qquad (2)$$

where $\bar{g}$ and σ are the mean grey-level value of the frame and its standard deviation respectively. g_i and g_{in} are the vector element values before and after normalisation. This normalisation reduces the effect of variation of illumination conditions between frames. For each segment in shot 1, the difference values between this segment and all the segments in shot 2 can be plotted out as a curve along the frames in shot 2. Potential matches in shot 2 for each segment will lead to local minima on this curve, which must be smaller than a threshold. Using the constraint that a reasonable replay will have at least two to three consecutive matching segments, local minima found on these curves are used to find a global match if they meet specific conditions. More specifically, for a local minimum at location f_i on the curve of ith segment, a replay is declared only if local minima are also found at the corresponding locations f_{i+25}, f_{i+50}, ... on the curves of $(i+1)th$, $(i+2)th$, ... segments. Suspicious short matching segments are eliminated by this constraint. This process is illustrated in Figure 2.

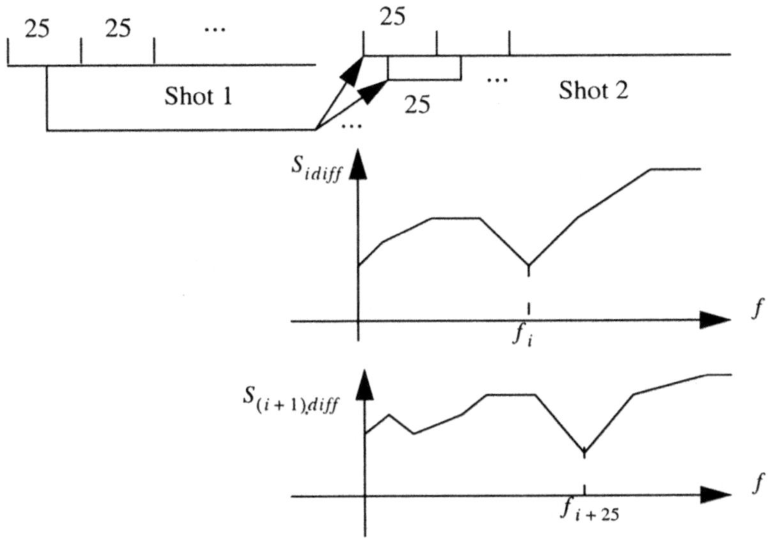

Figure 2. Illustration on details for finding exact replay from two shots

4 Detection of Slow Motion Replay

As described in Section 2, exciting events can also be shown as slow motion replays. Here we are interested in detecting a special slow motion replay, i.e. slow motion replay generated by inserting repeated frames into the original sequence. The number of inserted frames (or repeated frames) depends on the desired speed of the slow motion replay and can vary within a replay. This kind of slow motion replay generation requires no expensive high speed camera or equipment. Based on the characteristics of this frame repetition and the fact that the original highlight shots usually have a relatively large frame difference between two consecutive frames, the following algorithm is developed to detect this kind of slow motion replay.

As before, a video sequence is first segmented into shots. Within each shot, the difference between two consecutive frames is represented by the number of blocks, N_c, which change substantially in their luminance values from frame 1 to frame 2:

$$N_c = \sum_{i=0}^{N} B_i \tag{3}$$

where N is the total block number of the frame and B_i is calculated as following:

$$B_i = \begin{cases} 1, & if \ |g_{2i} - g_{1i}| > T \\ 0, & if \ |g_{2i} - g_{1i}| \le T \end{cases} \tag{4}$$

where g_{2i} and g_{1i} are the DC values of block i in frame 2 and frame 1 respectively and T is a threshold value, which is used to eliminate changes caused by noise. The measure N_c is better than the sum of the absolute block differences since it picks up only large changes between two frames. A typical curve of this measure for a shot containing this kind of slow motion replay is shown in Figure 3. We look for pattern on the curve, which is composed of a small value followed by a large value. This pattern results from the frame sequence (f_i, f_i, f_{i+1}), where the second f_i is the inserted frame. Several such patterns might appear on the curve for a shot containing a slow motion replay.Therefore, if several of this pattern are detected within a shot, this shot will be declared as a slow motion replay. The detected slow motion sequences can be slow motion replays from different cameras as long as they are generated by inserting some repeated frames. If the replay is a sequence from the same camera angle as that of the original sequence, the original sequence can be found by matching the sequence, extracted from the slow motion replay by deleting repeated frames, with other shots in the same video sequence. This can be easily achieved by using our algorithm for detecting exact replay.

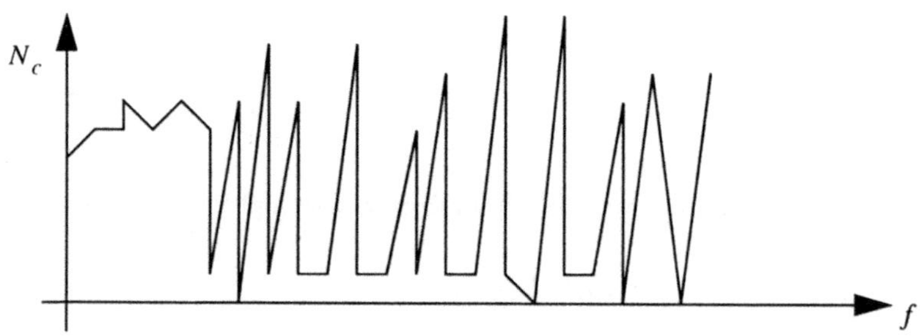

Figure 3. A typical curve of the measure N_c for a slow motion replay shot

5 Experimental Results

The above algorithms have been implemented in C++ on top of a general MPEG library which generates the corresponding DC image sequence from an MPEG-1/MPEG-2 video sequence.

The first test sequence is a tennis game which has 5 shots. Figure 4a shows the images of the first frames of these 5 shots with their frame numbers written under them. The first stage of the algorithm for detecting exact replay identifies two similar shot pairs (shot 1 and shot 4, shot 2 and shot 5). Shot 4 and 5 in this video are generated by the cut and paste function of an MPEG editing tool. Shot 1 does not include the first two frames in shot 4. In addition, the first several frames in shot 4 are re-encoded and thus are not exactly the same as the first frames in shot 1 in terms of actual signal. Shot 1 can be divided into five 25 frame-long segments. The corresponding 5 difference curves for finding their matches in shot 4 are shown in Figure 4b. The local minima corresponding to the segments of the replay all have a zero value except the first one. This is because shot 4 is almost a copy of shot 1 and there is only some difference caused by MPEG re-encoding at the beginning of the shot. The local minima are all 25 frames apart on subsequent curves. The algorithm can accurately detect the start and end frames of the matching segment both in the original and the replay shots, which are [0, 144] and [365, 509] respectively. The 6 curves for finding matches between shot 2 and shot 5 are also shown in Figure 4c and they have similar characteristics.

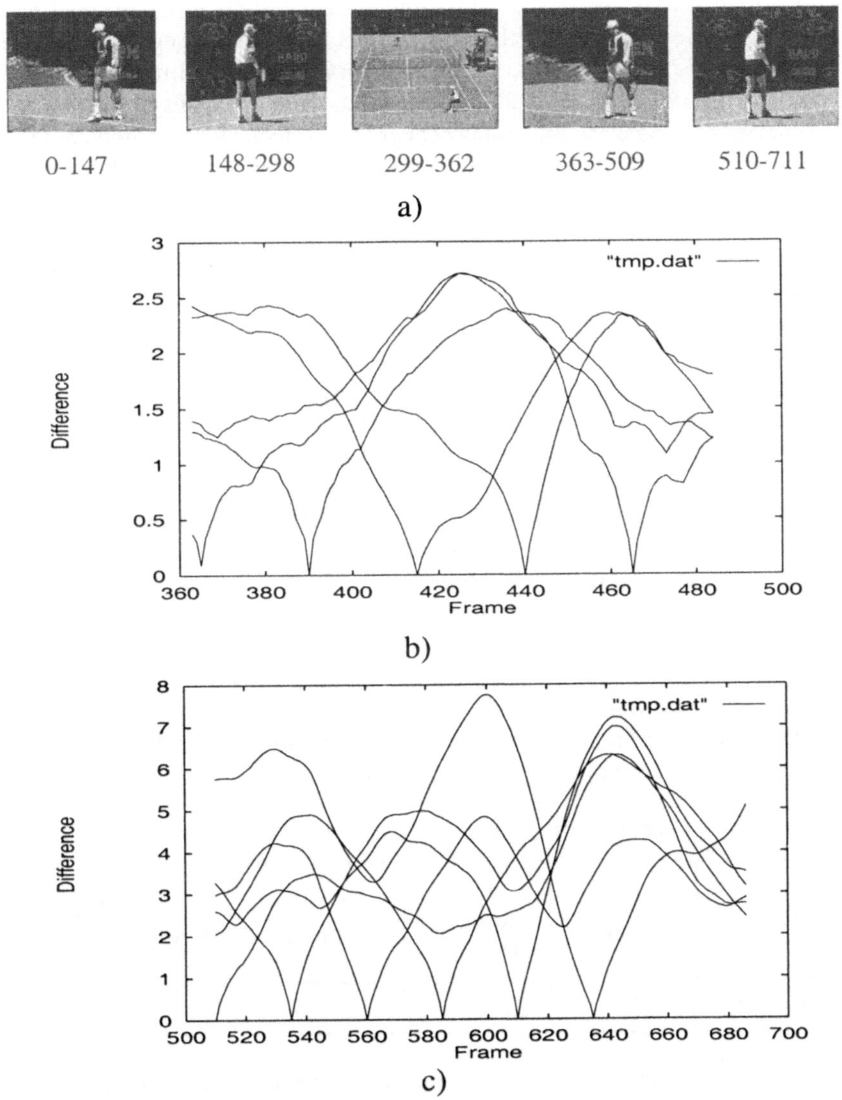

Figure 4. Two exact replays in a test video sequence

The second test sequence is a cricket game which contains a slow motion replay of 3 consecutive shots. This slow motion replay is obtained by playing the sequence captured by a high speed camera at the normal speed. To assess the performance of our algorithm for detecting noisy exact replays, we generate a noisy exact replay by manually extracting frames from the slow motion replay, which are interpolated, to approximately match the original shots. The mean frame grey-level curves of the original sequence and the replay are shown in Figure 6a. The original 3 shot sequence is 317 frames long and the replay is 170 frames long. From the figure, it can be seen that the two sequences are not exactly the same in terms of absolute values, but their temporal difference patterns are similar. The first frames of the 3 shots in the original sequence are shown in Figure 6b. The 12 difference curves in matching segments between the two sequences are shown in Figure 6c. Only 6 curves have local minima smaller than the threshold value, which is set to 2.0 in all the tests. This indicates that the other 6 segments do not have a match in the replay sequence. All these local minima are approximately 25 frames apart except that the third curve has a very flat area near the minimum. This is because shot 2 in the sequence changes very little temporally. This results in very small changes in difference values when the segment is moving along within sequence 2. In this case, the difference value which is smaller than the threshold value and the location of which is 25 frames apart from the minimum on the previous curve is taken as the corresponding minimum instead of the local minimum. This kind of interpolation is performed using the constraint of the global match criteria. The detected start and end frames of the matching segments in the original and replay sequences are [23, 192] and [5070, 5239] respectively.

To test the algorithm for detecting the special slow motion replay, a half hour of a cricket game video, which contains several slow motion replays, is used. The test result is listed in Table 1. All slow motion replays have been correctly detected. The detected false slow motion replay is a static scene with some camera shift. There are only two occurrences of the pattern of a small value followed by a large value on the curve of the measure N_c. As a result, it can be easily removed if the constraint of at least several frame repetitions in a slow motion replay is imposed. The curve of the measure N_c for one of the shots is shown in Figure 5. From the test, it was found that frame insertion is often used to adjust the frame rate for a sequence captured by a high speed camera. This indicates that our algorithm is also able to detect slow motion replay captured by a high speed camera where such adjustment has been made.

Table 1. The result of slow motion replay detection

Game	No of Shots	No of Replays Detected	No of True Replays	No of False/ Missed Replays
Cricket	103	16	15	1/0

Both algorithms run on the Sun Ultra machine. The average speed of the algorithm for detecting exact replays was about 27 frames per second, which consisted of the time taken for generating the frame feature vectors and the time for detecting the actual replays. If the feature vectors are generated off-line, the actual speed is much faster. The algorithm for detecting slow motion replays was able to process 33 frames per second. In summary, both algorithms could run faster than real-time.

6 Conclusions

In this paper, algorithms for detecting two special replays directly in the MPEG domain have been presented. As input, our algorithms take a DC image sequence reconstructed from an MPEG-1/MPEG-2 video sequence, which requires only minimal decoding. The algorithm for detecting exact replays takes a two-stage approach to further reduce the computational cost. Since the match process is performed by first finding sub-segment matches and then connecting detected sub-segments to a global match by a contiguity constraint, the algorithm is quite versatile and can be used to detect replays with any length. During testing, the algorithm for detecting slow motion replays was able to reliably detect all slow motion replays generated by repeating frames, whether they are from the same camera angle or not. Experimental results have shown that both algorithms are effective in detecting replays in sports footage.

References

1. G. Ahanger and T. D. C. Little, A Survey of Technologies for Parsing and Indexing Digital Video, J. of Visual Communication and Image Representation, **27** (1996) 28-43
2. Y. Gong, T.S. Lim, H.C. Chua, H. Zhang, and M. Sakauchi, Automatic Parsing of TV Soccer Programs, Second Int. Conf. on Multimedia Computing and Systems (May 1995) 167-174
3. F. Idis and S. Panchanathan, Review of Image and Video Indexing Techniques, J. of Visual Communication and Image Representation, **8** (1997) 146-166
4. S. Intille and A. Bobick, Visual Tracking Using Closed-Worlds, MIT Media Laboratory Perceptual Computing Section Technical Report No. 294 (November 1994)
5. D. LeGall, MPEG: A Video Compression Standard for Multimedia Applications, Commun. ACM **34** (1991) 46-58
6. J. Meng, Y. Huan and S.F. Chang, Scene Change Detection in a MPEG Compressed Video Sequences, IS&T/SPIE Symposium Proc., Vol. 2419, San Jose, California (February 1995)
7. T. Taki, J. Hasegawa and T. Tukumura, Development of Motion Analysis System for Quantitative Evaluation of Teamwork in Soccer Games, ICIP, Vol III (1996) 815-818
8. D. Yow, B.L. Yeo, M. Yeung and B. Liu, Analysis and Presentation of Soccer Highlights from Digital Video, Proc. 2nd Asian Conf. on Computer Vision (1995) II499-II503

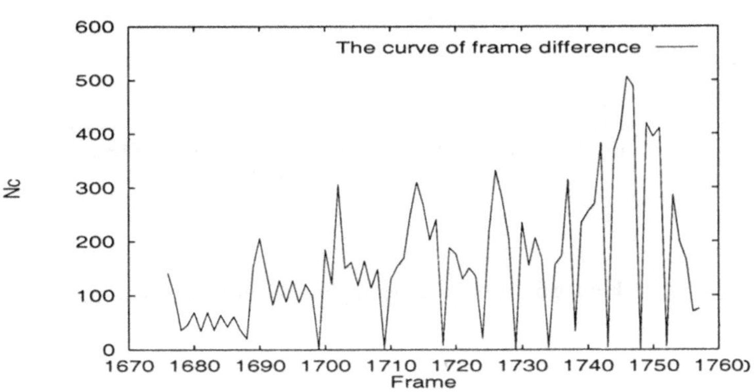

Figure 5. Temporal change of the measure N_c of a shot containing slow motion replay

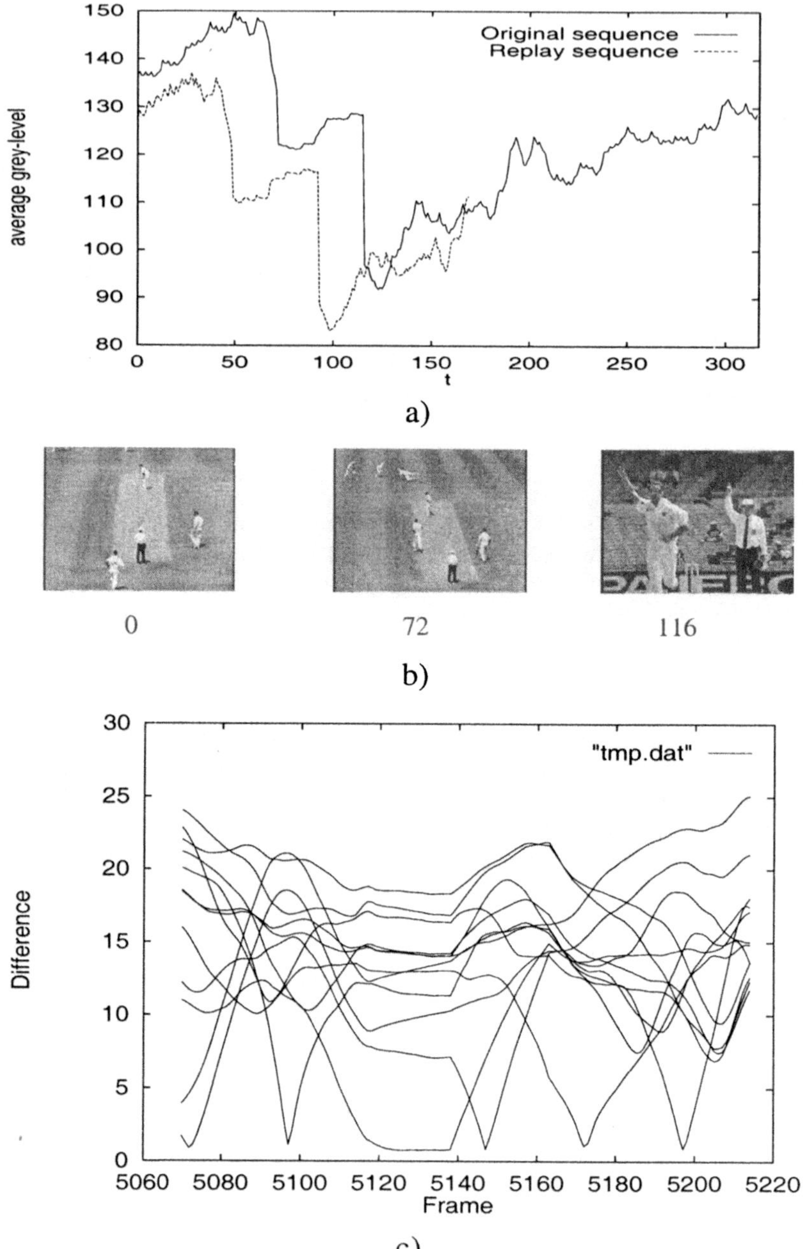

Figure 6. A noisy exact replay in another test sequence

Segmentation of Video Sequences using Volumetric Image Processing

Romildo José da Silva[†], Jonas Gomes[‡], and Luiz Velho [‡]

[†] Departamento de Matemática, UFCe, Fortaleza, Brazil
[‡] IMPA – Instituto de Matemática Pura e Aplicada, Rio de Janeiro, Brazil
{rjs|jonas|lvelho}@visgraf.impa.br

Abstract. This paper introduces an algorithm to detect cuts in a video sequence. The algorithm is based on volumetric processing of the video sequence, and uses techniques from differential geometry to classify the cut frames. The algorithm is very robust with respect to the presence of noise, and avoids the detection of "false cuts" in a video shot. We also describe an implementation of the algorithm that computes the video cut segmentation in real time.

1 Introduction

The area of image sequence processing [9] uses techniques from computer vision and image processing to analyze sequences of images, these sequences are generically called *digital video*, *video sequence*, or simply *video*. Video processing is of great importance in many applications such as video compression and transmission, video databases, surveillance videos, video editing, video mosaics, video morphing, movie restoration, movie colorization and so forth.

When processing a video sequence it is very important to exploit the temporal coherence of the images in the sequence. Video cuts destroy this temporal coherence, by joining together distinct camera shots. Therefore, the problem of video cut detection and segmentation is of great importance in order to obtain homogeneous sequences with high correlation between consecutive frames.

This paper introduces a new model for a cut frame in a video sequence. Our model provides a robust video cut segmentation algorithm which detects video cuts in real time.

2 Background

An *image sequence* is a one-parameter family of images $f\colon [a,b]\times U \to \mathbb{R}^3$ where $U \subset \mathbb{R}^2$, $[a,b]$ represents a time interval, and $\mathbb{R}^3$ is a representation of the color space. For black&white videos we have $f\colon [a,b]\times U \to \mathbb{R}$. An image sequence is also called a *video*, a *video sequence* or *digital video*. Note that the one-parameter family f describes a volumetric graphical object with domain $[a,b]\times U$. This fact will play a major role in our work.

When the time is discretized, the video reduces to a finite sequence of images $(f_0, f_1, \dots, f_n)$. Each image f_i is called a *frame*, and the sequence is naturally indexed by the *frame number.*

A *time segmentation* of the video sequence is a partition $a = t_0 < t_1 < \cdots < t_n = b$ of the time interval $[a, b]$. This partition induces a segmentation of the video sequence into n video sub-sequences $f_i \colon [t_i, t_{i+1}] \times U \to \mathbb{R}^3$, $i = 0, 1, \dots, n-1$.

A *shot*, [6], is an image sequence which presents continuous action from a single operation of the camera. In general, a *video sequence*, is produced from several shots in a process called *editing.* The editing process is based on several editing operations. A *cut* is the edit operation that consists of joining together two shots without the use of any transition effect. Cuts cause a sudden change of appearance in the content of the video frames. Besides the cut, there are other editing operations such as fade, dissolve and so forth.

The *video cut detection* problem can be posed as follows: *From a given video sequence $f \colon [a, b] \times \mathbb{R}^3$, determine a time partition $a = t_0 < t_1 < \cdots < t_n = b$, such that the video cuts occur precisely at times $t_1, t_2, \dots, t_{n-1}$.*

A generic strategy to solve the video cut detection problem uses frame comparison. This is a natural choice because consecutive frames in a single video shot have more features in common than frames that belong to different shots.

Frame comparison is nicely approached with the concept of a discriminant function. For a video sequence $(f_1, f_2, \dots, f_n)$, the *discriminant function*, $\mathrm{C} \colon \{f_1, \dots, f_n\} \to \mathbb{R}$, is defined on the set of video frames in such a way that a frame f_j is a cut frame if, and only if, $\mathrm{C}(f_j) > 0$. The discriminant function divides the set of frames $\{f_1, f_2, \dots, f_n\}$ into two classes: the classes of cut and non-cut frames.

Sometimes it is more efficient not to define discriminant functions directly on the frames of the video sequence, but use a *feature operator* instead. This is an operator $H \colon \mathcal{I} \to \mathbb{R}^n$, from the space of images to some euclidean space $\mathbb{R}^n$, $n > 0$. Feature operators transform a video sequence (f_n) into another sequence $(H(f_n))$ of vectors in $\mathbb{R}^n$. The rationale is that the features detected by the operator are insensitive to scene activities. Therefore it is easier, more efficient and robust to define discriminant functions using the feature sequence instead of the original video sequence. From a feature operator $H \colon \mathcal{I} \to \mathbb{R}^n$, and discriminant function d in $\mathbb{R}^n$, we obtain a discriminant function $\tilde{d}$ for the images of a video sequence by defining $\tilde{d}(f) = d(H(f))$. Since the feature operator is insensitive to scene activities, this discriminant function is constant on video shots, and changes values when a video cut occurs. Also, the discriminant function changes values when other editing activities occur. By properly modeling the changes of the discriminant function, it is possible to detect other editing operations.

When we have a discriminant function C, defined on the frames of a video sequence, an algorithm to solve the video cut detection problem can be easily attained: *Fix a threshold $\varepsilon > 0$, a cut occurs at frame f_j of an image sequence $(f_1, \dots, f_j, \dots, f_n)$, if $\mathrm{C}(f_j) > \varepsilon$.* In other words the frames f_j and f_{j+1} are discriminated within the scale of the given threshold ε.

In order to attain good results with the algorithm above, we must undertake three important steps:

1. Define the discriminant function;
2. Devise a good threshold ε;
3. Compute the discriminant function.

From the above actions we conclude that a robust video cut detection algorithm should have the following features:

- Perform a robust computation of the discriminant function in the presence of noise;
- Allow for the specification of a universal threshold that would work for different video shots in a video sequence;
- Make it possible an efficient implementation for use in real time applications.

Another important characteristic of a robust video cut detection algorithm is that it should not detect false cuts caused by scene activities.

Finally the discriminant function used by the algorithm should be invariant under changes of spatial scale. This invariance allows the use of the algorithm with videos of different resolutions, which can be exploited to increase the robustness and performance of the video cut segmentation algorithm.

3 Volumetric Video Segmentation

When processing video it is very important to take into account the continuous nature of the time component. This is beautifully grasped by the well known description of the essence of an animation given by Norman Mclaren from the National Film Board, Canada: *"Animation is not the art of drawings-that-move but the art of movements-that-are-drawn. What happens between each frame is more important than what exists on each frame. Animation is therefore the art of manipulating the invisible interstices that lie between frames"*.

From the signal processing point of view we can interpret Mclaren's statement to mean that the essence of a video sequence is captured when the signal is reconstructed as a full, three-dimensional, volumetric signal. Uses of volumetric techniques for video processing have appeared in the literature. In [1] techniques from tomographic processing are used for motion estimation in video sequences. In [4] it has been explored to construct multiresolution digital video.

One of the weaknesses of the existing methods to solve the video cut segmentation problem is that they process each video frame separately [10, 5, 8, 7] . We will introduce a new technique based on the volumetric representation of video. Thus the technique takes into account the intrinsic relationship between neighbor frames.

In this section we will give an overview of the method, with some examples. The algorithm will be described for black&white video sequences. Color video sequences can be processed by taking the luminance channel of the video sequence.

3.1 Geometric Classification

Point planarity is the basic concept underlying our discriminant function for the video cut segmentation algorithm.

Initially, we embed the volumetric video $f\colon U \times [a,b] \to \mathbb{R}$ on the four dimensional Euclidean space $\mathbb{R}^4$ as a hypersurface

$$M = \{(x, y, t, f(x, y, t))\,;\,(x, y, t) \in U \times [a, b]\}.$$

(This is the volumetric analogous to embedding an image as a surface in $\mathbb{R}^3$.)

Planar points are points contained in a flat neighborhood of the hypersurface M. In other words, a planar point is part of a piece of hyperplane contained in M. When a point is not planar, it is called *non-planar.*

On a Monge hypersurface, we can characterize a planar point p as a point where the matrix of the second derivatives of the function f (the *Hessian matrix*), has rank 0. This is proved in [2, 3]. Thus for a non-planar point p the Hessian matrix has rank values of either 1, 2 or 3.

The characterization of planar points allow us to define a feature operator C on each frame f_j of a video sequence:

$$\mathrm{C}(f_j)(x,y) = \begin{cases} 1 & \text{if } (x,y) \text{ is planar;} \\ 0 & \text{otherwise;} \end{cases}$$

Because of the characterization of the planar points using the rank of the Hessian matrix, it follows that the feature operator is a non-linear high-pass filter.

It is important to observe that volumetric neighborhoods are used in the classification of the pixels. This accounts for the intrinsic variation of pixel values along the time dimension. We also remark that, although the planar points sequence resembles a sequence obtained using an edge detecting filter, the nature of the computation Note that because of the presence of scene activities, the volumetric function varies linearly along the time for the frames of a video shot. Therefore, the non-planarity occurs because of the non-null values of the eigenvalues along the spatial x, y directions. This explains why the features detected on the video sequence of planar points resemble a two-dimensional edge processing.

3.2 Discriminant Function

When the volumetric object represents a video shot the volumetric segmentation is originated from the time evolution of the flat regions of the first frame in the shot, along with their boundaries. When scene activities in a shot are small the changes along time is linear, and the transformation from one frame to the next is well approximated by an isometry (rotation and translation). Therefore, the number of planar points between consecutive frames is constant. In practice, scene activities in a shot cause this number to vary, but the variation is very small. Therefore, the number of planar and non-planar points on each frame vary slowly. Additionally, volumetric video shots have in general a large number of planar points, because images in general have many flat areas when segmented. This fact, along with the variation of the number of planar points constitute the major cornerstone of our video cut algorithm.

In sum, for a video shot the volumetric function f varies linearly, on the average, along the voxel sequence $\ldots, (x, y, j-2), (x, y, j-1), (x, y, j)$. When a cut occurs at frame f_j, this linear variation is altered by the different values introduced by the frame f_{j+1} of the cut. In other words, the frame f_{j+1} of the new video shot introduces a separating face on the cubic segmentation of the volumetric video. As a result voxel (x, y, j) and $(x, y, j+1)$ are both non-planar. This causes a sudden and significant decay in the number of planar points of each frame of the video sequence.

This shows that we can define a discriminant function that associates to each frame of the video sequence the number of planar points of the frame. By fixing a threshold $\varepsilon > 0$, when the number of planar points decreases below ε a video cut occurs. As a matter of fact it is more convenient to use a normalized discriminant function

$$\mathrm{C}(f_k) = 100 \times \frac{\text{Number of planar pixels on frame} f_k}{\text{Number of pixels on frame} f_k},$$

which gives the percentage of planar points in each frame.

Figure 1(a) shows four frames of a sequence with 64 frames. A video cut occurs at frame 32. Figure 1(b) shows the corresponding feature sequence of planar and non-planar points. Figure 1(c) shows the graph of the associated discriminant function. As we expected, the graph shows that there is almost no variation in the number of planar points up to frame 31. At frame 32 the discriminant function decays to 27, and at frame 33 it assumes the value 28. The function jumps to 96 at frame 34, and remains constant until the end of the sequence.

The previous example contains two video shots with similar frames (a woman speaking). Now we will give an example where the two shots have dissimilar frames. Figure 2(a) shows 4 frames of a video sequence that contains a video cut. Figure 2(b) shows the corresponding feature sequence of planar and non-planar points. Figure 2(c) shows the graph of the discriminant function. Note that on the cut frames it decays from 97 to approximately 45.

4 Real-Time Implementation

In this section we describe the algorithm for video cut detection based on the techniques of volumetric image sequence processing described in the previous section. The algorithm is suitable for real-time video segmentation, even on low-end workstations equipped with a video capture board.

4.1 Algorithm

The algorithm is composed of three procedures that are applied to each frame: the feature operator; the classification function; and the discriminant function.

As we have seen in the previous section, the classification of planar and non-planar points can be attained using the Hessian matrix of the function f.

It is known that a matrix M has rank 0 if and only if its characteristic polynomial $P(x) = \mathrm{Det}(M - xI)$ is null. Straightforward computations show that the characteristic polynomial of the matrix $\mathrm{Hess}(f)$ is given by

$$P(x) = C_0 - C_1 x + C_2 x^2 - x^3, \tag{1}$$

where,

$$\begin{aligned} C_0 &= \mathrm{Det}(\mathrm{Hess}(f)) \\ C_1 &= \mathrm{Det}\begin{pmatrix} f_{xx} & f_{xy} \\ f_{yx} & f_{yy} \end{pmatrix} + \mathrm{Det}\begin{pmatrix} f_{xx} & f_{xz} \\ f_{zx} & f_{zz} \end{pmatrix} + \mathrm{Det}\begin{pmatrix} f_{yy} & f_{yz} \\ f_{zy} & f_{zz} \end{pmatrix} \\ C_2 &= f_{xx} + f_{yy} + f_{zz} \end{aligned}$$

Therefore, a point is classified as planar by computing the characteristic polynomial of $\mathrm{Hess}(f)$ and verifying if $C_0 = C_1 = C_2 = 0$. This is the planarity test used in our implementation. The main procedure is defined in algorithm 1:

Algorithm 1 : video_cut_detection (F)

```
for each frame f_i ∈ F do
   h_i ← feature(f_i)
   c_i ← classify(h_i)
   if discriminate(c_i) then
      mark_cut(i)
```

The feature operator is defined in algorithm 2. It calculates the rank of the Hessian matrix at each point of the volumetric image. The second derivatives, $f_{xx}, f_{yy}, f_{zz}, f_{xy}, f_{xz}, f_{yz}$, are computed using central differences. The formula for determining point planarity follows from equation 1.

Algorithm 2 : feature(f)

```
for each pixel f(u, v) do
   compute Hess(f)
   C_0, C_1, C_2 ← Hess(f) characteristic polynomial coefficients
   if C_0 < ε and C_1 < ε and C_2 < ε then
      h(u, v) ← planar
   else
      h(u, v) ← non-planar
```

The classification operator is defined in algorithm 3. It simply computes the percentage of planar points in the frame.

Algorithm 3 : classify(h)

---

for all pixels $h(u, v)$ **do**
  if $h(u, v)$ is planar **then**
    increment number of planar points
return percentage of planar points

One drawback of segmentation algorithms based on thresholding is the need to reliably find an appropriate threshold value for a given video sequence. The best option is to automatically determine the threshold based on the processed data. In our algorithm, we compute the threshold value dynamically, based on a statistical analysis of the feature vector (i.e. the percentages of planar points at each frame).

The discriminant function is defined in algorithm 4. It exploits the fact that when there is a temporal discontinuity in the image sequence, the percentage of planar points drops considerably for exactly 2 frames. (See Figures 1, 2 and 3) Based on this observation, it uses the average of the differences in absolute value of the percentage of planar points over four frames.

A video cut is detected whenever this quantity is greater than three times the variance σ of the percentage of planar points.

Algorithm 4 : discriminate(C)

---

compute σ over current interval
$d = \frac{1}{3}(|c_{i-1} - c_i| + |c_i - c_{i+1}| + |c_{i+1} - c_{i+2}|)$
if $d > 3(\sigma + \epsilon)$ **then**
  return TRUE
else
  return FALSE

This adaptive discriminant function is automatic since the variance in the number of planar points is computed over each continuous segment of the sequence. It is very robust because a temporal discontinuity will cause the discriminant value d to be approximately four times the variance. We add a small constant ϵ, to d in order to account for situations where the variance is zero.

4.2 Analysis

The basic fact behind the good behavior of the discriminant function we have defined is the slow variation of the number of planar points along the frames of a video shot.

This slow variance may be destroyed by textures and noise. Images with large areas of texture have a small number of planar points because of the high frequencies introduced by the texture (remember that non-planar points are points of high volumetric frequency). The decrease in the number of planar points makes it more difficult to obtain a good threshold for the discriminant function.

Most of the video sequences analyzed so far do not contain predominant textures. Now we will examine a video sequence with texture.

Figure 3(a) shows 4 frames of a video sequence with 64 frames. A video cut occurs between the football and the table tennis shots. Figure 3(b) shows the corresponding feature sequence of planar and non-planar points. Notice the smaller number of planar points because of the high frequencies introduced by the texture. Figure 3(c) depicts the graph of the discriminant function. As stated above, the discriminant function is not constant. Nevertheless, the sudden decay on the cut frame occurs, and this enables the algorithm to detect the cut reliably.

As the previous example shows, even in the presence of texture the discriminant function undergoes a sudden decay in a cut frame, which enables the algorithm to detect the cut. Experiments we have conducted showed that in spite of the noise introduced by the high frequencies of the texture the algorithm performs well. Certainly the automatic fine-tuning of the threshold for noisy sequences plays an important role.

5 Conclusions and Future Work

We have proposed to model a cut frame in a video sequence as a non-planar slice when we consider the video sequence as a volumetric object embedded as a Monge surface in $\mathbb{R}^4$. A mathematical characterization of planar points based on techniques from Riemannian geometry allows us to devise a robust algorithm to solve the problem of video cut segmentation.

We have also described some robustness criteria for a video cut detection algorithm. Our algorithm satisfies these criteria. Also, the algorithm allows for an implementation in real time.

Some directions for future work are discussed below.

- Our technique can be extended to obtain an algorithm to detect editing activities (fade, dissolve and so forth). For this we should use an editing model such as the one described in [5].
- Implementation of a scale space version of the algorithm to run in real time is an interesting direction to pursue. We remark that using scale space eliminates the noise influence in the computation of derivatives.
- Our algorithm is very robust with respect to the automatic definition of the discrimination threshold. Nevertheless it could perform even better if it could be trained to get the optimum threshold for different kinds of video sequences, such as, for instance, TV news.

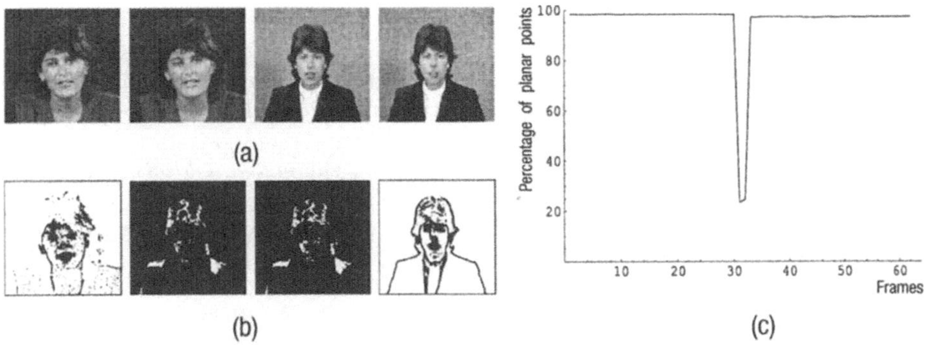

Fig. 1. Video sequence (a); feature sequence: planar points (b); discriminant function (c).

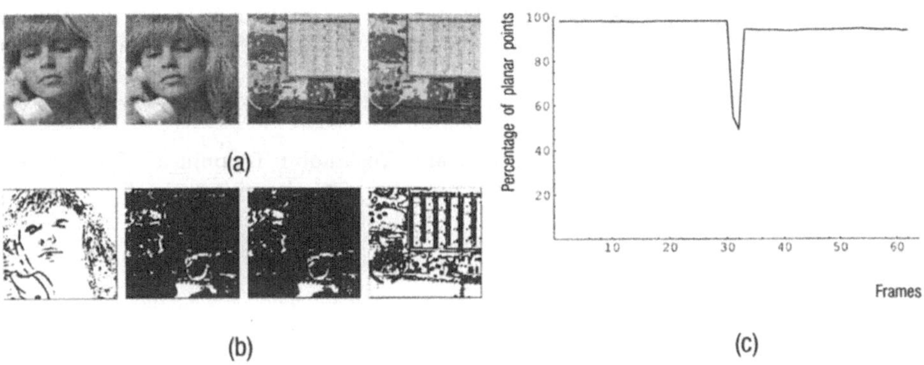

Fig. 2. Video sequence (a); feature sequence: planar points (b); discriminant function (c).

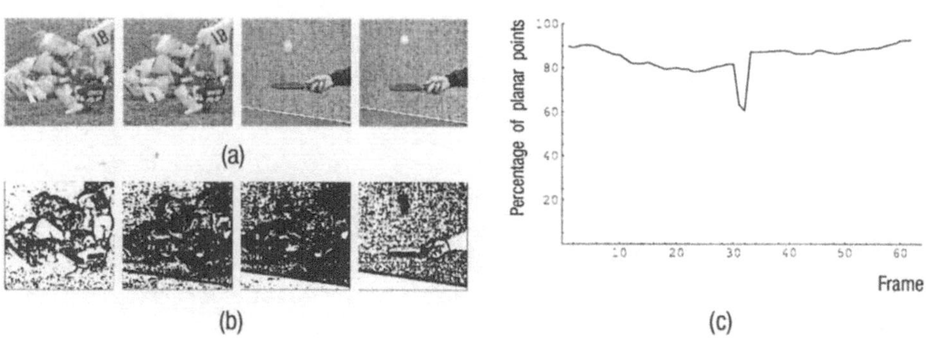

Fig. 3. Video sequence (a); feature sequence: planar points (b); discriminant function (c).

References

1. Akihito Akutsu and Yoshinobu Tonomura. Video tomography: An efficient method for camerawork extraction and motion analysis. In *Proceedings of ACM Multimedia Conference*, pages 349–356, 1994.
2. Romildo J. da Silva. *Geometric Processing of Volumetric Objects*. PhD thesis, IMPA, Rio de Janeiro, Brazil, September 1998 (in Portuguese).
3. Romildo J. da Silva, J. Gomes, and L. Velho. Video cut detection using volumetric image sequence processing, 1999. (IMPA preprint).
4. Adam Finkelstein, Charles E. Jacobs, and David Salesin. Multiresolution video. *SIGGRAPH '96 Conference Proceedings*, pages 281–290, 1996.
5. Arun Hampapur, Ramesh Jain, and Terry Weymouth. Digital video segmentation. In *Proceedings of ACM Multimedia Conference*, pages 357–364, 1994.
6. Ira Konigsberg. *The Complete Film Dictionary*. Penguin Books, 1989.
7. A. Nagasaka and Y. Tanaka. Automatic video indexing and full-video search for object appearances. In *Proc. of the IFIP Second Working Conference on Visual Database Systems*, pages 119–133, 1991.
8. K. Otsuji and Y. Tonomura. Projection-detecting filter for video cut detection. *Multimedia Systems*, 1:205–210, 1994.
9. M. Igrahim Sezan and R. L. Lagendijk. *Motion Analysis and Image Sequence Processing*. Kluwer Academic, 1993.
10. Yukinoby Taniguchi, Akihito Akutsu, and Yoshinobu Tonomura. Panoramaexcerpts: Extracting and packing panoramas for video brwosing. In *Proceedings of ACM Multimedia Conference*, pages 427–436, 1997.

Visual Speech Analysis for Spoken Chinese Training of Oral Deaf Children

Xiaodong Jiang[1], Qianghua Qiang[1], Zhisong Zhou[1], Yunlai Wang[2]

[1] Department of Computer Science, Nanjing University, Nanjing, P.R. China, 210093
xdjiang@public1.ptt.js.cn, qiangqh@263.net
[2] Nanjing Oral School, Nanjing, P.R. China, 210026

Abstract. This paper presents a novel vision-based speech analysis system STODE which is used in spoken Chinese training of oral deaf children. Its design goal is to help oral deaf children overcome two major difficulties in speech learning: the confusion of intonations for spoken Chinese characters and timing errors within different words and characters. It integrates such capabilities as real-time lip tracking and feature extraction, multi-state lip modeling, Time-delay Neural Network (TDNN) for visual speech analysis. A desk-mounted camera tracks users in real-time. At each frame, region of interest is identified and key information is extracted. The preprocessed acoustic and visual information are then fed into a modular TDNN and combined for visual speech analysis. Confusion of intonations for spoken Chinese characters can be easily identified, and timing error within words and characters also can be detected using a DTW (Dynamic Time Warping) algorithm. For visual feedback we have created an artificial talking head directly cloned from user's own images to generate correct outputs showing both correct and wrong ways of pronunciation. This system has been successfully used for spoken Chinese training of oral deaf children in cooperation with Nanjing Oral School under grants from National Natural Science Foundation of China.

1 Introduction

The deaf people in China account for more than 0.5% of the entire population, i.e., more than 60 million Chinese are profoundly deaf. Statistics also show that many others are profoundly hearing impaired. It has long been agreed upon that the communication and academic learning demands placed on deaf children in school require small class size and intensive one-to-one instruction. Unfortunately, the cost of resources and energy makes it impractical, if not impossible, for such instruction to be offered to the vast majority of deaf children in China.

The recent developments in interactive technologies have offered a very promising and cost-effective way of increasing the quality of education for deaf children, particularly as it pertains to developing and refining spoken communication skills. In cooperation with teachers and students from Nanjing Oral School, we are developing a novel system STODE (Speech Training For Oral Deaf Education) based on visual speech analysis and synthesis to improve the speaking ability of oral deaf children. STODE assists the children in combating two major problems in speech learning: the confusion of intonations for spoken Chinese characters and timing errors within different words and characters.

And three major technical challenges arise from this scenario:
(1) how to perform lip tracking and feature selection in real time;
(2) how to combine the acoustic and visual input for dynamic visual speech analysis;
(3) how to detect timing errors within words and characters.

To address these issues, we have proposed a parametric lip model and performed model fitting based on the results of lip tracking and feature extraction. A neural network is employed to classify lip shapes into one of the five classes and select additional model parts for fine-tuning of lip models. The extracted acoustic and visual features are fed into a TDNN (visual features that belong to different classes are processed by different input layers) and combined for Chinese visual speech analysis, which provides the basis for detection of confusion of characters which differ only in intonations. The timing error within characters can be easily identified at the same time using Dynamic Time Warping algorithm. For visual feedback to the user, we create an artificial talking head cloned directly from the user images and animate it in real-time. It is controlled by results from the visual speech analysis system and can then produce output in both ways, the way that the child spoke and the way he/she should speak.

2 System Overview

Figure 1 gives an overview of different modules in our system and the communication between them. We use a microphone and a desk-mounted camera to record the acoustic and visual data. After the ROI Detection module detects and tracks ROI (Region of Interest) in real time, the Lip Model Fitting module performs model adaptation offline. Both acoustic and visual features extracted are fed into a combined TDNN recognizer for Chinese visual speech analysis.

Unlike most western languages, spoken Chinese words are sequences of characters which are spelt continuously. And spoken characters are in turn sequences of phonemes. While there are no more than 30 phonemes in Chinese, they combine to make more than 6,000 frequently used characters. Each character corresponds to one of the four intonations and many words could be identified only by using intonations of the characters in it. Basically, hearing impaired children must overcome two major difficulties in speech learning: the confusion of characters which differ only in intonations and timing errors within different words and characters. For most Chinese speech recognizers, it is very difficult to identify these two problems during the recognition. However, we have found that this task can be greatly simplified in the language training. We are not interested in recognizing what was spoken (we already know it since it's a training process). We are only interested in identifying whether the intonation pronounced is wrong and whether a certain phoneme is spoken too fast or too slowly. And we find that the Dynamic Time Warping algorithm is very suitable for solving these problems.

In our system, words in the sample are two characters long on average, and they could form a simple Subject-Action-Object sentence which typically is 3 words long. The acoustical signal is sampled at 16KHZ. The resolution of the image is 180x240 pixels. And it allows uninterrupted capturing of color images at 25Hz (PAL system in China) on our system.

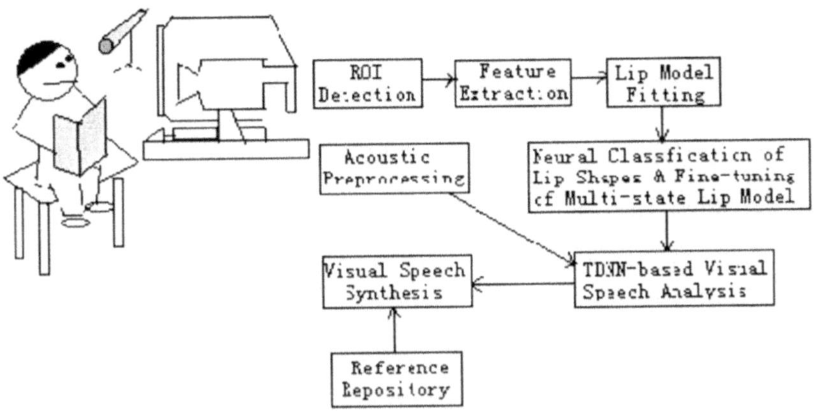

Figure 1. STODE System Overview

3 Lip Model Fitting

3.1 Detection of Region of Interest (ROI)

One major drawback of using gray-level images is that the external borders of lips is not very marked in them when taken under diffuse light conditions. Previous research work also shows that the information carried by color seems to suffer these limitations much less than pure gray-level images. Since we are interested in describing the lips region (where the red hue is dominant), we first transform the original RGB image to HSI (hue, saturation, intensity) space, in which information related to colors and luminance are disentangled. Here we use only the HS components for segmentations of lip regions by assuming that HS values of lip colors follow a two-dimensional

Gaussian distribution. And we find that the parameters of the distribution for different people and different lighting conditions are different. Therefore, we try to integrate in our system the ability of handling lighting changes by adapting parameters of the two-dimensional Gaussian distribution. Because the Gaussian distribution only has very few parameters, it is possible to adapt these parameters in real-time. Here we use a linear combination of the known parameters to predict the new parameters.

After identifying the HS distribution at each frame, we can obtain its mean vector and covariance matrix. Then we can use the maximum likelihood criterion to obtain the best set of coefficients for prediction. Figure 2 shows the ROI extracted.

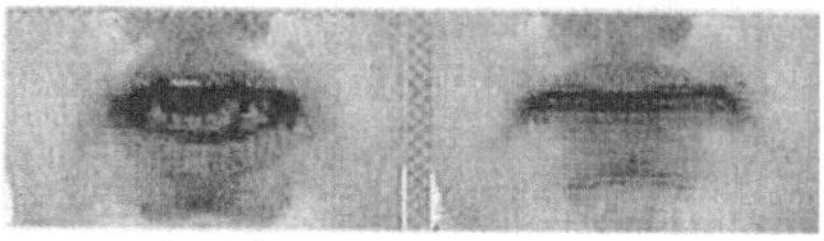

Fig. 2. Region of Interests Extracted

3.2 Feature Points Extraction

Fig. 3. 7-parameter Lip Model

After the ROI has been detected, the six feature points we intend to find for model fitting are (see Figure 3):

- The left and right lip corners
- The two feature points where the vertical symmetry axis of the mouth intersects the external boundaries of the upper and lower lips
- The two feature points on the external boundary of the upper lip which define D in Figure 3.

First we find the line between the lips by using a horizontal integral projection of the image in the ROI. We then apply a horizontal edge detector to the ROI to find out the external boundaries of the upper and lower lips. The lip corners are found by looking for the darkest pixel along the two columns in the ROI located at the horizontal boundaries. And the next two feature points can be found by intersecting the middle vertical line orthogonal to the line between the lips onto the external boundaries of the upper and lower lips. The last two feature points defining D also could be easily found by finding the point with the largest Y coordinate on the external boundary of the upper lip. The other point on the symmetric side of the vertical symmetry axis of the mouth can be found by simple transformation after taking into consideration the inclination angle •, which is the angle between the horizontal axis of the image plane and the line connecting two lip corners.

3.3 Lip Modeling Fitting

We have adopted a 2D lip model to describe the mouth of the subject which consists of 3 parabolic arcs, closely reproducing the boundaries of the lips. This 7-parameter model is shown is Figure 3.

As illustrated by Figure 3, our model has seven parameters (Xo, Yo, θ, W, Hu, Hl, D). The whole mouth is positioned at O (the middle point of the segment joining the two vertices) and is rotated by θ (the inclination angle). The parobolic arcs are defined as follows:

- The external boundary of the upper lip is defined as a pair of parabolic arcs of height Hu, laterally translated, with respect to O by D, and having semiamplitude W-D.
- The external boundary of the lower lip is defined as a parabolic arc of semiamplitude W and height Hl.

Here lip model fitting involves finding optimal values for the seven parameters using detected feature points – making the resulting parabolic arcs as "close" as possible to the external boundaries of the lips. And the optimality of parametric values is established by maximizing a global energy function, which accounts for two dimensional information coming from the chrominance analysis of the image, as well as a priori knowledge about lip shapes.

3.4 Neural Classification of Lip Shapes and Fine-tuning of Lip model

Neural classification of lip shapes is essential for fine-tuning of lip models and selection of different input layers in TDNN-based visual speech analysis. In addition to the 6 feature points detected, we select another 12 feature points along the parabolic-model external boundaries of upper and lower lips. As is shown in Figure 3, six of the twelve points are the middle and quadripartite points on the pair of parabolic arcs which model the external boundary of upper lip. The other six points are the octapartite points of the parabolic arc which models the external boundary of lower lip excluding the middle point. The HSI values for these 18 feature points are accumulated, forming a 54-dimensional input vector. Based on these input, a 54-h-5 neural network is employed to classify the lip shapes into one the following 5 classes (states):

- lips closed
- lips open but teeth invisible
- lips open and teeth visible, but teeth are clenched so that no dark region is visible
- lips open and only the upper teeth and a dark region below are visible
- lips open and both upper and lower teeth and a dark region are visible

The neural classification of lip shapes into 5 distinct classes provides critical information for modeling lip opening and teeth edge detection. After the classification, optional lip features (internal boundary of upper and lower lips, lip closing edge, teeth edge, etc.) are selected for each shape model state and fine-tuning of the resulting multi-state lip model is performed by maximizing the local and global energy functions. These newly selected features are included into the model description for later use by the TDNNs.

4 TDNN-based Visual Speech Analysis

4.1 Analysis Task and Network Architecture

For visual speech analysis we use a modular TDNN (Time-delay Neural Network). Figure 4 shows the general architecture of the network. We do not call this task a 'recognition' task because it differs from traditional speech recognition task in that we are not interested in identifying what was spoken by the child (we already know it in advance). What we are interested in is to isolate each spoken Chinese character from a continuous speech sequence and check if it is what's supposed to be spoken and if it has been spoken with the correct intonation and timing. We find the modular TDNN is very suitable for our tasks.

As can be seen from Figure 4, the visual features identified above together with the preprocessed acoustic features are fed into the TDNNs. The TDNN is composed of two input layers (acoustic and visual input layer), one hidden layer and one phoneme layer. Backpropagation was applied to train the networks in a bootstrapping phase to fit phoneme targets.

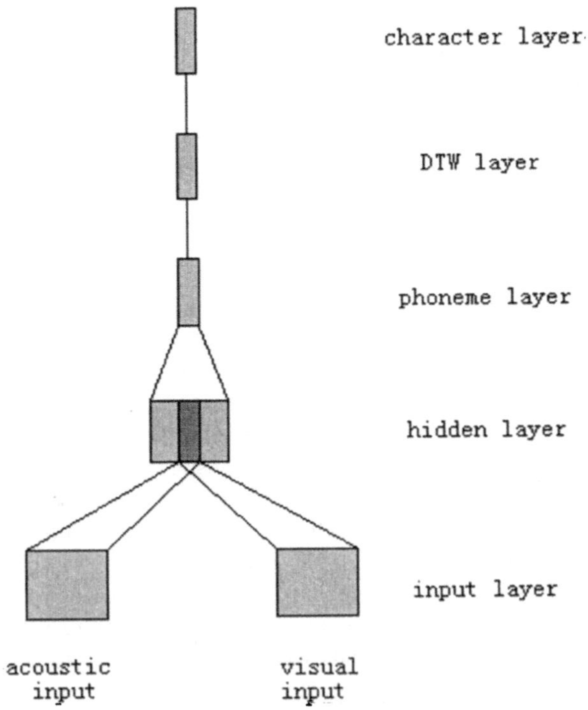

Figure 4. TDNN Architecture

Please note that in the multi-state lip shape model described above, images of different lip shapes deliver different kinds and different amount of data into the Visual Input Layer in the TDNN. To deal with this problem, we have proposed a multi-state TDNN which uses 5 kinds of visual input layers, each handling visual input corresponding to one of the five shape models.

Please note that in our system the combining of visual and acoustic data is done at the input layer. Above the phoneme layer, the Dynamic Warping Algorithm is applied (DTW layer) to find the optimal path of combined phoneme hypotheses to identify spoken Chinese characters which differ only in intonations and to detect possible timing errors within characters.

4.2 Acoustic and Visual Input Representation

In our system the acoustic data is sampled at 16KHZ rate and 8 bit precision. For acoustic data representation, we have followed the well-established approach to apply FFT on the Hamming windowed speech data to get 16 Melscale Fourier coefficients as input to the Acoustic Input Layer. For visual data representation, we have performed the lip-tracking and feature points extraction task by applying our 2D multi-state lip shape model. Then we use both the color profile of the feature points on external and internal boundaries and position and movement of lip boundaries for feature extraction using principle component analysis (PCA). The extracted feature vectors are then fed to the Visual Input Layer.

4.3 Combination of Visual and Acoustic Data

Combining visual and acoustic data is done at the input layer. There are several advantages for this approach as compared to combination at a higher layer. Firstly, if the acoustic and visual data are combined at the phoneme layer, then we have to precisely define a complete set of visemes. However, we find that unlike phonemes, visemes are usually hard to define unless restricted to a very small set. Secondly, combination of visual and acoustic data at the input layer allows the network to take full advantage of lower correlation between acoustic and visual events such as intermodal timing relationships. The combined input takes the form of a weighted sum of the acoustic and visual input data. And the weights for this combination depend partly on the quality of the acoustic data. If the acoustic quality is high, the weight for it should be high. However, in the presence of considerable acoustic noise, a higher weight should be assigned to visual input to yield better results. When assigning weights for acoustic and visual signals, we must also take into account the fact that some phonemes are easy to recognize acoustically while some can be more reliably distinguished from the visual input.

4.4 Dynamic Time Warping for Speech Error Detection

After the phoneme hypotheses are generated by the phoneme layer in TDNN, it is directly input to DTW layer for further processing. First and foremost, we must make sure that what was spoken by the child is just what he's supposed to speak, although it may differ in intonations and timing. This task is mainly a recognition task. The DTW layer is also employed to detect two kinds of speech errors which occur frequently in speech learning by hearing impaired children: the confusion of intonations for spoken Chinese characters and the timing error in them. The detailed approach using Dynamic Time Warping algorithm is explained below.

Speech is a time-dependent process. Several utterances of the same word are likely to have different durations, and utterances of the same word with the same duration will differ in the middle, due to different parts of the words being spoken at different rates. These are where the two kinds of speech timing errors occur: timing between characters in a word, and timing between phonemes in a word. To detect the timing error is to find out the difference between the input speech pattern and the reference speech pattern. A specific example of timing error detection using the Dynamic Time Warping algorithm is illustrated in Figure 5.

Figure 5 shows a 'time-time' matrix used to visualize the time alignment to detect the

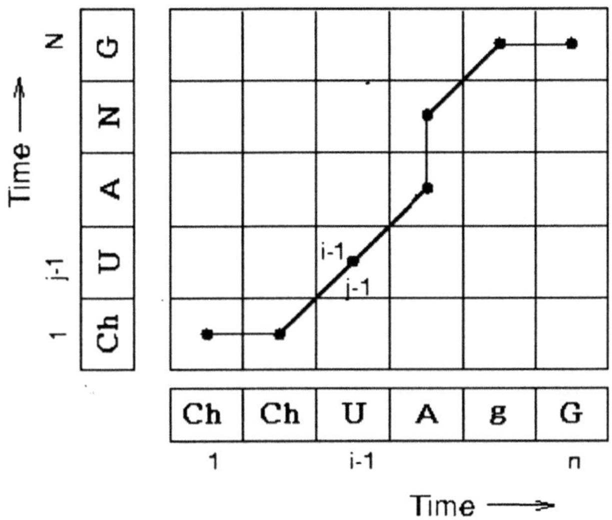

Figure 5. Illustration of a time alignment path between a template pattern 'ChUANG' and a noisy input 'ChChUAgG'

timing error for the Chinese character corresponding to window. To better illustrate its pronunciation, we use Chinese PiYing (ChUANG) here to represent the character. In the matrix, the reference pattern (template) goes up the side and the input pattern goes along the bottom. In this illustration, the input 'ChChUAgG' is a noisy version of the template 'ChUANG'. The idea is that 'g' is a closer match to 'G' compared with anything else in the template. The input will be matched with all templates in the system's repository. The best matching template is the one for which there is the lowest distance path aligning the input pattern to the template (here we use the Euclidean Distance). A simple global distance score for a path is simply the sum of local distances that go to make up the path. The warping path found by the system is also shown in Figure 5. Using this Dynamic Time Warping technique, the timing error could be easily detected.

Another possible speech error to identify is the confusion of different intonations. We have prepared reference samples with all four kinds of intonations for all characters in our system. If at the highest level of the modular TDNN, i.e., the character level, the character recognized differs from the supposed character only in intonation, the system then concludes that the child has confused the intonation and this information is then recorded for later use.

5 Visual Feedback Generation

In order to provide proper visual feedback to the child, we create an artificial talking head cloned from the user's own images and animate it in real-time. It is controlled by the results from the visual-speech analysis system and can then produce output in both ways, the way that the child spoke and the way he/she should speak. Repeating and emphasizing the audio-visual frames when speech errors occur could benefit directly from the results of the output of the TDNN-based visual speech analysis system. Generation of correct lip motions will rely on successful speech-to-lip movement synthesis techniques, which exceeds to scope of this paper.

6 Conclusion

In this paper we present a novel vision-based speech analysis system STODE for use in spoken Chinese training of oral deaf children. Its design goal is to help oral deaf children overcome two major difficulties in speech learning: the confusion of intonations for spoken Chinese characters and timing errors within different words and characters. This system has been successfully used for spoken Chinese training of oral deaf children in cooperation with Nanjing Oral School under grants from National Natural Science Foundation of China. We will continue to improve and refine our techniques and apply them to other contexts in the future, such as the foreign language training for normal people.

References

1. A. Waibel, T. Hanazawa, G. Hinton, K. Shikano, and K. Lang. Phoneme Recognition Using Time-Delay Neural Networks. IEEE Transactions on Acoustics, Speech and Signal Processing, 37(3):328-339, March 1989
2. Vogt, M. Fast Matching of a Dynamic Lip Model to Color Video Sequences under Regular Illumination Conditions. In Stork & Hennecke, 1996
3. Yullie, A, Cohen, D, Hallinan, P. Facial feature extraction by deformable templates, Harvard Robotics Laboratory, Technical Report No.88-2, 1988
4. David G. Stork, Greg Wolff, and Earl Levine. Neural Network Lipreading for Improved Speech Recognition. In IJCNN, June 1992
5. P. Haffner, M. Frannzini, and A. Waibel. Integrating Time Alignment and Connectionist Networks for High Performance Continuous Speech Recognition. Proc. International Conference on Acoustics, Speech and Signal Processing, 1991
6. B. Dodd, R. Campbell. Hearing by Eye: the Psychology of Lip-reading. Lawrence Erlbaum Assiciates, Hillsdale, New Jersey. 1987
7. R. Cole et al. Intelligent animated agents for interactive language training, Speech Technology in Language Learning, ESCA Workshop, 1998
8. D. W. Massaro. Perceiving Talking Faces: From Speech Perception to a Behavioral Principle. Cambridge, MA: MIT Press, 1998

Extracting Bimodal Representations for Language-Based Image Retrieval[1]

Thijs Westerveld, Djoerd Hiemstra, Franciska de Jong

University of Twente, Centre for Telematics and Information Technology,
PO Box 217, 7500 AE Enschede, The Netherlands
{westerve, hiemstra, fdejong}@cs.utwente.nl

Abstract This paper explores two approaches to multimedia indexing that might contribute to the advancement of text-based conceptual search for pictorial information. Insights from relatively mature retrieval areas (spoken document retrieval and cross-language retrieval) are taken as a starting point for an investigation of the usefulness of the concept of bimodal dictionaries and of clustering features from multi-modal documents into one semantic space. One of the advantages of the presented techniques is that they are domain independent.

1 Introduction

Among the various types of objects that one could want to search for in the multimedia domain, image content seems to be one of the more challenging types. Speedy and easy access to image content in the general domain is not supported by today's search tools and technology, and in spite of progress in content based image retrieval or advances in the area of video logging (a technique which reuses subtitles or speech transcripts for the automatic indexing of video fragments [13]), it is unlikely that on short notice general purpose technology will become available for indexing images on a conceptual level.

In this paper we will investigate parallels for image content retrieval with retrieval areas that have already reached a certain level of maturation (text retrieval), or where a breakthrough is imminent (spoken document retrieval and cross-language retrieval) and where the incorporation of the available technology in digital workflow processes can already be shown at several places.

In order to address the parallelism at a proper level of abstraction, section 2 will first discuss the retrieval problem in a very general way, based on the classical paradigms for information retrieval. Then we will analyse two more complex retrieval tasks. In both cases the complexity is not matching the complexity of the image case, but still it is complex enough to be able to generalise the findings in such a way that it offers a useful baseline for a conceptual exploration of the problem of developing automatic indexing tools for the image domain. In section 3 the notion of deriving

---

[1] Part of the research for this paper has been funded by the Dutch organisation for Scientific Research NWO.

bimodal dictionaries from parallel corpora will be shown to be very useful in modelling an approach for image retrieval which will eventually support text based querying of images. In section 4 the construction of one semantic space for both text and image features via *Latent Semantic Indexing* will be shown to offer a useful basis for concept-based retrieval.

Research in computer vision can be argued to advance the search for pictures in comparison to text-based search using manual annotations to pictures [15]. The research described in this paper explores the possibility to reuse *all* textual material that accompanies a picture for the purpose of automatic indexing. The concluding section 5 will argue that because of the parallelism with more matured retrieval technology and because of the fact that textual queries can be linked to the conceptual level there is room for confidence that the approaches described may facilitate a next advancement in cross-modal retrieval.

2 Learning from other IR areas

The goal of an information retrieval system is to present the user a set of documents that satisfy the user's information need which is expressed by a query. Every approach to information retrieval has three basic components: (1) a method for representing documents, (2) a method for representing queries and (3) a method for comparing the two representations [14]. Figure 1 graphically displays the basic components of an IR system.

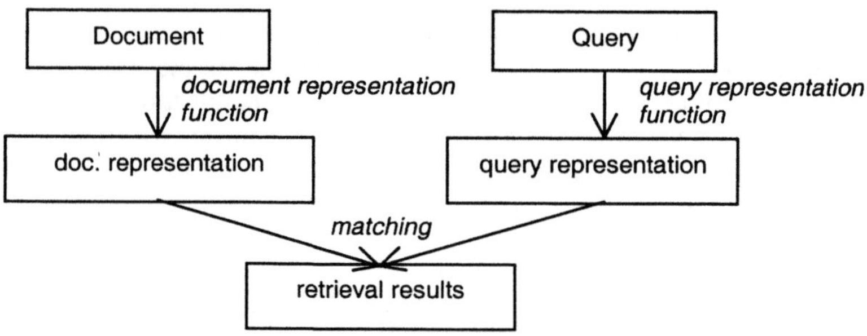

Fig. 1. The information retrieval paradigm

In the case of textual documents in a specific language and textual queries in the same language, both the query and document representation functions can be kept relatively simple. Still, an important problem in text retrieval is the fact that the same concept can be formulated in many different ways. Because of that, it is very hard to predict which query will yield relevant documents on a given concept. People search for documents discussing certain issues and are less interested in the specific words used in the documents to convey this information. This problem is known as the paraphrase problem [14]. Cross-modal IR, cross-language IR and spoken document retrieval can be viewed as special instances of the paraphrase problem. Queries and documents necessarily use different vocabularies because of differences in language or modality.

The following sections will go deeper into approaches and resources for cross-language information retrieval (CLIR) and spoken document retrieval (SDR).

2.1 Approaches to CLIR and SDR

A CLIR system supports the use of textual queries to search documents in other languages. A SDR system supports the use of textual queries to search audio documents containing speech. In systems that support CLIR or SDR, either the document representation function or the query representation function (or both) need to be much more complicated than in the classical text retrieval case.

In the case of CLIR the system can either translate all of the documents to the language of the query (off-line document translation) [10], or translate the query to the language of the documents (query translation) [8], or translate both to some intermediate language. Document translation has the advantage that it can be done off-line during indexing. Furthermore, the quality of document translation will in principle be better because the full document context is available for disambiguation. In the case of query translation there is often very little context. Latent semantic indexing (LSI) is an approach to CLIR in which both documents and queries are represented in a format that is in some sense intermediate between the two languages [4,16].

In the case of SDR, one option is to apply large-vocabulary speech recognition on the spoken documents to generate a textual representation [13]. Another option is phone-based retrieval. Just like in speech recognition, the system extracts discrete features from the continuous speech signal: so-called phones, but the final recognition step in omitted. During searching the query is also converted into a phone representation [11]. Phone-based retrieval is much faster during indexing and is less sensitive to out of vocabulary words.

2.2 Resources for CLIR and SDR

Both CLIR and SDR may rely on research areas that have proven to be commercially successful: machine translation and speech recognition. In addition, CLIR systems might also be built using machine-readable human dictionaries [8], parallel corpora (two texts that are translations of each other) [16] or comparable corpora (texts in two languages on the same subject which are not direct translations) [1]. SDR systems typically use speech recognition software [13], but might also use pronunciation dictionaries and transcribed speech, which are used to train the speech recognition software, directly [11].

2.3 Language-based image retrieval

In the sections above a brief overview was given of approaches and resources for CLIR and SDR. Drawing the parallel with language-based image retrieval, three basic approaches can be identified: (1) off-line image recognition, (2) on-line 'query visualisation' and (3) the use of an intermediate representation. If the available resources are taken into account it becomes apparent that the first option will not be realised in the near future. Unlike machine translation systems for CLIR and speech recognition systems for SDR, the state of the art in computer vision does not permit the automatic full interpretation of an arbitrary scene [15].

However, there are annotated image collections. In a sense these resources are resembling manually produced dictionaries for CLIR and pronunciation dictionaries for SDR. Such collections can be searched using textual queries, but new pictures should always be annotated by hand.

Systems that support CLIR or SDR can be trained on parallel corpora and transcribed speech respectively to interpret new or unseen data. We argue that the same applies to language-based image retrieval if large image/text corpora are available. Such corpora might be acquired from the Internet by using complete web pages plus images or e.g. from newspapers by using complete articles plus corresponding photos. This paper suggests two approaches to language-based image retrieval using large mixed image/text corpora. The first approach is the automatic extraction of a bimodal dictionary from the corpus. The second approach is based on clustering of both text and image features into one conceptual space using LSI.

3 Extracting a Bimodal Dictionary from a Parallel Corpus

If we have a parallel corpus of documents in the modalities text and images (i.e. a set of pictures with reasonably complete descriptions), we could extract a bimodal 'translation' lexicon from this corpus using techniques developed for cross language information retrieval [9]. Such a translation lexicon can be extracted by looking at the number of times language elements and image elements co-occur. If this number is relatively high, the elements are probably related. For example, if image descriptions contain the word *sun* and the corresponding images often contain a yellow circle, we could conclude that the two elements (the word *sun* and a yellow circle) are related in a way that is similar to the relation between *sun* and *soleil.*

3.1 Pre-processing

In order to be able to extract such relations from a parallel corpus of images and text, both the images and the descriptions need to be pre-processed.

The pre-processing of images consists of the determination of the objects or features present. In practice, low-level features like e.g. colour-histograms, textures and hue and saturation values are used to describe images. Low-level image features proofed to be useful for image retrieval systems that use query-by-example [5,7,12]. For the sake of our example, we assume that some basic shapes and colours like e.g. 'yellow circle' are identified.

A tree in the park on a sunny day

Fig. 2. Example image and description

For the pre-processing of textual objects we assume the application of a statistical part-of-speech tagger for lemmatising the words in the text, thereby following the approach taken in NLP-enhanced retrieval systems such as Twenty-One [10]. Suppose we have a picture of a tree in a park with the accompanying description "A tree in the park on a sunny day" (**Fig. 2**). The features detected for this image might be: a green circle, a yellow circle, a brown rectangle, a green rectangle and a blue rectangle. The information elements from the text might be *tree*, *park*, *sun* and *day*.

3.2 Counting Co-occurrences

Once the images and descriptions have been pre-processed, we can start counting the number of co-occurrences for the various text and image elements. Suppose we have a small example corpus, consisting of three pictures on the one hand, and corresponding descriptions on the other hand. (**Fig. 3**).

A **tree** in the **park** — A **tree** — A **sunny day** in the **park**

Fig. 3. Example corpus[2]

To compute co-occurrence frequencies from the corpus, a table will be constructed in which the columns represent the words in the captions, whilst the rows represent the features in the pictures. Since the mapping between words and image features will not always be one-to-one, the number of words in a description might differ from the number of features in the corresponding image. When this happens, null-terms will be introduced, to balance the two.

Initially all cells in the table will be set to zero. Each time a word and a feature co-occur, the corresponding cell in the table will be increased. The counts for the co-occurrences are distributed equally over all possibilities. For example, in the last image, *yellow circle* might be a translation of either, *park*, *sun* or *day*, so the three cells corresponding to these translations are all increased by 0.33.

When all three pictures from our example corpus have been processed, the table looks like this:

	tree	park	sun	day	(null)
green circle	0.75	0.25	-	-	1.0
yellow circle	-	0.33	0.33	0.33	-
brown rectangle	0.75	0.25	-	-	1.0
blue rectangle	0.25	0.58	0.33	0.33	0.5
green rectangle	0.25	0.58	0.33	0.33	0.5

[2] The information elements in the captions are in bold face

The following bimodal dictionary can be inferred automatically by applying the EM-algorithm as described in [9]. The algorithm eliminates certain word image-feature combinations and infers for example that trees basically consist of green circles and brown rectangles.

	tree	park	sun	day	(null)
green circle	1.0	-	-	-	1.0
yellow circle	-	-	0.5	0.5	-
brown rectangle	1.0	-	-	-	1.0
blue rectangle	-	1.0	0.25	0.25	0.5
Green rectangle	-	1.0	0.25	0.25	0.5

The algorithm that is used to infer the bimodal dictionary can easily be generalised for non-discrete lower level features. Future experiments have to point out if in fact the resulting bimodal dictionaries are effective in cross-modal search situations.

4 Using LSI for Cross-Modal Information Retrieval

Another way to find relations (or translations) between words and image features is building a semantic space with LSI. The idea of using LSI for multi-modal indexing is not completely new. In another study [2], images from the world wide web were indexed, analysing both the image features and the surrounding text (alt-tags, title, near text) of an image. In this study, words and image features are analysed separately building two separate spaces that are merged afterwards. LSI is used to analyse the textual part. A more integrated approach, in which the two modalities are combined from the start will yield a semantic space in which text and images are firmly interwoven.

As stated above, LSI can be used for Cross-Language Information Retrieval. After a short introduction to LSI this section will explain how the same techniques can be used for Cross-Modal Retrieval. For a more detailed description of LSI, cf. [3].

4.1 Latent Semantic Indexing

LSI uses a matrix in which each term is represented as a vector of document occurrences. The elements in the vector can be binary, natural or real-valued, indicating either *if* a term occurs, *how often* a term occurs or what the *weight* of the occurrence is (e.g. tf/idf).

From this matrix, the most meaningful linear combinations of terms and documents are computed using Singular Value Decomposition (SVD) [6], a form of two-mode factor-analysis that is similar to eigen-value/eigen-vector decomposition. The original term-document-matrix A is decomposed into three matrices containing linearly independent components that together represent the original term document matrix:

$$A = T\, S\, D' \qquad \textbf{(1)}$$

T and D are matrices with left and right-singular vectors, representing respectively terms and documents. S is a diagonal matrix with singular values that are ordered in decreasing magnitude.

When the smaller singular values in S are ignored (i.e. set to zero), the product of the three matrices is an optimal approximation of the original matrix in a lower dimension. In this lower dimensional space, documents that contain different, but similar[3] terms are mapped onto the same vector. This way, the underlying, latent semantics of the documents are uncovered. The similarity between two documents is computed using the cosine measure of the transformed documents. The documents are transformed using the singular value matrices:

$$\mathrm{sim}(d_1,d_2) = \cos(T^{t}d1, T^{t}d_2) \qquad \textbf{(2)}$$

where T is the matrix with the singular vectors representing the terms.

4.2 Building a Cross-modal Semantic Space

To use LSI for cross-modal indexing and retrieval, a term-document matrix has to be constructed. Analogous to cross-language retrieval with LSI, documents from the two modalities are treated as the same document. So along the rows of the matrix we will have both text and image features.

Suppose we use the example corpus from **Fig. 3** to build the matrix, then the matrix will look like this:

		doc 1	doc 2	doc 3
	tree	1	1	0
Terms from the text:	park	1	0	1
	sun	0	0	1
	day	0	0	1
	green circle	1	1	0
	brown rectangle	1	1	0
Terms from the images:	blue rectangle	1	0	1
	green rectangle	1	0	1
	yellow circle	0	0	1

Singular Value Decomposition is used to decompose this matrix into three matrices of a lower dimensionality. The semantic space that is constructed from this small example corpus via reduction to two dimensions is shown in **Fig. 4.**

In a way, the semantic space can be regarded as a bimodal dictionary. In this space, related terms from the two modalities (translations) are located close to each other.

---

[3] similar terms is, in this case, terms that often occur together in documents.

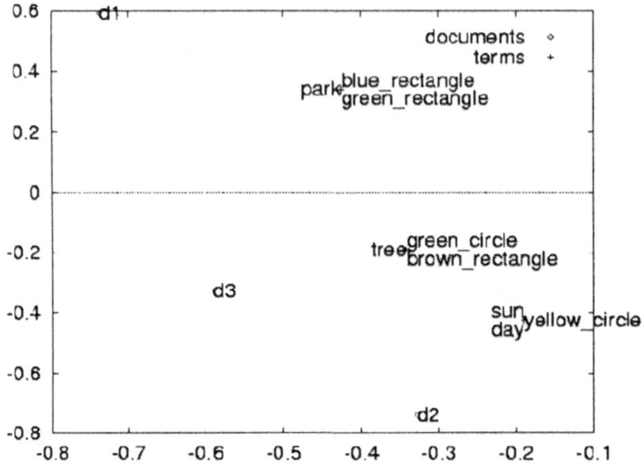

Fig. 4. 2-dimensional semantic space of example corpus from **Fig. 3**

4.3 Using a mixed corpus

Application of the described approach is hindered by the fact that parallel corpora of text and images are not widely available. However, it is also possible to build a similar semantic space using a mixed corpus. A mixed corpus is a corpus consisting of documents that contain text or images or both (**Fig. 5**). In a mixed corpus, at least a number of documents need to contain both text and images, but the text and the images don't need to be translations of one another, they only need to be *about* the same subject. Mixed corpora are much easier to obtain. We could take for example documents from the World Wide Web.

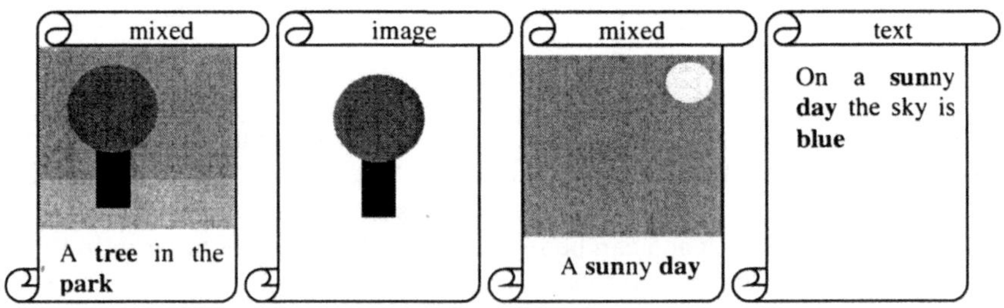

Fig. 5. Mixed corpus

Once we have a corpus, we can apply proven techniques developed for conceptual monolingual information retrieval to build multi-modal and even cross-modal indices.

In concept-based retrieval, the assumption is that documents can communicate the same information in various wordings. The same assumption can be made on multi-modal documents. These documents can communicate the same information using different words, different images or even words instead of images and vice versa.

So, from a mixed corpus, again, a term-document matrix can be constructed in which *terms* from both text and images are represented. This matrix can then be decomposed using SVD and in the resulting space related terms will be close to each other. Both textual and visual queries, as well as multi-modal ones, can be mapped onto this space to find documents about a specific concept in any modality.

5 Concluding Remarks

In this paper, we have addressed the problem of cross-modal and multi-modal indexing. We have shown that multi-modal indexing can be regarded as just another case of multi-lingual indexing. Just like in cross language information retrieval and in spoken document retrieval, we are dealing with a set of documents and queries that cannot be compared in a trivial way because they differ in language or modality.

In order to be able to retrieve documents in one modality using a query in another modality, we need a suitable mechanism to map both query and documents to a common representation language. We have presented two methods for mapping documents in different modalities to the same common language:

1. deriving a bimodal dictionary
2. multi-modal indexing using LSI

Both methods use the fact that the co-occurrence of two terms (visual or textual) in a text is not purely coincidental. Both methods automatically derive the relationships between terms from a parallel (1) or mixed (2) corpus. Therefore, both methods heavily depend on the availability of such a corpus.

Since, corpus based methods have proven to be successful in both CLIR and SDR, and indexing images based on low-level image features works fairly well, we are confident that extracting bimodal representations from multi-media corpora may be useful for language based image indexing and retrieval.

References

1. Brachsler, M. and Schäuble, P. *Multilingual Information Retrieval Based on Document Alignment Techniques*, Proceedings of the second European Digital Libraries Conference, 1998.
2. Cascia, M. La, Sethi, S., Sclaroff, S., *Combining textual and visual cues for content-based image retrieval on the world wide web*, In: IEEE Workshop on content-based access of image and video libraries, 1998
3. Deerwester, S., Dumais, S.T., Harshman, R., *Indexing by Latent Semantic Analysis*, In: Journal of the American Society for Information Science, 41 (6), pp391-407, 1990.
4. Dumais, S.T., Landauer, T.K., Littman, M.L., Automatic Cross-Linguistic Information Retrieval using Latent Semantic Indexing, In: Proceedings SIGIR96, Workshop On Cross-Linguistic Information Retrieval, 1996.

5. Flickner, M., Sawhney, H., Niblack, W. Ashley, J., Huang, Q., Dom, B., Gorkani, M., Hafner, J., Lee, D., Petkovic, D. Steele, D. and Yanker, P. *Query by image and video content: the QBIC system*, In: Maybury, M.T. (ed.) Intelligent multimedia information retrieval, pages 7-22, 1997.
6. Forsythe, G.E., Malcolm, M.A. and Moler, C.B., *Least squares and the singular value decomposition* In: Computer Methods for Mathematical Computations, (Chapter 9), Englewood Cliffs, NJ: Prentice Hall, 1977.
7. Gevers, T. and Smeulders, A.W.M., *PicToSeek: A content-based image search engine for the WWW*, In: Proceedings of VISUAL'97, 1997
8. Hiemstra, D. and W. Kraaij, *Twenty-One at TREC-7: Ad-hoc and Cross-language track*, In: Proceedings of the seventh Text Retrieval Conference TREC-7, Nist Special Publications, 1999.
9. Hiemstra, D., *Multilingual domain modeling in Twenty-One: automatic creation of a bi-directional translation lexicon from a parallel corpus*, In: Peter-Arno Coppen, Hans van Halteren and Lisanne Teunissen (eds.), Proceedings of the eighth CLIN meeting, pages 41-58, 1998.
10. Jong, F. de, *Twenty-One: a baseline for multimedia retrieval*, In: Proceedings of the 14th Twente Workshop on Language Technology TWLT-14, pp 189-195,1998.
11. Kraaij, W., J. van Gent, R. Ekkelenkamp, and D. van Leeuwen, *Phoneme-based Spoken Document Retrieval*, In: Proceedings of the 14th Twente Workshop on Language Technology TWLT-14, pp 141-153, 1998.
12. Marsicoi, M., Clinque, L. and Levialdi, S., *Indexing pictorial documents by their content: a survey of current techniques*, In: Image and vision computing 15, pages 119-141, 1997
13. Netter, K. and F. de Jong, *Olive: speech based video retrieval*, In: Proceedings of the 14th Twente Workshop on Language Technology TWLT-14, pp 187-189, 1998.
14. Oard, D.W. and Dorr, B.J., *A Survey of Multilingual Text Retrieval*, Technical report TR-96-19, University of Maryland, http://www.ee.umd.edu/medlab/mlir/mlir.html
15. Smeulders, A.W.M., T. Gevers and M.L. Kersten, *Computer vision and image search engines*. In: Proceedings of the 14th Twente Workshop on Language Technology TWLT-14, pp 107-116, 1998.
16. Yang, Y. Carbonell, J.G., Brown, R.D., Frederking, R.E., *Translingual Information Retrieval: Learning from Bilingual Corpora*, Artificial Intelligence 103 (1-2), pp 323-345, 1998.

A Dissimilarity Measure for Query by Example Retrieval

Folco Banfi, Rolf Ingold
Institute of Informatics
University of Fribourg
Chemin du Musée 3
CH-1700 FRIBOURG
Fax: +41.26.300.97.31
{folco.banfi, rolf.ingold}@unifr.ch

Abstract. In this paper we present a method for computing the dissimilarity between a digital image and a sketch produced with a simple paint tool. Images are roughly segmented and region information (size, position, color and shape) is extracted. Multiple segmentation results are then obtained by iteratively merging pairs of regions. The dissimilarity is computed according to the region information. Experiments show that this dissimilarity measure can be used to perform similarity searches.

Keywords: digital libraries; image content analysis; content-based indexing/ retrieval.

1 Introduction

Over the last few years, the amount of digital images produced daily has been steadily growing, thanks to the availability of better image compression techniques, as well as cheaper scanners, digital cameras and storage devices. Furthermore, the increasing popularity of the Internet has led to a huge quantity of images available to the public in digital form.

In order to be useful, these images must be easily retrievable from the collections they are stored in. To achieve this goal, descriptive data must be extracted from the images; for large document spaces, this task is too much time-consuming to be performed by humans [1]. Efficient methods for extracting such image features, as well as methods for indexing and querying image databases, must be developed.

We present a work in which the database is queried using an incomplete sketch of the sought image (see Figure 1), a task which requires efficient (dis)similarity measures. In this paper we present a way of computing the dissimilarity between a sketch and a digital image based on local features extracted after segmentation. Features are stored in a hierarchical data structure.

Fig. 1. Examples of sketches, along with their target images

The context of our work is presented in Section 2, while the extraction of the image features is explained in Section 3. The dissimilarity measure is the subject of Section 4, while in Section 5 we list some experimental results. Conclusions and future developments are discussed in Section 6.

2 Looking for an Image

In order to search for an image in a database, some information about the images contained therein must be available. This information can be primitive (colors, shapes, boundaries, ...) or logical (semantic) [2]. Since logical information must generally be extracted by hand, current research focuses on primitive information (henceforth "features"), extracted either from the whole image [3][4][5] or after partitioning it, for example with a segmentation algorithm [6][7][11]. Progress in the extraction of features has led to similarity-based retrieval systems, in which images are ranked according to the similarity to a given query image, among which we can list QBIC [8], Photobook [9], PICASSO [6] and Blobworld [11].

Back in 1996, when we started to work in this field, the majority of the few available content-based retrieval systems were based on global features (average color, average texture, etc.), like in CANDID [12] and JACOB [14]. The discriminatory power of such features is limited, since details are in general lost.

We believe that, in order to obtain better retrieval results, the querying process should be as intuitive as possible. This is why we asked the users to query the database using hand-drawn sketches of the sought images. Our first experiments [20] with sketches depicting the whole target image showed that areas considered as less relevant by the users were drawn with less precision, generating sketches that weren't really similar to the target image. This is only natural considering that when presented with an image human beings tend to focus on a few areas of it [19]. This problem, along with the desire to speed up the sketch production process, led us towards incomplete sketches (i.e., sketches containing only the areas the user considered as relevant).

Sketches, which are produced using a paint tool, contain color blobs that must be compared to the database images' content. We decided to extract features after segmentation into regions, and to store several segmentation results in order to maximize the chances of finding regions that are similar to the blobs in the sketch.

Currently we suppose that the user is looking for an image which is in the collection, and that he/she remembers at least some parts of it or has a low-quality print of it. The sketch is made with a paint tool that allows freehand drawing but has a limited choice of tools (typically, only "pencil" and "bucket"). The sketch is done "quickly" (about one minute) and must not cover the whole available surface, what we call an "incomplete sketch".

3 Feature Extraction and Data Organization

In our system, images are segmented into regions. The regions are then organized in a hierarchical data structure: an image I contains n_I layers $(I = \{I_1, \ldots, I_{n_I}\})$. Every layer I_i represents a segmentation result and contains I_i regions.

$$I_i = \left\{I_i^1, \ldots, I_i^{I_i}\right\}$$

I_{i+1} is generated by merging exactly two regions of I_i, hence I_1 is the layer containing the most regions, while I_{n_I} contains the smallest number of regions. An example can be seen in Figure 2. A similar approach is used in [6].

Fig. 2. From left to right, original image and segmentation results for 1, 2, 3, 4 and 5 regions.

Layer I_1 is obtained by segmenting I into connected regions with the segmentation algorithm developed by Comaniciu and Meer [18]. For every extracted region, a set of features is then computed. These features are: the centroid, the size, the average color (in the L*u*v* color space [15]), and the shape. Shape is coded as an ellipse, whose axes correspond to the eigenvectors of the region's covariance matrix multiplied by the corresponding eigenvalues and normalized so that the ellipse's surface is equal to 1. Position of the region's centroid and region's size are normalized so that they lie between 0 and 1.

Generating a new layer I_{i+1} requires the selection of two regions of I_i that will be merged. To achieve this goal, we had to develop a dissimilarity measure d_{Reg} between regions. In our case, we want d_{Reg} to satisfy the following criteria:

- $d_{Reg}(I_i^j, I_i^k) = f(D_M(I_i^j, I_i^k), d_{Col}(I_i^j, I_i^k))$,
  where D_M is Mahalanobis' generalized distance [17] between the regions' geometric covariance matrices and d_{Col} is the euclidean distance between the average colors of the two regions in the L*u*v* color space.
- $d_{Reg}(I_i^j, I_i^k) \in [0, 1]$
- $(D_M(I_i^j, I_i^k) = D_M(I_i^j, I_i^l)) \wedge \langle d_{Col}(I_i^j, I_i^k) > d_{Col}(I_i^j, I_i^l)\rangle \Rightarrow d_{Reg}(I_i^j, I_i^k) > d_{Reg}(I_i^j, I_i^l)$
- $(d_{Col}(I_i^j, I_i^k) = d_{Col}(I_i^j, I_i^l)) \wedge \langle D_M(I_i^j, I_i^k) > D_M(I_i^j, I_i^l)\rangle \Rightarrow d_{Reg}(I_i^j, I_i^k) > d_{Reg}(I_i^j, I_i^l)$
- When two regions are totally dissimilar according to D_M or d_{Col}, d_{Reg} should not lie below a given value:
  $d_{Col}(I_i^j, I_i^k) = 1 \Rightarrow d_{Reg}(I_i^j, I_i^k) \geq \omega_{Col}, \omega_{Col} \in [0, 1]$
  $D_M(I_i^j, I_i^k) = \infty \Rightarrow d_{Reg}(I_i^j, I_i^k) \geq \omega_M, \omega_M \in [0, 1]$

The dissimilarity measure d_{Reg} we used is the following:

$$d_{Reg}(r_i^j, r_i^k) = \omega_M \cdot \tanh\frac{D_M(r_i^j, r_i^k)}{10} + \omega_{Col} \cdot d_{Col}(r_i^j, r_i^k)$$

Color being extremely important for merging regions belonging to the same object, since geometrically compatible regions can be totally unrelated, the weight associated to d_{Col} should be much bigger than the one associated to D_M. Experimentally, we set ω_M and ω_{Col} to, respectively, 0.1 and 0.9.

The two regions r_i^j, r_i^k which minimize d_{Reg} are merged, while all the other regions aren't affected. Due to the nature of d_{Reg}, new regions are not necessarily connected. This fact, despite being contrary to the usual definition of segmentation (like the one given in [16]), is not disturbing, since we believe that a non-connected cluster can represent a single entity (like a cluster of yellow flowers in a field). Allowing only connected clusters would be counter-productive (we would have to match every yellow spot in the sketch with every single flower in the image, which would increase computing time significantly). Once r_i^j, r_i^k are merged, the current segmentation result is stored in layer l_{i+1}. This process is repeated until the minimum dissimilarity between two regions of the current layer exceeds a threshold τ.

This method is used on both digital images and sketches. In the case of the digital images, τ is set to 0.1 (small enough to prevent completely unrelated regions from merging, see Figure 3) and only the last m layers are kept, since the information contained in the first layers is in general too detailed, if compared to that extracted from the sketch; in fact, it is not uncommon for l_1 to contain well over 100 regions. This way we obtain $I = \{l_{n_I - m}, \ldots, l_{n_I}\}$. For the sake of simplicity, in this paper we will consider that no image has more than m layers, hence $I = \{l_1, \ldots, l_{n_I}\}$, with $n_I \leq m$. In our experiments, m was set to 10. Sketches, on the other hand, are segmented using $\tau = 0.02$ (due to their different nature), and only their last layer is kept.

0.09 0.10 0.13 0.18 0.23

Fig. 3. Different segmentation results, along with the minimum dissimilarity between two regions. A threshold of 0.10 stops the merging process before completely unrelated regions begin to merge.

4 Comparing a Sketch With an Image

Comparison of a sketch S with a digitized image I returns a dissimilarity score $d(S, I)$, whose computation requires the computation of a dissimilarity $d_L(S, l_i)$ between the sketch S and a layer l_i of the image, which in turn requires the computation of a dissimilarity $d_R(S^k, r_i^j)$ between a region of the sketch S^k and a region r_i^j of the layer l_i.

The smallest dissimilarity score between the sketch and the image's layers $\{I_1, ..., I_{n_I}\}$ corresponds to $d(S, I)$.

$$d(S, I) = \min_i d_L(S, I_i)$$

Prior to the comparison between the sketch and the image's layers, all the dissimilarities $d_R(S^k, I_i^j)$ are computed and stored. Because of the few changes between layers (see Section 3), this task isn't too much time-consuming.

4.1 Comparison Between the Sketch and a Layer of the Image

The dissimilarity between the sketch S and a layer of the image I_i is computed using the following formula:

$$d_L(S, I_i) = \frac{\min_{\sigma, q}\left(\sum_{j=1}^{q} d_R(S^{\sigma(j)}, I_i^{\rho(j)}) \cdot size(S^{\sigma(j)}) + \sum_{j=q+1}^{s} p(S^{\sigma(j)}, I_i) \cdot size(S^{\sigma(j)})\right)}{\sum_{j=1}^{s} size(S^j)}$$

where d_R is the dissimilarity between a region of the sketch and a region of the layer, $(S^{\sigma(1)}, I_i^{\rho(1)}), ..., (S^{\sigma(q)}, I_i^{\rho(q)})$ are couples of regions whose dissimilarity is below a given threshold υ, σ is a permutation of $\{1, ..., s\}$, ρ is a function of $\{1, ..., q\}$ towards $\{1, ..., l_i\}$ (which implies that a region of I_i can be associated to only one region of S and vice versa) and $p(S^{\sigma(j)}, I_i)$ is a penalty attached to every region of the sketch such that the dissimilarity between it and every region of the current layer exceeds the threshold υ.

$$p(S^k, I_i) = \gamma \cdot \min_j d_R(S^k, I_i^j)$$

The penalty p is designed in such a way that sketches containing regions that are totally dissimilar to the regions in the image obtain higher dissimilarity scores. γ has been experimentally set to 1.5.

The dissimilarity $d_L(S, I_i)$ is normalized by dividing it by the surface covered by the sketch's regions in order to obtain comparable results even when different sketches are used.

The minimum dissimilarity is obtained by computing all possible solutions. Since all the region dissimilarities have been computed beforehand and are known, the number of solutions (hence the complexity) can be reduced by setting a low value of υ. In fact, if we set $\upsilon = 1$ (the maximum value taken by d_R), we will have $l_i!/(l_i - s)!$ possibilities; on the other hand, experiments have shown that if $\upsilon = 0.2$ less than 20% of the couples satisfy the condition, and in the worst case (every region of S has $\lceil l_i/5 \rceil$ regions of I_i that are similar to it) we will have to explore $(\lceil l_i/5 \rceil)^s$ possible solutions, a value significantly smaller. Table 1 shows the effect that can be obtained on the number of solutions by setting $\upsilon = 0.2$.

Table 1. Number of possible solutions for $s = 5$ and different values of υ.

solutions	$l_i = 5$	$l_i = 6$	$l_i = 7$	$l_i = 8$	$l_i = 9$	$l_i = 10$	$l_i = 11$
$\upsilon = 1$	120	720	2520	6720	15120	30240	55440
$\upsilon = 0.2$	1	32	32	32	32	32	729

4.2 Comparison Between a Region of the Sketch and a Region of the Image

The dissimilarity between a region of the sketch and a region of the image is a weighted sum:

$$d_R(S^k, I_i^j) = \omega_s \cdot d_s(S^k, I_i^j) + \omega_c \cdot d_c(S^k, I_i^j) + \omega_p \cdot d_p(S^k, I_i^j) + \omega_h \cdot d_h(S^k, I_i^j)$$

where d_s is the dissimilarity between the sizes of the two regions, d_c is the euclidean distance between their average colors in the L*u*v* color space, d_p is the euclidean distance between the regions' centroids and d_h is the dissimilarity between the regions' shapes. d_s, d_c, d_p, d_h all return values between 0 and 1 and $\omega_s + \omega_c + \omega_p + \omega_h = 1$; hence $d_R(S^k, I_i^j)$ is also between 0 and 1. While d_c and d_p are trivial, computation of d_s and d_h deserves some words of explanation.

4.2.1 Dissimilarity Between Regions' Sizes

Let us suppose that $s_1, s_2 \in [0, 1]$ are the sizes of the two regions to be compared. Such a dissimilarity measure f should, in our opinion, satisfy the following criteria:

- be bounded between 0 and 1;
- reach 0 if and only if $s_1 = s_2$;
- reach 1 if and only if s_1 and s_2 are totally dissimilar;
- grow in a monotonous way when moving away from the $s_1 = s_2$ axis, in any direction;
- given two pairs of regions whose size differences are the same, return a larger value for the pair containing the smallest regions.

These criteria led us to the following dissimilarity measure:

$$d_s(S^k, I_i^j) = \frac{|size(S^k) - size(I_i^j)|}{\delta + (1 - \delta) \cdot \max(size(S^k), size(I_i^j))}$$

δ has been set experimentally to $1/3$, so that small regions that are slightly different in size are not considered as too much dissimilar (see Figure 4)

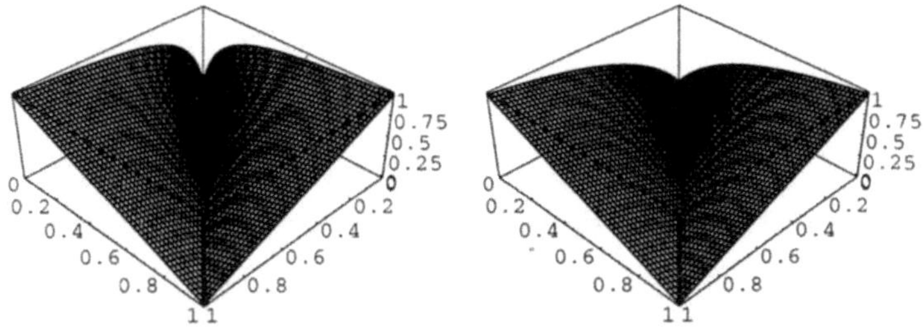

Fig. 4. With $\delta = 1/10$ (left) little differences between small regions generate high dissimilarity scores; $\delta = 1/3$ (right) avoids this problem.

4.2.2 Dissimilarity Between Regions' Shapes

As we said in Section 3, the shape of the regions is represented by an ellipse. The most intuitive way to compute the dissimilarity between two ellipses is compute the surface of the overlapping area when the centers are superposed. Let a_1, b_1 be the axis lengths of the ellipse representing S^k, a_2, b_2 the ones of I^j_i's axes and α the angle between the main axes of the two ellipses. The shape dissimilarity is computed as follows:

$$
\begin{aligned}
d_h(S^k, I^j_i) = 1 - min(&\\
&min(a_1, \sqrt{(a_2 \cdot \cos(\alpha))^2 + (b_2 \cdot \sin(\alpha))^2}) + \\
&min(b_1, \sqrt{(b_2 \cdot \cos(\alpha))^2 + (a_2 \cdot \sin(\alpha))^2}), \\
&min(a_2, \sqrt{(a_1 \cdot \cos(\alpha))^2 + (b_1 \cdot \sin(\alpha))^2}) + \\
&min(b_2, \sqrt{(b_1 \cdot \cos(\alpha))^2 + (a_1 \cdot \sin(\alpha))^2}))/ \\
&max(a_1 \cdot b_1, a_2 \cdot b_2)
\end{aligned}
$$

d_h is based on an approximation of the surface of the overlapping area.

5 Experimental Results

Experiments were performed by asking three subjects to draw sketches of an image using Photoshop with only the "pencil" and "bucket" tools enabled. The subjects had a printed copy of the image before them and were asked to draw only the areas they considered as relevant. Drawing of the sketch was done in a relatively short time (about one minute). Dissimilarity between the sketches and all the images in the collection was then computed, and the images were sorted according to it. The collection consisted of 685 images collected randomly from various Internet sites, all sharing the same orientation (landscape) and proportions (4x3). The features were extracted from the images scaled down to 160x120 pixels. For every sketch, we recorded the position obtained by the target image after sorting the collection according to the dissimilarity to the sketch.

Table 2. Position obtained by the target image when ranking the database images according to the dissimilarity with the corresponding sketch.

1st	Top 5	Top 10	Top 25	Top 50	Beyond
5	4	0	3	1	2

As it can be seen in Table 2, 9 images out of 15 ranked in the first 5 retrieved images (hence inside the top 1%), while 12 out of 15 were in the top 25 matches, which correspond to the top 4% of the database. Very good results were obtained also with extremely simple sketches (see Figure 5).

1st 2nd 3rd 4th 5th

Fig. 5. A sketch and the top five images of the collection sorted according to the dissimilarity to the sketch.

The cases where the image appeared outside of the top 25 depended on:

- poor quality of the sketch (colors not faithful to the image, badly drawn shapes, not enough relevant information); this is the worst possible situation, as there are no chances of retrieving the right image;
- segmentation problems: I_1 (the image's first layer) does sometimes suffer from undersegmentation. This is not a frequent case and it could be solved by replacing the Comaniciu-Meer algorithm with another kind of segmentation.

It should be said that the merging order can provoke disappointing results, too. In fact, despite the fact that the ω_M weight is remarkably smaller than the ω_{Col} one (see Section 3), sometimes the Mahalanobis distance dominates the color distance and provokes the merging of two regions that form a geometrically "good" region, even though their average colors are very different. This affects only the database images, since the threshold used to stop the merging process is quite large; furthermore, this problem is rather rare.

6 Conclusions and future work

In this paper we have presented a way to compute the dissimilarity between an incomplete sketch drawn with a simple paint tool and a digital image using local information extracted from both images. This measure depends on the dissimilarity between regions of the sketch and regions of the digital image. Regions are extracted by segmentation and are organized in a hierarchical way.

Our experiments, in which we sorted a 685-image collection according to the similarity between a sketch depicting one of the collection's images and the images themselves, showed that most of the time the target image can be found in the top 1% of the sorted collection. This suggests that our approach can be useful for query by sketch retrieval. More extensive testing, with a larger database, is needed in order to confirm this impression.

Furthermore, our results suggest that the idea of comparing a partial sketch with a digital image using region information extracted from a segmentation is a good one. Better results could be obtained by keeping the general framework and changing the segmentation algorithm that generates the first layer of the image data, the function that controls the region merging and/or the dissimilarity measure itself.

References

1. Philippe Aigrain, Hongjiang Zhang, Dragutin Petkovic, Content-Based Representation and Retrieval of Visual Media: A State-of-the-Art Review, Multimedia Tools and Applications, No. 3, pp. 179-202, 1996
2. Venkat N. Guivada, Vijay V. Raghavan, Content-Based Image Retrieval Systems, IEEE Computer, Vol. 28, No. 9, pp. 18-22, 1995
3. Suresh K. Choubey, Vijay V. Raghavan, Generic and Fully Automatic Content-Based Image Retrieval Using Color, Pattern Recognition Letters, Vol. 18, pp. 1233-1240, 1997
4. Anil K. Jain, Aditya Vailaya, Image Retrieval Using Color and Shape, Pattern Recognition, Vol. 29, No. 8, pp. 1233-1244, 1996
5. D.P. Huijsmans, M.S. Lew, D. Denteneer, Quality Measures for Interactive Image Retrieval with a Performance Evaluation of Two 3x3 Texel-Based Methods, Proceedings of International Conference on Image Analysis and Processing, pp. 22-29, 1997
6. A. Del Bimbo, M. Mugnaini, P. Pala, F. Turco, L. Verzucoli, Image Retrieval by Color Regions, Proceedings of International Conference on Image Analysis and Processing,, pp. 181-187, 1997
7. Colour Image Retrieval Fitted to "Classical" Querying, José Martinez and Sylvie Guillaume, Proceedings of International Conference on Image Analysis and Processing, pp. 15-21, 1997
8. Myron Flickner, Harpreet Sawhney, Wayne Niblack, Jonathan Ashley, Qian Huang, Byron Dom, Monika Gorkani, Jim Hafner, Denis Lee, Dragutin Petkovic, David Steele and Peter Janker, Query by Image and Video Content, the QBIC System, IEEE Computer, Vol. 28, No. 9, pp. 23-32, 1995
9. A. Pentland, R.W. Picard and S. Sclaroff, Photobook: Content-Based Manipulation of Image Databases, International Journal of Computer Vision, Vol. 18, No. 3, pp. 233-254, 1996
10. Alberto Del Bimbo, Pietro Pala, Visual Image Retrieval by Elastic Matching of User Sketches, IEEE Transactions on Pattern Analysis and Machine Intelligence, Vol. 19, No. 2, pp. 121-132, 1997

11. Chad Carson, Serge Belongie, Hayit Greenspan and Jitendra Malik, Region-Based Image Querying, Workshop on Content-Based Access of Image and Video Libraries, associated with the Conference on Computer Vision and Pattern Recognition, June 20, 1997, San Juan, PUR

12. Patrick M. Kelly, Michael Cannon, Query by Image Example: the CANDID Approach, Los Alamos National Laboratory White Paper, 1995

13. Virginia E. Ogle, Michael Stonebraker, Chabot: Retrieval from a Relational Database of Images, IEEE Computer, Vol. 28, No. 9, pp. 40-48, 1995

14. Marco La Cascia, Edoardo Ardizzone, JACOB: Just a Content-Based Query System for Video Databases, in Proc. ICASSP-96, 1996

15. R.W.G. Hunt, Measuring Color (second edition), 1992, Ellis Horwood, Chichester, UK

16. Nikhil R. Pal, Sankar K. Pal, A Review on Image Segmentation Techniques, Pattern Recognition, Vol. 26, No. 9, pp.1277-1294, 1993

17. Samuel S. Wilks, Mathematical Statistics, 1962, Wiley, New York, USA

18. Dorin Comaniciu, Peter Meer, Robust Analysis of Feature Spaces: Color Image Segmentation, Proc. IEEE Conf. on Computer Vision and Pattern Recognition (CVPR '97), pp. 750-755, 1997

19. Laurent Itti, Christof Koch and Ernst Niebur, A Model for Saliency-based Visual Attention for Rapid Scene Analysis, IEEE PAMI Vol. 20, No. 11, pp. 1254-1259, 1998

20. Folco Banfi, Rolf Ingold, Computing Dissimilarity Between Hand-Drawn Sketches and Digitized Images, in Proceedings of VISUAL99, 3rd International Conference on Visual Information Systems, Amsterdam, 1-4 June 1999

Content-based Video Retrieval by Example Clip on WWW

Xiaoming Liu Yueting Zhuang Yunhe Pan,

Institute of Artificial Intelligence, ZheJiang University
HangZhou, 310027, P.R.China
{Liuxm,Yzhuang}@icad.zju.edu.cn Panyh@sun.zju.edu.cn

Abstract. The similarity measure of two video clips is a key issue in video retrieval. In the development of our www-oriented video retrieval system, we propose a new model of video similarity. Comparing to existing algorithms, it proposes many influencing factors, such as order factor, speed factor, disturbance factor, etc, on the basis of human's subjectivity in visual judgement. Thus this algorithm embodies the degree of similarity completely and systematically. On the other hand, it has resolution adaptation because it can be applied to every level of video structure. In the retrieval system, it is used to process video query by example clip on the World Wide Web. This paper introduces this algorithm in detail and presents experiment results at the end of the paper.

1 Introduction

With the development of computer technique and the flourishing of multimedia applications, the study of multimedia information retrieval has received attention from more and more researchers ever since 1990's. In the image retrieval domain, many research fruits have been achieved ranging from feature extraction to retrieval model[7]. As to the video retrieval, researchers usually focus on how to represent the content of video for its abundance and complexity[1]. But the work on the retrieval subsystem, which is the key to embody the efficiency and performance of system, has been overlooked relatively. To satisfy the user's query by example video clip, we propose a new video similarity model.

Currently the video retrieval is carried out in three steps: 1) segment a video stream into a sequence of shot, and construct a hierarchical video structure based on shots; 2) extract the visual feature of keyframe, motion information and camera parameter, then store them into database; 3) the system process the user's query and return results to the user. Let us focus on step 3. Young-II Choi et. al[6] has proposed a video data model, which integrated visual feature and annotated keyword, and a video retrieval language on the semantic level. But this language is not convenient to the user. To facilitate the user to build up a query, a visual interface between the user and this language is still needed at end. Now the widely accepted query mode of video is keyword and example query. Keyword query can be implemented by traditional information retrieval technique as soon as video is annotated by text. Example query occurs when a user submits a video or image and wants to find similar video. In the area of measuring the similarity between videos, Dimitrova et. al[3] regarded the average distance of corresponding frames between two videos as similarity measure, and took the temporal order of the frames into account. Lienhart et. al [5]considered the video similarity from different hierarchies, and defined the measure by different degrees of aggregation based on either a set or sequence representation. But they did not consider other influences existed in the similarity measure.

In this paper, we introduce the design of our www-oriented video retrieval system and propose a new model to measure the similarity between videos. As known from the research of psychology[4], the human's visual judgement has a lot of criterion. The similarity measure has significance only if it can simulate human's judgement. So our model should comprise many sorts of influencing factors to embody the subjectivity of human. This paper is organized as follows. Section 2 introduces the construction of video database. The similarity model of video is detailed in section 3. Section 4 shows the experiment results. Finally we give the conclusions and future directions.

2 The Construction of Video Database

Video, a frame sequence on the temporal coordinate, contains abundant information. In our opinion, there are two sorts of features, the local and the global one, to represent the content of video. Firstly, the name, production date, director and some description texts of video belong to the global feature, which indicates the general attribution. On the other hand, a video can be regarded as a sequence of continuous shots. The structure of video, i.e. the relationship between the shots, manifests the manner used in the production of video. This attribution of style also pertains to global feature. Secondly, because video has a long temporal duration, every shot describes distinct content at different time. So such contents embody the local feature of video, which is not only of the temporal, but also of the space.

The architecture of our video retrieval system is shown in figure 1. In the video fetch subsystem, the spider automatically searches the videos on the internet, and fetches them to our local computer. So the video source of our system comes from the internet. While the system downloads the video, the web page contained it is also obtained. From this HTML file, we could use syntax parsing technique to extract some useful information about this video, such as what this video tells about, when it is produced, etc. Except for these, we have implemented the work to find the type of video from the URL string of the video source based on a predefined type tree. On the other hand, the close caption of video also provides some themes about the content of video[9]. All these three methods help us to annotate the video by the system, which is often done by the people previously. And we also store the URL string of the video the database, thus resolve the question of limited physical disk space, and regard internet as the video container and backup device.

The storage subsystem is designed by the theme of global and local feature. We do shot-boundary detection by the integration of color histogram and edge extraction[10], and construct the structure of scene according to semantic information. Within the shot, unsupervised clustering technique is used to do adaptive keyframe extraction[8]. After that, a video is represented as a hierarchical video structure consisted of the video, scene, shot and keyframe, which can be used not only in retrieval, but also to provide preview of video's content. According to the technique introduced in this section, it is clear that all the work of video indexing, to add a new video record to the database, can be automatically implemented by our system. It is really beneficial for acquiring a abundant, general testbed, and freeing the human's labor at the same time. After our system runs several days, we have obtained a testbed to test our retrieval algorithm.

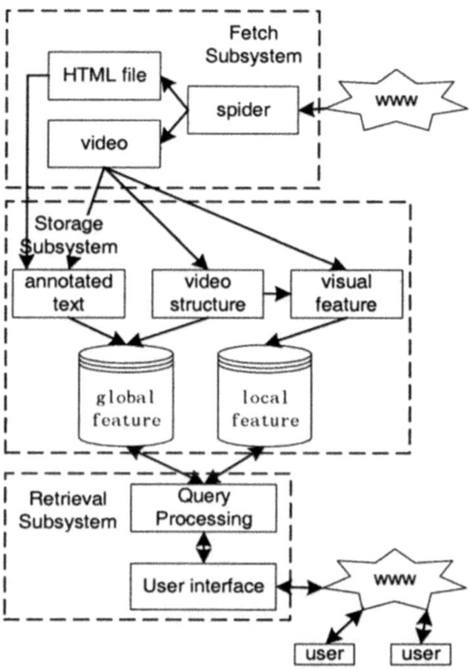

Fig. 1. The architecture of www-oriented video retrieval system

The construction of local feature database is based on the work of video organization. For every keyframe, we extract its visual features and storage them to database. Currently the visual features we utilize are color and texture. As to the color feature, we convert the color of every pixel from *RGB* space to *HSV* space, then calculate histogram using *H* and *S* weights in a two-dimension space, and finally regard 32 normalized values as features. We use the coarseness, contrast and direction defined by Tamura[2] to represent texture feature. Conclusively, the visual feature of every keyframe is represented as a vector, which is composed of 35 values.

From the database design, we can see that there are various features of video in our local database. Based on it, we can process the user's query and let him to preview all these videos through our video structure. When the user needs a certain video for sure, he can obtain it by the stored URL.

3 A Video Similarity Model

From the above work, the construction of video database has been completed. Firstly we introduce how the retrieval subsystem processes the user's query. At present we provided two query modes: keyword and example. Keyword query occurs when a user wants to find video by typing in some interested subjects, such as director, film name, etc. To process this style of query we will utilize traditional information retrieval technique based on the annotated global feature database. Example query is a representative retrieval mode in content-based retrieval, in which a similarity model and the distance calculation of feature vector are needed.

For the hierarchical structure of video, its similarity can be measured by its lower layer, such as scene and shot. Here we do it based on the similarity of shots. As mentioned before, the judgement of visual similarity is a behavior related to human subjectivity and manifested many criterions. So let us see the criterions used in the human's subjective judgement of video similarity.

- Visual similarity. Two similar videos should be similar in the lower visual feature, such as color, texture, etc. Usually it is a most important criterion. For example, in a video depicting the sun rising, the red keynote of color, the partition between the sky and the ground, and the circular shape are usually presented.
- Temporal order similarity. In two videos, some corresponding shots may have different temporal order though their contents are the same entirely. For example, the temporal order of three shots in $video_1$ is ABC, but in $video_2$ it is CBA, which means the first and last shot exchange their positions. This situation is named as the reorder of shots. Generally the human's preference about the temporal order will be manifested in the overall similarity measure.
- Temporal duration similarity. Some films may have editions of different lengths after montage, within which there is the case that a shot has a long temporal duration in the long edition while relative short one in the short edition. In fact it is the discrepancy of video content on speed. Generally when all the other conditions are the same, the more alike the speeds are, the more similar the videos are.
- Granularity similarity. Ideally when $video_1$ are similar to $video_2$, the same number of their shots has the correspondence of one-to-one. But the reality is not always the case. There will be a great diversity of the structure of correspondence, which influences the overall similarity measure.

Suppose the video submitted by user is named as *query video*, denoted as V_q, and segmented into n shots. So V_q is represented as

$$V_q = \{S_{q1}, S_{q2}, \ldots, S_{qn}\} \tag{1}$$

where S_{qi} means the ith shot of V_q. The temporal duration of S_{qi} and V_q is denoted as P_{qi} and T_q respectively. There are h video clips in the video database. Anyone of them is named as *database video* and denoted as V_d, which has m shots shown as:

$$V_d = \{S_{d1}, S_{d2}, \ldots, S_{dm}\} \tag{2}$$

The means of S_{di} and P_{di} are all the same as before. And any shot, S_{di}, is represented by a keyframe, f_{di}, within itself. The objective of video retrieval is to find several video clips similar to V_q from h shots and return to the user in a descending order of similarity. This process is carried out in four steps:

3.1 The construction of corresponding graph between similarity shots

For every shot of V_q, S_{qi}, , firstly we will find the most similarity shot in V_d respectively. Because we represent a shot as a keyframe, the similarity measure between shots converts to the one between images. Now let us consider the latter. We convert the final similarity value in the range [0,1]. 1 means they have the most similarity, and 0 means they do not similar entirely. Because the attributions of two vectors composed the visual feature vector are different, we should distinguish them while calculating the vector distance.

As to the color vector, we can use histogram intersection as follow for it has been normalized in the range [0,1] and defined over the same physical domain.

$$Similarity_{Color} = \sum_{i=0}^{31} Min(ColorHist_{f1}(i), ColorHist_{f2}(i)) \tag{3}$$

As to the vector-based feature representation, such as texture, every value does not in the same range. So we should convert all these values into the same range before the utilization of distance measure. By the example of *contrast* in texture feature, let us see how to use Gaussian normalization method. Suppose there are k keyframes, denoted as $Contrast_i(i=1\sim k)$, in video database. Firstly we calculate the mean m and standard deviation σ of $Contrast_i$, and then normalized k values into range [-1,1] by

$$Contrast'_i = \frac{Contrast_i - m}{3\sigma} \qquad i=0,..,k \tag{4}$$

As known from Gaussian distribution, the probability of $Contrast_i$ in the range [-1,1] is approximately 99%. So we should mapping the out-of-range values to either –1 or 1. The normalization of *coarseness* and *direction* is same as before. Then we can accumulate the distance of three values as the texture vector distance.

Now the respective distances of two vectors have been achieved. But only the color distance is in the range [0,1]. So we have to normalize the texture distance by Guassian normalization also. But after we use formula like (4) to get $similarity_{texture}$, the below liner transformation is needed for converting it to the range [0,1].

$$Similarity'_{Texture} = 1 - \frac{Similarity_{Texture} + 1}{2} \tag{5}$$

At last, we can get the similarity between two images according to two weights W_c, W_t as follow.

$$Similarity = W_c \bullet Similarity_{Color} + W_t \bullet Similarity'_{Texture} \tag{6}$$

After this section, for V_q and V_d, we can get a corresponding graph such as figure 2. The connected solid line means this correspondence has the most similarity for V_{qi}.

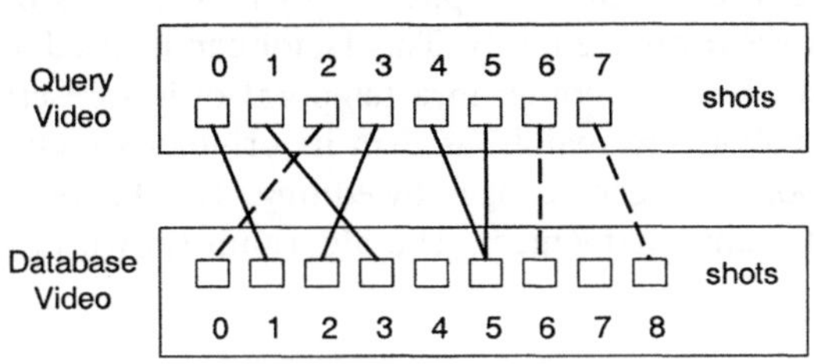

Fig. 2. A corresponding graph of similar shot

3.2 Clustering-based similarity distinguish

After above calculation, we have obtained $n \times h$ similarity value, $Similarity_i$, between shots. But some of these values are very small, which means some shots of query video can not find similar shot in some database video. If we still include these small values in the future calculation, the efficiency will be affected. So we want to distinguish a portion of values as similar values, others as no similar values, and remove the latter from the corresponding graph. But of these $n \times h$ values in the range [0,1] which value pertains to the similar values? In fact, it equals to find a *cut* value in the range [0,1], and regard all the values as similar ones if they are larger than *cut*, other as no similar ones if smaller. Traditionally it is implemented by predefining a threshold. But here we use a clustering based algorithm to get the *cut* value. *Cut* is one value of the ascending order sequence of $n \times h$ $Similarity_i$, which can divide the sequence into two portions and let the centroids of two portions have the largest distance. The formula is shown as follow:

$$cut = \{ Similarity_i \mid Max\,(\frac{\sum_{j=i+1}^{n \bullet h} Similarity_j}{n \bullet h - i} - \frac{\sum_{j=1}^{i} Similarity_j}{i}) \} \qquad i=1,2,....,n\ h \qquad (7)$$

Comparing to the method of predefining threshold, this algorithm has a high flexibility. It can dynamically distinguish what is similar or not according to current situation of shot similarity. It is intuitionistic because similarity is a relative conception in nature. In figure 2, we use dashed line to represent shot correspondence of no similarity. In the further calculation, their similarity values will be skimmed. On the other hand, if all the corresponding shots of V_d to V_q are no similarity, the V_d can not be the possible result returned to the user, which further facilitates the future calculation. The above two sections embody the visual similarity of human judgement.

3.3 Calculation of factors

Based on other criterions of human subjective judgement, we proposed several influencing factors to measure similarity.

The order factor is used to judge whether the corresponding shots of two videos appear in the same temporal order. As shown in figure 2, in database video, the corresponding shot of $shot_1$ and $shot_3$, $shot_3$ and $shot_2$, are in a reverse order comparing to query video. We use a value to represent the degree of this reversion in the range [0,1]. 1 means the temporal order of shot appears in two videos is the same. In the worst case, 0 means they are reverse entirely. This factor can be used to judge whether some shots of video have been compiled in a temporal order-preserving manner. A high value indicates the shots are mainly used in its original structure; a low one signals that the order of shots has been changed by editing. This factor embodies the temporal order similarity of human judgement. The algorithm shown in figure 3 calculates it.

The main theme of this algorithm is to calculate the percentage of reverse correspondences to all the ones based on the corresponding graph.

```
SimilarityShotOrder(Correspondence)
Input: Correspondence(i)=j : the shot i of query video has the most similarity with
shot j of database video. Correspondence(i)=-1 means shot i has no correspodence
   Output: [0,1]:the order factor of this correspondence graph
order= reOrder =0
submitShotIndex=queryShotIndex=0
while ( submitShotIndex < n ) {
  while ( Correspondence(submitShotIndex) = -1 )
    submitShotIndex=submitShotIndex+1
if(Correspondence(submitShotIndex)>=queryShotIndex)
    order=order+1
  else
    reOrder=reOrder+1
 queryShotIndex=Correspondence(submitShotIndex)
 submitShotIndex++
}
Return order/(order+reOrder)
```

Fig. 3. Algorithm for order factor calculation

After the calculation in section 3.2, suppose there are *n'* and *m'* similar shots in V_q and V_d respectively. We define the speed factor as follow:

$$Speed = 1 - \frac{\left| \sum_{i=1}^{n'} P_{qi} - \sum_{i=1}^{m'} P_{di} \right|}{\sum_{i=1}^{n'} P_{qi}} \tag{8}$$

In the range [0,1], this value describes the temporal duration discrepancy of similar shots in two videos. 1 means their duration is the same. The closer to 0 the factor value is, the more discrepancy their speeds have. It can be used to measure the discrepancy degree of different film editions in speed. This factor embodies the temporal duration of human judgement.

In the list of *n'* and *m'* corresponding shots, there are some shots do not have corresponding shot. For example, in figure 2, $shot_2$ of query video and $shot_4$ of database video pertain to this case, whose presentation indicates the discontinuousness of corresponding shots. So we utilize disturbance factor to measure the occurrence frequency of such shots. Suppose there are *x* and *y* such shots in *n'* and *m'* shots respectively. This factor is calculated as follow:

$$Disturbance = 1 - \frac{x+y}{n+m} \tag{9}$$

At last, we use the congregate factor shown as follow to measure the degree of one-to-many correspondence in corresponding graph. For example, in figure 2, the $shot_4$

and $shot_5$ of query video all correspond to $shot_5$ of database video. This factor indicates the discrepancy of depiction degree of similar shot in different video. The last two factors manifest the granularity similarity of human judgement.

$$Congregate = \frac{m'}{n'} \tag{10}$$

3.4 Calculation of overall similarity

Now we can calculate the overall similarity between V_q and V_d as follow:

$$Similarity = W_1 \bullet \sum_{i=1}^{n'} \left(\frac{P_{qi}}{T_q} \bullet Similarity_i\right) + W_2 \bullet Order + W_3 \bullet Speed + W_4 \bullet Disturbane$$

$$+ W_5 \bullet Congregate \tag{11}$$

where $W_1,\ldots,W_5$ indicate the preference of human regard to every judgement criterion. So the initial weights can be determined not only by the system, but also by the user through indicating his preference about these four criterions on the user interface. The fraction before $Similarity_i$ is the percentage of $shot_i$ duration to the video duration. This weight manifests that long duration shot will have more contribution to the overall video similarity, which is according to the mental judgement of human. When the calculation of similarity between V_q and any video V_d in database is finished, we can return several V_d to the user in a descensive order of similarity. Thus the query processing is finished.

From it we can see that our algorithm can be applied to any layer of the video hierarchical structure although we show its utilization in video similarity calculation. It is generally and has a resolution adaptation. For example, we can use this algorithm to calculate shot similarity based on the frame sequence of lower level. On the other hand, if a user submits an image as an example query, this algorithm can still work well because an image can be regard as a special form of video.

4 Experiment Results

Recently, We have implemented a video retrieval system, *vilib*, on personal computer. As shown in figure 1, this system is divided into two parts. Based on the SQL Server database, the storage subsystem is implemented with visual C++, and the retrieval subsystem is done with Active Server Pages. Our video database consisted of 5 hours of video from various sources. Within it, there are films such as "Forest Gump" and "True Lies", the series, several TV commercials, and live recordings. For each video clip, we calculate its features and storage them to database.

We test our system by submit several video clips as example query. One of the query results is shown in figure 4. In every row, we use keyframe to represent the video clip. The clip in first row is the one submitted by the user, and others are the similar clips found by our system. As we can see, in such a big video testbed, all these results are relevent to the query video and they listed in a descensive similarity order. Based on the human's relevance judgement, we get the *recall* and *precision* value for four example query, and show them in table 1. From it we can see the excellent performance of our system. We also observed that our algorithm is especially appropriate for small clip retrieval.

Fig. 4. A retrieval result of our system

Table 1. Retrieval performance of our system

Query	Video content	Recall	Precision
1	Gump talks with someone	0.9	0.84
2	Someone is playing Ping-Pong	0.7	0.6
3	Sun is rising	0.7	0.65
4	A man is walking on the meadow	0.8	0.6

5 Conclusions

The similarity measure of video clip is a key point in video retrieval. In this paper we presented a new similarity model. Comparing to existing algorithms, it proposes many influencing factors, such as order factor, speed factor, interfere factor, on the basis of human's subjectivity in visual judgement. So this algorithm embodies the similarity degree completely and systematically. On the other hand, it has granularity adaptation because it can be applied to every level of video structure. In the retrieval system, it can be used to process video query by example clip successfully, which is proved in our system. By our system, anyone can find interested video similar to an example clip on www, which is really a good application in multimedia information retrieval. At present, we are doing further work on the relevance feedback. Then the weights of every factor in this algorithm can be adjusted according to the user's feedback. In such a mechanism, this algorithm can embody the user's preference better and return better retrieval results to the user.

6 Acknowledgments

Our work was sponsored by the National Natural Science Foundation of China. We would like to thank Yi Wu, Yi Mao for fruitful discussions.

References

1. H. J. Zhang, J.H. Wu, D. Zhong and S. W.Smoliar. An Integrated System for Content Based Video Retrieval And Browsing. Pattern Recognition, Vol.30, No.4,1997.
2. H.Tamura, S.Mori, T.Yamawaki, "Texture features corresponding to visual perception," IEEE Trans. on Sys, Man, and Cyb, vol.SMC-8, no.6, 1978.
3. Nevenka Dimitrova and Mohamed Abdel-Mottaled, content-based Video retrieval by example video clip. In:SPIE 3022,1998.
4. S. Santini,R.Jain.. Similarity Matching. submited to : IEEE transactions on Pattern Analysis and Machine Intelligence. URL:ftp://vision.ucsd.edu/pub/simone/vision/SimPaper.ps.Z
5. Rainer Lienhart, Wolfgang Effelsberg, Ramesh Jain, "VisualGREP: A systematic methord to compare and retrieval video sequences". In: SPIE Vol.3312, p.271-282,1997.
6. Young-Il Choi,Yoo-Mi Park,Hun-Soon Lee,Seong-Il Jin, "An Integrated Data Model and A Query Language for Content-Based Retrieval of Video", In: Proceedings of 4th International Workshop, MIS'98, Istanbul, Turkey, p.192-198, Sept. 1998.
7. Yong Rui, Thomas S. Huang, Shih-Fu Chang, Image Retrieval: Current Techniques, Promising Directions and Open Issues, Journal of Visual Communication and Image Representation , 10, 1999.
8. Yueting Zhuang, Yong Rui, Thomas S.Huang. Adaptive Key Frame Extraction Using Unsupervised Clustering, In: proceeding of IEEE ICIP'98, Oct.1998, Chicago,USA.
9. Yueting Zhuang, Yong Rui, Thomas S. Huang, Applying Semantic Association to Support Content-based Video Retrieval, In: proceeding of Int.Workshop on Very Low Bitrate Video Coding,Oct.1998, USA.
10. Zhuang Yueting, Wu yi, Pan Yunhe. Video Catalog--A New Approach To Video Organization, accepted by Pattern Recognition and Artifical Intelligence.1999.

Digital Sound Watermarks Based on Improved Sinusoidal Analysis/Synthesis Model

Zhe Song[1] , Zhigeng Pan[2] , Jiaoying Shi[1]
[1] Department of Computer Science and Engineering, Zhejiang University
Hangzhou 310027, P.R.China
zsong@trident.com.cn; jyshi@cad.zju.edu.cn
[2] Department of Computing, Hong Kong Polytechnic University
Kowloon, Hong Kong
cszgpan@comp.polyu.edu.hk

Abstract. In this paper, a simple and efficient algorithm for designing digital sound watermark is presented. The main idea is by hiding the secret information in the amplitude of a certain frequency under 20Hz. This approach improved the sinusoidal analysis / synthesis model. Our approach can improve the sound watermark detection even after the signal has been compressed by MEPG lay-3. The experimental results illustrated the efficiency of our algorithm.

1 Introduction

Digital representation of media facilitates access and potentially improves the portability, efficiency, and accuracy of the information presented. Undesirable effects of facile data access include an increased opportunity for violation of copyright and tampering with or modifications of content [1]. Data hiding represents a class of processes used to embed data, such as copyright information, into various forms of media such as image, audio, or text with a minimum amount of perceivable degradation to the "host" signal, i.e., the embedded data should be invisible and inaudible to a human observer. Nowadays more attention has been paid to this research field. Recently, some methods have been taken employing cryptography and steganography [2].
There are some differences between cryptography and steganography in the way of hiding data [1]. Cryptography mainly focuses on how to translate a secret message into a version that can only be read by the key holder. Everyone knows that the secret message does exist. However, steganography cancels the existence of the secret message. No one knows the existence of the secret message except the sender and the receiver. Steganography gives more protection to the secret message and has been used widely.

1.1 Related Work

There are a lot of research results on data hiding in formatted text data, images, and

video [1,2,3], while little attention has been paid on data hiding in audio signals. Data hiding in audio signals is especially challenging, since the human auditory system operates over a wide dynamic range. Sensitivity to additive random noise is also acute [1]. In addition, compared to images and video, audio signals are presented by much less samples per time intervals. The sound watermarking, which employs steganography, is a piece of secret information hidden in the original sound and inaudible to the human hearing. More details of sound watermark features can be found in [2,3,4,5].
The prior research work on sound watermarking includes the followings. Stego[6], one of several widely available software packages, simply encodes data in the least-significant bit of the original sound. Although this technique can be easily implemented and needs no original sound to detect the secret message, it suffers from most of the typical digital processing. It also creates an additional problem of degrading audio quality. Statistic method [7,8] gives good results on the tightness with the original sound, however its information hiding capacity is too small. Bender et al. [1] propose several techniques for watermarking which are applicable to audio signals. They call the techniques spread-spectrum coding, echo coding, and phase coding.
Spread-spectrum [1,4,9,10,11,12] is a promising technology for data hiding. However, it often introduces perceivable distortion into the original sound. Boney et al. [10] propose a spread-spectrum approach for audio watermarking. They use a PN sequence that is filtered in several stages to exploit long-term and short-term masking effects of the human audio system. Bassia et al. [11] apply a very straightforward time-domain spread spectrum watermarking method to audio signals. Ikeda et al. [12] propose the use of band-limited random sequence to introduce further flexibility in the spread spectrum based audio data hiding.
In addition, Yardimici et al. [13] employ the phase-coding using all-pass filtering. Wang's watermarking solution [14] is a transformed permutation watermark, it permutes the host audio signal in time domain. Tilki et al. [15] developed a system for an interactive TV application where they embed information into the audio of TV signals.

1.2 Design Methodology of Sound Watermarking

There are two trade-offs for development of sound watermarking method. The first trade-off exists between the quantity of embedded data and the degree of immunity to original sound modification. By constraining the degree of original sound degradation, a watermarking method can operate with either high embedded data rate, or high resistance to modifications, but not both. As one increases, the other unavoidable decreases. While this can be shown mathematically for some data-hiding systems such as spectrum, it seems to hold true for all data-hiding systems. In any system, you can trade bandwidth for robustness by exploiting redundancy. The quantity of embedded data and the degree of original sound modification vary from application to application. Accordingly, different techniques are employed for different applications.
The second one is the trade-off between the watermark inaudibility and the resistance to compression. Compression is one of the most typical digital processing operations. To achieve inaudibility, most watermarking algorithms hide secret information by

adding message to those insignificant parts within the original audio signal. For example, spread-spectrum algorithm translates protected information as pseudo-noise of which amplitude must under sound masking threshold. However, most of audio compression algorithms mainly employ perceptual model and reduce the data redundancy by removing the insignificant part in original sound. In fact, using either statistical or perceptual method, the watermark is very likely the target of removal by lossy compression algorithms. If the watermark power added to original sound is large enough to avoid being removed by compression algorithm, then consumers may hear it. But when it decreases under sound masking threshold, it will be removed or destroyed by the compression.

We notice that when the amplitude of frequency is under 20Hz or beyond 20,000Hz, the modification to sound signals cannot be noticed because it locates in an inaudible area of spectrum. It brings the idea that if the watermark can be added to spectrum under 20Hz, the modification can be large enough to avoid being removed by compression algorithm without notice. The spectrum above 20,000 Hz is not considered since some typical signal processings will affect this region of spectrum significantly.

The basic idea of sound watermark designing in this paper is to select a specific frequency under 20Hz as the watermark frequency, and replace its amplitude –watermark amplitude (named for simplicity), with the protected information. We present a novel sound watermark-designing method. It is mainly based on the sinusoidal analysis/synthesis model, which is first put forward by [16]. Our approach can improve the sound watermark detection even after the signal has been compressed by MEPG lay-3.

The paper is organized as follows. In Section 2, an improved sinusoidal analysis/synthesis model is presented. In Section 3, we discuss the design of the sound watermarking in detail. In Section 4, we give some experimental results of the digital sound watermarking performance and the last section includes conclusion.

2 An Improved Sinusoidal Analysis/Synthesis Model

The first problem to be solved in designing the digital sound watermark is to replace the watermark amplitude with the secret information. There are several possible methods to perform this work. The first method is using digital filter to remove the amplitude of watermark frequency from the original sound, then add the watermark generated by the watermark amplitude. However, it is not an ideal way because the watermark frequency is very small compared with the sampling frequency. Such a filter will affect the amplitude of adjacent frequency significantly. Another method is to replace the amplitude of the watermark frequency with given amplitude after applying FFT to the original sound, and use IFFT to generate the watermarked sound. But this method gives obvious alias between adjacent frames in the synthesized sound. The best method to do the replacement is to synthesize the sound by using synthesis equation discussed below. The watermark amplitude is replaced with the secret information while synthesizing.

Based on a sinusoidal model [16], an analysis/synthesis technique is developed that characterizes sound signal in terms of the amplitudes, frequencies, and phases of the component sine waves. These parameters are estimated by applying a peak-picking algorithm to the short-time Fourier transform of the original sound. Rapid changes in the highly resolved spectral components are tracked by using a frequency-matching algorithm and the concept of "birth" and "death" of the underlying sine waves. For a given frequency track, a cubic phase function is applied to the sine-wave generator, whose output is amplitude-modulated and added to sine waves for other frequency tracks. The resulting synthesized sound preserves the general waveform shape and is nearly perceptually indistinguishable from the original.

The authors propose some extensions on sinusoidal analysis/synthesis model for sound watermark designing [17,18]. The first extension is the frequency-matching algorithm. Based on the matching rules, a couple of frequencies are matched when they are very near to one another within a small area of spectrum (Δ). It can be described as:

$$\left|f_n^k - f_m^{k+1}\right| < \Delta \qquad \text{(1-a)}$$

$$\left|f_n^k - f_m^{k+1}\right| < \left|f_n^k - f_i^{k+1}\right| \qquad \text{(1-b)}$$

$$\left|f_n^k - f_m^{k+1}\right| < \left|f_i^k - f_m^{k+1}\right| \qquad \text{(1-c)}$$

Where f_n^k is the nth frequency of the kth frame, f_m^{k+1} is the mth frequency of the k+1th frame. A specific frequency can only be matched once. If there is no frequency locating in the area of Δ, the frequency will be declared "birth" or "death".

In the previous sinusoidal model, the frequency-matching operation proceeds as follow (suppose f_n^k is the next frequency that will be matched in the k+1th frame):

First find the nearest frequency to f_n^k in the k+1th frame, if it is found (assume it is f_m^{k+1}), then f_m^{k+1} is a candidate of f_n^k match. Next, we check whether the nearest frequency to f_m^{k+1} is f_n^k. If not, f_n^k has to match some other unmatched frequency which is the second nearest to f_n^k within ($f_n^k - \Delta, f_n^k + \Delta$), otherwise, it will be declared "death" when no other frequency is found, and these finished the matching operation of f_n^k.

There may exist a case that will lead to improper "death" and "born" using this algorithm. Consider the following condition, f_m^{k+1} is the only unmatched frequency locating in ($f_n^k - \Delta, f_n^k + \Delta$), but f_n^k is not the best match of f_m^{k+1}, that means there exist another frequency which is closer to f_m^{k+1} than to f_n^k. If it is f_{n+1}^k, then f_n^k is declared "death". Furthermore, when matching f_{n+1}^k, the closest frequency to f_{n+1}^k is not f_m^{k+1}, assume it is f_{m+1}^{k+1}. Then f_m^{k+1} will be declared "born" and matches itself. In fact f_n^k and f_m^{k+1} should be matched according to matching rules.

To solve such a problem, a second scan should be added to the matching process. When a frame's matching work is over, a second scan will check (i) whether there exist adjacent "death" and "born" matches and (ii) whether they can match to each

other based on the matching rules. If they can be matched to each other, then remove them from the "death" and "born" pair, match them in this second scan.
The synthesis equation in sinusoidal analysis/synthesis model can be expressed as:

$$y(t) = \sum_{l=1}^{L} \sum_{t=0}^{T} A_l(t) \cos\theta_l(t) \tag{2}$$

Where $A_l(t)$ is the interpolated amplitude, and $\theta_l(t)$ is the interpolated phase. The $A_l(t)$ is linear interpolated:

$$A_l^k(n) = A_l^k + (\frac{A_l^{k+1} - A_l^k}{N}) \cdot n \tag{3}$$

Where A_l^k is the amplitude in the lth match of the kth frame and A_l^{k+1} is the amplitude in the lth match of $k+1$th frame. We substitute the amplitude interpolation equation by employing logarithmic method [10]. The equation can be written as:

$$A_l^k(n) = 2^{(1-\frac{n}{N})\log_2 A_l^k + \frac{n}{N}\log_2 A_l^{k+1}} \tag{4}$$

Logarithmic interpolation can give better simulation to the original sound.

3. Sound Watermark Designing

3.1 Representation of the Watermark

The digital sound watermark has many representation forms such as a segment of descriptive text or a segment of sound signal. In our method, the descriptive text is chosen as the representation form because of its less redundancy.
Besides the descriptive information of sound data owner, some other information about the data user can also be included in the watermark so that the unauthorized piracy can be traced to the right person. For the sake of giving more protection to the watermark, cryptography can combine with steganography usage. It means that watermark is first encrypted before being translated into a binary bit stream.

3.2 The Watermark Designing Algorithm

The basic idea of sound watermark designing is to analyze the original sound using FFT, and then select a frequency under 20Hz as watermark frequency. The watermark amplitude will be replaced with secret information, and the watermarked sound will be synthesized by using the sinusoidal synthesis equation described in Section 2.

The flowchart of the sound watermark designing and detection is shown in Fig. 1. The detailed algorithm is described below.

Step 1: Calculate short time Fast Fourier transform (FFT) of each frame. The ith FFT coefficient of the kth frame A_i^k can be represented as:

$$A_i^k = \sum_{n=0}^{N} s(n) * w(n) * \exp(-2\pi jni / N) \tag{5}$$

Where $s(n)$ is the original sound signal and $w(n)$ is the window function (the window length must be longer than 2 watermarking period). Compute the total energy of each frame, which will be used in step 2. The total power level of the *k*th frame E_k can be written as:

$$E_k = \sum_{n=0}^{N-1} [s(n) * w(n)]^2 \tag{6}$$

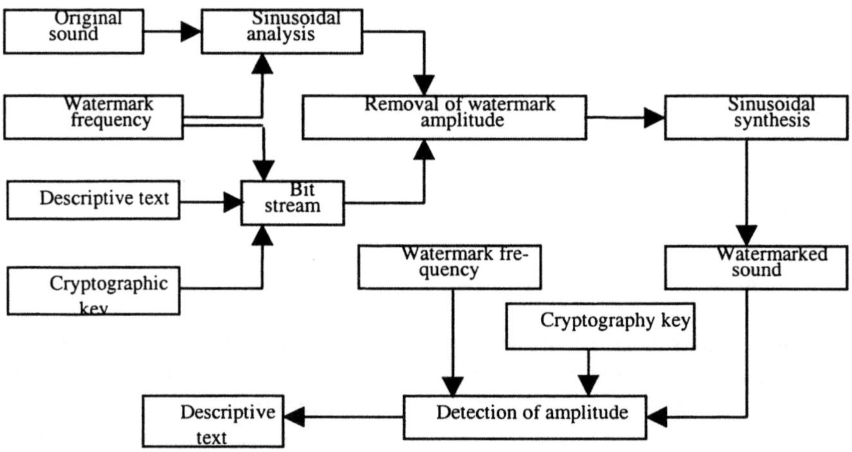

Fig. 1. Flowchart of watermark-design and detection

Step 2: Translate the watermark information into binary streams, each bit corresponding to a frame. The value of the sound watermark amplitude represents the binary bit '0' or '1'. If the bit corresponding to the *k*th frame is '0', the value of the watermark amplitude A_w^k is set to zero, otherwise A_w^k is set to:

$$A_w^k = \begin{cases} 3E \cdot \delta & 3E \cdot \delta > E_q \\ E_q & 3E \cdot \delta \leq E_q \end{cases} \tag{7}$$

E_q is a minimum energy threshold. δ is an experimental value. A_w^k should be set to a value which is big enough to avoid being removed by the compression algorithm. E_q is used to guarantee the value of A_w^k is big enough even if E is very small during a tranquil section of the original sound.

Step 3: Synthesize the watermarked sound using the interpolation equation in sinusoidal analysis/synthesis model described. The $\theta_l(t)$ is calculated as:

$$\theta_l(t) = a_0 + a_1 t + a_2 t^2 + a_3 t^3 \quad (8)$$

Where a_0 and a_1 are:

$$\begin{cases} a_0 = \theta_l^k \\ a_1 = 2\pi f_l^k \end{cases} \quad (9)$$

θ_l^k is the lth phase of the kth frame, f_l^k is the lth frequency of the kth frame. It is quite time consuming to compute a_2 and a_3, therefore, we use the equations:

$$\begin{bmatrix} a_2(M) \\ a_3(M) \end{bmatrix} = \begin{bmatrix} \frac{3}{T^2} & -\frac{1}{T} \\ -\frac{2}{T^3} & \frac{1}{T^2} \end{bmatrix} \cdot \begin{bmatrix} \theta_l^{k+1} - \theta_l^k - 2\pi f_l^k T + 2\pi M \\ 2\pi f_l^{k+1} - 2\pi f_l^k \end{bmatrix} \quad (10)$$

Where T is the total time of one frame, θ_l^{k+1} is the lth phase of $k+1$th frame, f_l^{k+1} is the lth frequency of $k+1$th frame. M is the integral of x, which is given below.

$$x = \frac{1}{2\pi}\left[\left(\theta_l^k + 2\pi f_l^k T - \theta_l^{k+1}\right) + (f_l^{k+1} - f_l^k)\pi T\right] \quad (11)$$

The phase of watermark frequency is set to zero because of its good performance in the watermark detection.

3.3Watermark Detection

The watermark detection can be easily implemented because only the watermark frequency and the window length are required. First apply FFT to the watermarked sound, then locate A_w^k based on the given watermark frequency. By comparing the value of A_w^k with $2E \cdot \delta$ (We do not use $3E \cdot \delta$ since the interference introduced in signal processing operation should be considered), we can decide the watermark bit '0' or '1'. By concatenating the bits into a stream, we can recover the information from it.

4. Implementation and Experimental Results

Some experimental results are given below. In the first experiment, the original sound is a piece of music, which lasts 9 seconds, the second is a model sound of hornpipe, which last 22 seconds. Both are sampled at 22.05kHz, 16 bits per sample. The watermark frequency is chosen at 10Hz, using 4096 points' FFT analysis. The little difference between (1.c) and (1.d) is generated by the frequencies leakage adjacent to watermark frequency. 2.a-2.d are the result of another example. We implement our algorithm using MATLAB 5.0 on a PC Pentium II 350. The MPEG layer-3 compression program is l3enc/l3dec [19].

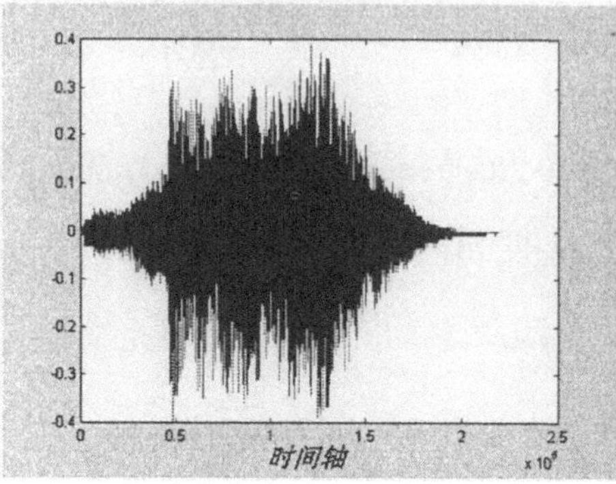

(1.a) Original sound

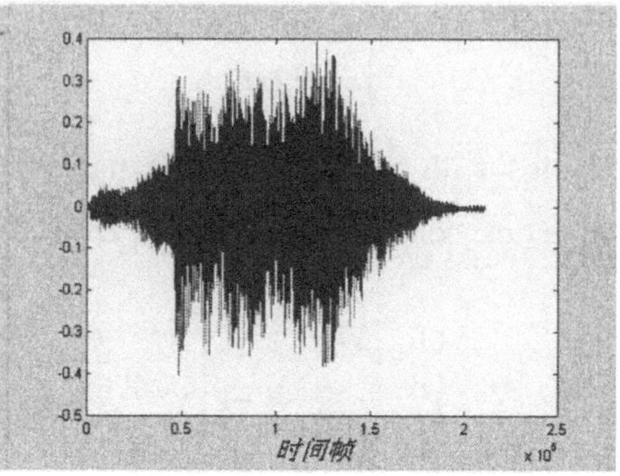

(1.b) Watermarked sound

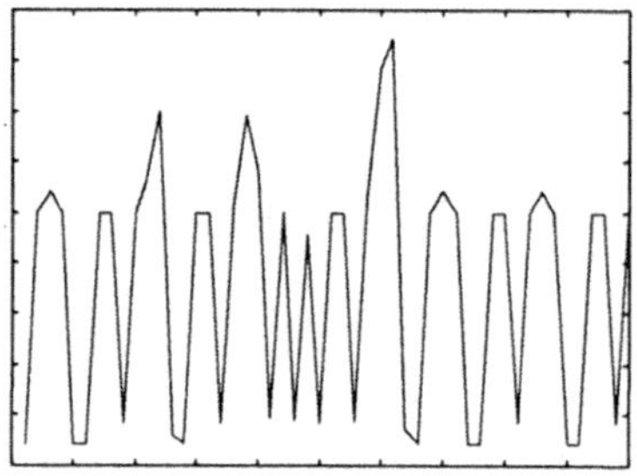

(1.c) Watermark amplitude of each frame

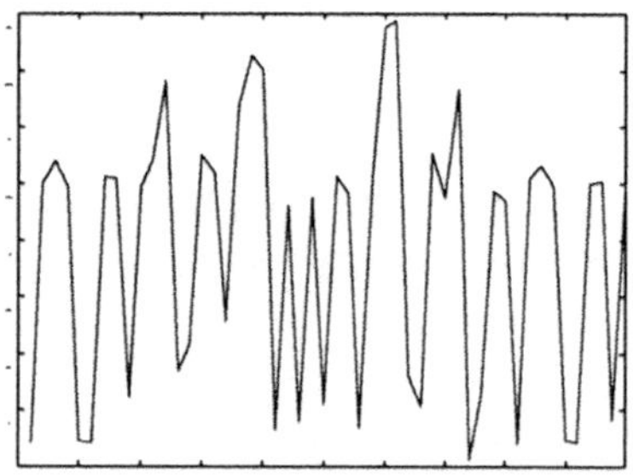

(1.d) Watermark amplitude of detection added to original sound

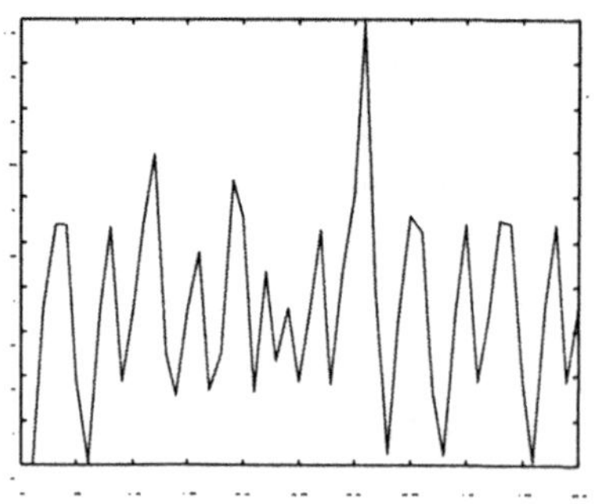

(1.e) Watermark amplitude detected after compression/decompression of MEPG lay-3

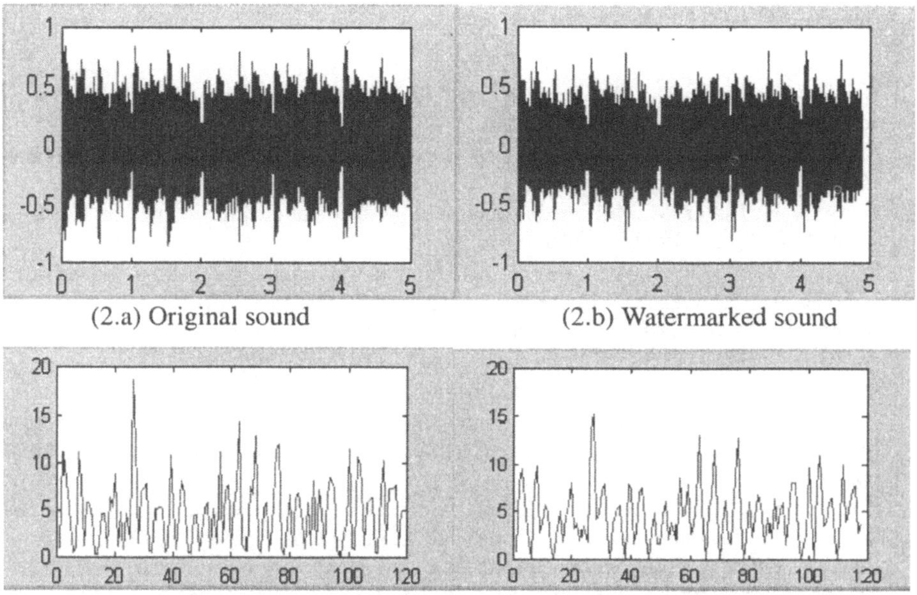

(2.a) Original sound (2.b) Watermarked sound

(2.c) Watermark amplitude of each frame (2.d) Watermark amplitude detected after compression/decompression of MEPG lay-3

Fig. 2. Experimental results of sound watermark performance

5 Conclusion

A novel method for designing digital sound watermark is presented in this paper. By hiding the information in the amplitude of a certain frequency under 20Hz, the lengthy computation of sound mask threshold can be avoided. In addition, it performs well even after the watermarked sound was compressed by MPEG layer-3 method. In the future, we will add error correction (e.g. Cyclic Redundancy Code, CRC) and self-clocking information into our watermark designing. The CRC will enhance the watermark resistance to modifications of the original sound signals. The self-clocking information will ensure that the embedded data can be recovered when only fragments of the original sound are available, e.g., if a sound bite is extracted from an interview, data embedded in the audio segment can be recovered. This additional self-clocking feature will facilitate automatic decoding of the hidden data, since there is no need to refer to the original sound.

Acknowledgements: This research work is supported by Natural Science Foundation of China. The authors would like to thank Dr. Qiong Zhang and Dr. Hui Xiang for interesting discussion and valuable suggestion. The authors would further like thank Dr. Simon Shiu, Ms. Kangkang Ying, and the anonymous reviewers for their comments and suggestions, which helped to improve the quality of the paper.

References

1. Bender, W.; Gruhl, D.; Morimoto, N. et al. Techniques for data hiding. IBM Systems Journal, Vol. 35(1996) pp313-320
2. Kahn, D. The history of Steganography. First International Workshop on Information Hiding, Cambridge, U.K.(May/June, 1996) pp1-5
3. Hartuma, F.; Kutter, M. Multimedia watermarking techniques. Proceedings of The IEEE , Vol87, No.7(July, 1999) pp1079-1107
4. Schyndel, R. V.; Tirkel, A.; Osborne, C. A digital watermark. Proceedings of the IEEE International Conference on Image Processing, Vol.2(1994)pp86-90
5. Jessop, P. The busniess cases for audio watermarking. Proceedings of IEEE Conf. on Acoustic, Speech, and Signal Processing, Vol.4(1999) pp2077-2078
6. Machado, R. "Stego", http://www.nitv.net/~mech/Romana/stego.html (1994).
7. Gruhl, D.; Bender, W. Information Hiding to Foil the Casual Counterfeiter. Second International Workshop on Information Hiding, Portland, Oregon, USA(April, 1998) pp1-15
8. Cox, I.; Kilian, J. Et al. A Secure, Robust Watermark for Multimedia. First International Workshop on Information Hiding, Cambridge, U.K. (May/June, 1996) pp183-205
9. Cox, I.; Kilian, J. Et al. Secure Spread Spectrum Watermarking for Multimedia. NECI Technical Report 95-10, NEC Research Institute, Princeton, NJ, (1995)
10. Boney, L.; Tewfik, A.H.; Hamdy, K.N. Digital watermarking for audio signals. Proceedings of IEEE Multimedia'96 (1996) pp483-490
11. Bassia, P.; Pitas, I. Robust audio watermarking in the time domain. EUSIPO'98, Rhodes, Greece.(Sept., 1998)
12. Ikeda, M.; Takeda, K.; Itakura, F. Audio data hiding by use of band-limited random sequences. Proceedings of IEEE International conference on Acoustic, Speech and Signal Processing, Vol.4(1999)pp2315-2318
13. Yaidimci, Y. et al. Data hiding in speech using phase coding. Eurospeech'97(1997) pp1679-1683
14. Wang, Y. A new watermarking method of digital audio content for copyright protection. Proceedings of ICSP'98, Vol.2 (1998) pp1420-1423
15. Tilki, J.F.; Beex, A.A. Encoding a hiding digital signature onto an audio signal using psychoacoustic masking. Proceedings of 7th Inter. Con. On Digital signal Processing Application & Technology, Boston(1996) pp476-480
16. McAulay, R.J.; Quatieri, T.F. Speech analysis/synthesis based on a sinusoidal representation. IEEE Trans. Acoust. Speech Signal Processing, Vol. ASSP-34 (1986) pp744-754
17. Song, Z.; Zhang, Q.; Shi, J.Y. An improved Sinusoidal Analysis/ Synthesis model. Proceeding of 7th China Computer Conference, China (1998) pp936-941
18. Song, Z. The presentation and application of audio signal feature parameters", Master Thesis, Zhejiang University, China (March, 1999)
19. Fraunhofer Institut Integrierte Schaltungen, "l3enc/l3dec: layer-3 encoder/decoder ", http://www.iis.fhg.de/departs/amm/layer3/sw/
20. Ptzmann, B. Information hiding terminology. In: R. Anderson, editor, Information Hiding, First International Workshop, Volume 1174 of Lecture Notes in Computer Science, Springer-Verlag, Berlin(1996) pp347-350

Video on Demand Servers: Storage Architecture with Disk Arrays

Putra Sumari[1], Madjid Merabti[1], Rubem Pereira[1]

[1] Distributed Multimedia System Group, Liverpool John Moores University, Byrom St., Liverpool, England, L3 3AF
{P.Sumari, M.Merabti, R.Pereira}@livjm.ac.uk

Abstract. The storage organisation of Video on Demand (VOD) servers is an important issue in the design of VOD systems. VOD servers are responsible for storing videos in disks and feeding them to users on request. The strategy used for storing movies in multiple disks affects the overall server performance, especially when a large number of concurrent streams are supported. The existing phase based striping method used in VOD server tends to lead to areas of unutilised disk. This spare area becomes more significant as the number of disks in the server becomes large. In this paper we propose the *Spare Phase Based Striping Method* to utilise the spare area and further reduce the waiting time. In this method, we group together the spare disk space of each individual disk into one large single spare area and use it to duplicate the most popular movies. We also present the *Half Reverse Phase Based Method* for use as a data layout in the spare area. This method guarantees a maximum waiting time for popular movies, reducing RAM dependency in comparison with the *Replication Scheme* and improving the average waiting time. We evaluate our scheme by carrying out a simulation study to compare it with other schemes, particularly with regard to the usage of RAM and the average waiting time.

1 Introduction

Video-on-demand(VOD) is a service that has received much attention recently[1-5]. It provides video services to users on request with interactive VCR functionality (play, forward, rewind, pause and resume). One important component of this application is the VOD server. VOD servers are responsible for video distribution to users. The design of such VOD server is not an easy task due to the nature of video data. Video data is voluminous and requires real time transmission[6]. An hour of MPEG II playback video with transfer rate of 4 Mbps requires approximately 1.8 GB of storage space. The real time characteristics of video data require the system to support Quality of Service (QoS) guarantees, which requires careful resource allocation, especially RAM, transmission bandwidth, and disk bandwidth. It is important that all the resources are utilised appropriately for achieving acceptable performance.

Efficient video data storage schemes, along with some striping technique, can help the server achieve good performance[2, 4, 7-12] and increase the number of concurrent users that can be supported with low waiting time. Striping techniques improve disk utilisation and enforce load balancing[4, 9-12]. One of the existing disk storage schemes is the *Phase Based Striping Method*, which views movies as groups of small segments and organise them into rows and columns. The physical storage in disk is in column major form. The first column is stored first followed by the second column and so on until the last column. The disk head begins reading at the first column and proceeds up to the last column before returning to the first column and repeating the process. Since the disk space is generally bigger in size when compared to the size of the stored movie, there usually exists some spare area at the disk.

In this paper we propose the *Spare Phase Based Striping Scheme* to utilise the spare disk space and further improve the waiting time. In this scheme we group together the spare disk space of each individual disk into one large single area and use it to duplicate the more popular movies. We present the *Half Reverse Phase Based Scheme* for storing movies in the spare area. Thus, popular movies will no longer depend on RAM for extra replicated streams, as in existing schemes. This scheme guarantees 50% reduction in waiting time for popular movies in comparison with the *Replication Scheme*. More RAM is thus made available for supporting other less popular movies. The deterministic waiting time for popular movies and the freed RAM created by the scheme will have a considerable effect on the overall average waiting time of the system. We conduct simulation study to look at the relation of RAM size and average waiting time.

The remainder of the paper is organised as follows: Section 2 reviews some related studies. Section 3 explains some existing disk striping method before presenting our proposed striping scheme. Section 4 is the description of the simulation study and results. Finally, section 5 presents some conclusions and future work.

2 Background and Related Studies

The VOD server is an important component of VOD systems. It can store a large number of digitised movies and serves requests for the same or different videos on demand. In other words, the VOD server accesses different parts of various movies and feeds them to different users requesting them. Due to the large volume of data associated with videos, it is necessary that the VOD server has multiple disks for storing movies. Disk arrays (RAID)[13, 14] and disk farms [9] are example of multiple disks systems. One method of storing movies in these types of multiple disks is using striping techniques[2, 11, 13, 14], which can be further divided into either fine-grained striping or coarse-grained striping. The striping method simply folds multiple disks address spaces into a single unified space seen by the host. This is accomplished by distributing consecutively logical units (called stripes) among the disks in round robin fashion. To play back the file, each disk in the array operates synchronously (i. e. each disk head is located at the same position and transfer data together). The striping on multiple disks exploits the transfer parallelism and also improves disk utilisation and load balancing, and hence increases the number of concurrent streams. Many existing allocation strategies available(i. e. contiguous, random, constraint) can apply the striping technique in order to deal with multiple disks. In [2], the striping technique with data interleaving on a disk array is used for their Per-storage device buffering technique. In [11], the *Random Duplicated Assignment* striping technique is introduced. It assigns pieces of each data to randomly chosen disks instead of striping a single copy across many disks. It resulted in smaller waiting time and lower disk and RAM requirements.

To further improve the performance of VOD services some efforts have focussed on combining the usage of RAM with striping techniques with the aim of increasing the number of concurrent streams and further reducing the waiting time[2, 9-11]. In [10] a comprehensive simulation on striping of 64 movies onto 16 disks supported by 4 GB RAM is discussed. It was shown that the use of the priority disk scheduling algorithm coupled with real time prefetching for buffer management offers the best performance. In [15], the special constraint allocation scheme called *Phase Based Method* is introduced. It stripes an entire movie onto a single disk in order to serve multiple users with guaranteed waiting time. This scheme divides the movies into segments of predetermined size and organises them in matrix form and physically stores them onto disk in column major form. An enhancement was presented in [9] by striping all segments onto multiple disks and distributing the segments evenly into different disks with the aim not to have the disks under-utilised due to their different popularity. They presented three different striping strategies with the aim to further reduce the waiting time. With support of 4 GB RAM, they simulated a large scale environment consisting of a 24-disk disk farm with 36 ninety minutes movies with different popularity.

3 Striping Method

In this section we first describe two of the commonly used strategies for storing videos in multiple disks: the *phase based striping method* and the *phase based striping with replication method.* We then discuss our proposed *spare phase based striping method.*

3.1 Phase Based Striping Method

The original phase based scheme [15] divides the entire movie into blocks and can be represented as matrix *(m x n)* as shown in figure 1a. The movie has *m*n* blocks (*m* rows and *n* columns). The matrix is physically stored on a disk in a column major form as in figure 1b. In column major form, the first column is stored first, followed by the second column and so on until the last column. The disk head will read the first column, which contains block *1*, up to block *(m-1)n + 1*, and then read the next column, which contains segment 2 up to segment *(m-1)n+2* and so on until the last column which contains segment *n* up to segment *mn*. Then reposition takes place where the disk head returns to segment *1* of the first column. The time taken for the disk head to read from segment *1* of the first column to segment *mn* of last column is known as a *phase time*. Phase time is also known as *cycle time*. The number of rows(m) is derived by

$$m = (D_{rate}/M_{rate}). \tag{1}$$

Phase time(T) is obtained by

$$T = (M_{length}/(D_{rate}/M_{rate})). \tag{2}$$

The number of columns(n) is derived by

$$n = (T * M_{rate})/d. \tag{3}$$

← *Phase time* →

$$\begin{pmatrix} 1 & 2 \ldots\ldots n \\ n+1 & n+2 \ldots\ldots 2n \\ 2n+1 & 2n+2 \ldots\ldots 3n \\ \cdot & \cdot \quad\quad \cdot \\ (m-1)n+1 & (m-1)n+2 \ldots\ldots mn \end{pmatrix}$$

(a)

← *Phase time(T)* →

$$\left[(1,n+1,\ldots,(m-1)n+1),\ (2,n+2,\ldots,(m-1)n+2),\ \ldots\ ,\ (n,2n,\ldots,mn) \right]$$

(b)

Fig. 1. General case for phase based method

Symbol	Meaning of symbol
m	Number of rows
n	Number of columns
d	Segment/block size
$D_{capacity}$	Disk capacity
D_{rate}	Disk transfer rate
M_{rate}	Movie display rate
M_{length}	Length of movie
N_{disk}	N disks
N_{movie}	N movies
T	Phase time

Fig. 2. Meanings of symbols used

This scheme stores the entire matrix on a single disk and columns are retrieved consecutively from disk. There is no overhead for the disk seek and latency times. Thus the main I/O disk overhead is the transfer time. With this scheme m different streams can be supported concurrently. Details of interactive VCR operation for this scheme can be found in[15]. This scheme requires three buffers of size $m*d$ to operate. The first two buffers are used for a double-buffering scheme and the third is for storing the first column in order to give time for the disk to make reposition at the beginning of column 1 after reading column n.

VOD servers that support a large number of movies must rely on several disks. It uses phase based striping methods to store movies in multiple disks. Phase based striping represents movies in matrix form as shown in figure 3a. In this example two movies are used with each one divided into a (3 x 5) matrix The first movie is shown by segments 1, 2, ... , 15 and the second movie is shown by segments a, b, ... , o. The segments in each column are distributed evenly onto multiple disks in round robin manner as in figure 3b. In this example the segments are striped into a two-disk configuration where each has bandwidth of three segments per second. Every second, six segments(three segments from each disk) are read and sent to the network.

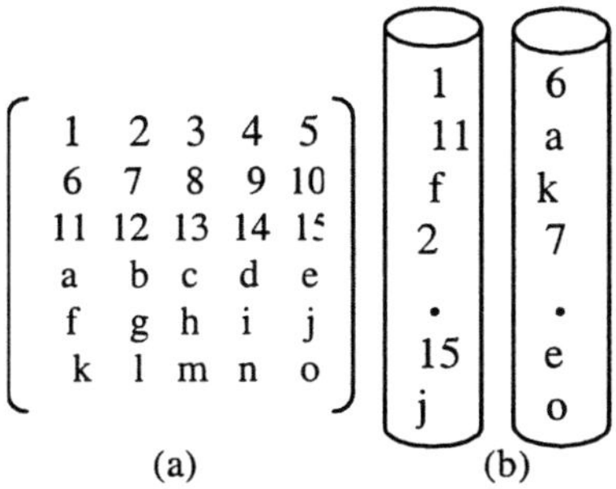

Fig. 3. The phase based striping.

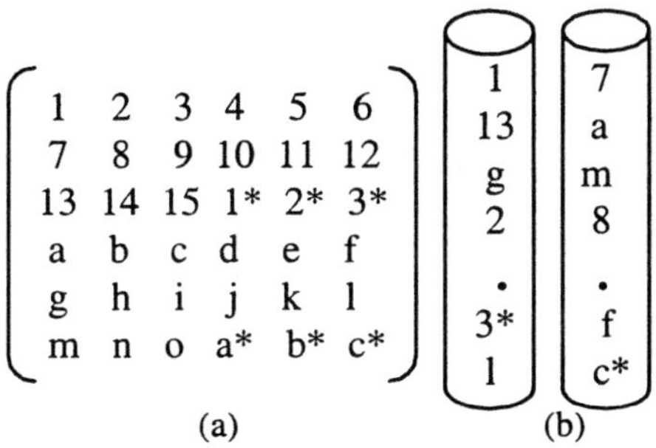

Fig. 4. The phase based striping with replication

3.2 Phase Based Striping with Replication

The phase based striping method described above offers regular starting of videos at fixed intervals and limits the maximum waiting time of new users to phase time. A further enhancement[9] is achieved by replicating a few segments at the second half of the last row as in figure 4a. By replicating some segments (shown by asterisks) starting at the middle column, the disk is only required to travel half of the phase time, to encounter segment 1 and initiate a new playback(known as replicated stream). This scheme cuts the waiting time by 50%. Note that this increases the number of columns while the number of rows remain fixed. This leads to longer phase time(6 seconds instead of 5 seconds without replication). The waiting time, however, is limited to 3 seconds. In order to support each replicated stream, RAM of the size of half of the row is required. This RAM is called sustainable playback RAM.

The striping of segments under this scheme is shown in figure 4. The example shows two movies, each divided into (3 x 6) matrix. The first movie is shown by segment 1, 2 up to segment 3* and the second movie is shown by segment a, b, up to segment c* (shown in figure 4a). The segments of each column are distributed evenly on multiple disks in round robin manner as shown in figure 4b. In this example the movies are striped onto a two-disk configuration where each disk have transfer rate of three segments per seconds. So at every second six segments (three segments from each disk) are read and sent to the network. The advantages of this scheme are that it reduces the average waiting time by around 50% and replicated streams can be started whenever sufficient RAM is available.

3.3 Spare Phase Based Striping with Replication

Disks can also be represented as a set of rows and columns and furthermore the capacity of a disk normally exceeds the size of the movie. Since the number of rows of the movie is equal to the number of rows of the disk, the number of columns of the movie will be manually smaller than the number of column of the disk. The remaining columns are left as spare area. For example let $D_{capacity}$ = 2.25 GB, D_{rate} = 75Mbps, M_{rate}=4Mbps, d = 4 Mb and M_{length}= 60 minutes. Each movie has 18 rows(m=75/4) and 200 columns(n= 3600/18). A disk with 2.25 GB can have n_{new} = 250 columns:

$$n_{new} = (D_{capacity}/d)/m. \tag{4}$$

and 18 rows. 50 columns out of 250 are not being used. With N_{disk} disks, N_{disk} * 50 columns are wasted. If there are ten disks then about 4.5 GB of disk storage is being wasted (equivalent to two movies storage).

The disk head cannot read the spare area of the disk due to the reposition factor. The disk head has to return to the first column after reading the last column of the movie. Hence the spare area becomes unavailable for use. The total spare area become significant as the number of disks increases. Thus it is important the spare area be used. The spare area can be made available by the following scheme. We increase the number of columns of the movie to be equal to the number of columns of the disk and decrease the number of rows of the movie. The new number of row m_{new} of the movie is derived by

$$m_{new} = [(M_{length} * M_{rate})/d] / n_{new} . \tag{5}$$

1	2	3	4	5	6	7	8
9	10	11	12	13	14	15	16
a	b	c	d	e	f	g	h
i	j	k	l	m	n	o	p
5	6	7	8	1	2	3	4
13	14	15	16	9	10	11	12

(a)

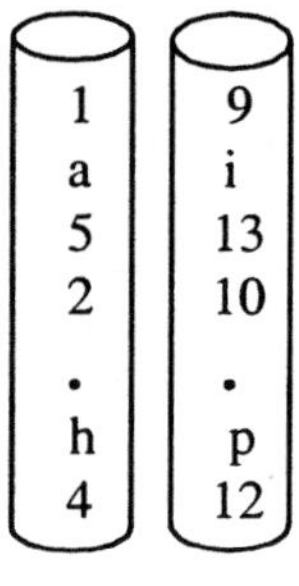

(b)

Fig. 5. Spare phase based striping method

5	6	7	8	1	2	3	4
13	14	15	16	9	10	11	12

Fig. 6. Reverse phase based method

This will leave the spare area as empty rows instead of columns. This spare area then can be used for other purposes and in this paper we propose the use of this area to further reduce the waiting time(figure 5). Figure 5a shows two movies, each divided into (2 x 8) matrix after adaptation to the new scheme. The first movie is shown by segments 1, 2, .. , 16 and the second movie is shown by segments a, b, .. , p. This first movie, which we identified as more the popular movie is duplicated and stored in the spare area. This proposed new data layout is called *reverse phase based method* for use in the spare area. In this layout the first half and the second half of the same movie are switched which is shown in figure 6. Figure 6 shows an example of a movie with 15 segments. We see that the first segment is stored starting at the middle row. In figure 5a the last two rows of the matrix contains duplication of movie stored in reverse phase based method.

In figure 5b, we show the segments are striped across two-disk configuration. The total number of movie that can fit disks generally satisfy equation (6).

$$N_{movie} = [(D_{rate} * N_{disk})/d] / m_{new} \tag{6}$$

In the previous example we can have each movie with 15 rows and 240 columns instead of 18 rows and 200 columns.

4 Simulation Study

In order to carry out the evaluation and comparison of these three strategies in terms of their mean waiting time and the size of RAM required, three separate simulation have been conducted. We use five Seagate Baracuda 4LP[18] with 2.25 GB of storage and 75 Mbps minimum transfer rate. We use five 60 minutes movies with MPEG-II 4 Mbps transfer rate. We assume the server has a large common buffer with capacity 0.5 GB. The detail of each simulation is as follows:

(1) The phase based striping simulation. Each movie is divided into 18 rows and 200 columns. There are 3600 segments each 4 Mb in size. Five movies are striped onto five disks. The phase time is 200 seconds(3.3 minutes). There is no RAM for sustainable playback storage

(2) The phase based striping with replication. Each movie is divided into 18 rows and 206 columns. The number of columns is slightly larger than the first case due to replication. Five movies are striped onto five disks. The phase time is 206 seconds(3.4 minutes). The size of RAM for the sustainable playback storage is 0.5 GB.

(3) The spare phase based striping scheme. Each movie is divided into 15 rows and 240 columns. The number of columns is increased to 240 and the number of rows is decreased to 15. This leads to extra storage space of 1.8 GB. This extra storage is used to duplicate the most popular movie in reverse phase based method. Overall six movies, including the duplicated one, are striped onto five disks. The phase time is 240 seconds(4 minutes). The size of RAM for sustainable playback storage is 0.5 GB.

The simulation was developed using the CSIM/C++ discrete event simulation language[16]. The popularity of each video is determined based on Zifpian distribution[9, 10, 17] and the distribution to characterise the users arrival rates is based on Poisson distribution. The popularity of each video can be varied by changing the distribution factor, z and similarly for the arrival rate by changing the Poisson distribution factor, p. We adopt the default value of [9] for the Zipfian and Poisson parameter which are z = 0.2 and p = 8. The total number of incoming users is 1000.

Since the amount of RAM is limited we only allowed two top movies to be replicated for a new playback. The results are as follows.

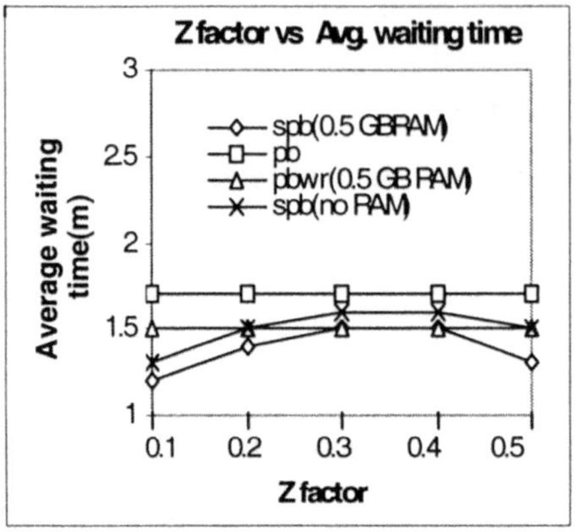

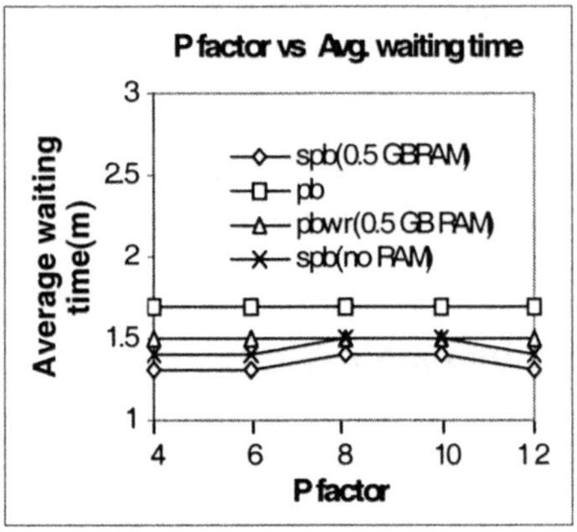

Fig. 7. Access pattern Vs avg. waiting time. **Fig. 8.** Arrival rate Vs avg. waiting time

Figure 7 shows the effect of different access pattern to the movies against the average waiting time. Overall, figure 7 shows that our scheme, (the spb striping) gives the lowest average waiting time compared to other schemes(phase based stripping(pb) and phase based striping with replication(pbwr)) for all access pattern studied. In the case of default value(z = 0.2) with 0.5 GB RAM the average waiting time for phase based striping with replication(pbwr) scheme is reduced by 10%. This is because the most popular movie is duplicated in the disk. The duplication used reversed phase based method. This means that every replicated stream created from the most popular movie is guaranteed. Furthermore, RAM, which is thus freed from the most popular movie, is used for replicated stream of other less popular movies. This affects the average waiting time. Figure 7 also shows us that at z with 0.1, the smallest average waiting time occurred. This is because as the z parameter becomes smaller, the access pattern becomes more localised with a small number of movies receiving most of the accesses. The pattern is quite similar when z is 0.5 where one of the movies is being accessed the most and is duplicated at the spare area.

The most interesting result in figure 7 is that the average waiting time of spare phase based striping(spb) with no RAM is less than the phase based striping with replication(pbwr) with 0.5 GB RAM.

Figure 8 shows the effect of different users arrival rate on the average waiting time. The results are similar to those in figure 7. Overall, the spare phase based striping(spb) gives the smallest waiting time when compared to other schemes. Again, the average waiting time of spare based striping(spb) with no RAM is less than the average waiting time of phase based striping with replication(pbwr) with 0.5 GB RAM.

5 Conclusion

In this paper we have presented a new scheme for storing videos in VOD servers using disk arrays to further improve the waiting time and reduce disk space wastage. We called this *spare phase based striping scheme.* In this scheme we group together the spare disk space of each individual disk into one large single spare area and use them to duplicate the most popular movies. We also present the *half reverse phase based scheme* for use as a data layout in the spare area. This method guarantees a maximum waiting time for popular movies, eliminating RAM dependency as found in *replication scheme* and hence affecting the system average waiting time. The scheme also eliminates RAM dependency on most popular movies. Simulation study has been conducted and comparison has been made regarding the relation of RAM usage and average waiting time for the new and existing schemes. The average waiting time is reduced by 10 %. Interestingly, the average waiting time using *spare based striping* with no RAM is less than the average waiting time of *phase based striping with replication* with 0.5 GB RAM.

References

1. Chang, E., Garcia-Molina, H., : Reducing Initial Latency in Media Servers. IEEE Multi media. (1997) 50–61
2. Martinez-Garcia, A., Conde, F., Vina, A., : Efficient Memory Management in VOD Disk Array Servers Using Per-Storage-Device Buffering. Proceeding of the 24th EUROMICRO Conference, Sweden. (1998)
3 Liao, W., Li, V. O. K., : The Split and Merge(SAM) Protocol for Interactive Video-On-Demand. IEEE Infocom. (1997)
4 Barnett, S. A., Anido, G. J. : Performability of disk-array vifro servers. Multimedia System. 6(1998) 60-74
5 Sumari, P., Merabti, M., Pereira, R., : Video-on-demand Server: Strategies for improving performance. IEE Proceeding Software. 146(1999) 33-37
6 Gemmel, D. J., Vin, H. M., Kandlur, D. D., Rangan, P. V., Rowe, L. A. : Multimedia storage server: A tutorial. Computer. 28(1995) 40-49
7 Chen, P. M., Lee, E. K., Gibson, G. A., Katz, R. H., Patterson, D. A. : RAID: High Performance, Reliable Secondary Storage. ACM Computing Surveys. 26(1994) 146-185
8 Chen, P. M., Lee, E. K., : Striping in a RAID Level 5 Disk Array. SIGMETRIC 95 Otawa, Ontario, Canada. (1997)
9 Chua, T. S., Li, J. Ooi, B. C., Tan, K. L., : Disk stripping Strategies for Large Video-on-Demand Servers. The fourth ACM International Multimedia Conference, Boston, MA. (1998)
10 Freedman, C. S., Dewitt, D. J., : The SPIFFI Scalable Video-on-Demand. ACM SIGMOD. (1997)
11 Korst, J., : Random Duplicated Assigment: An Alternative to Striping in Video Servers. The fifth ACM International Multimedia Conference. (1997)
12 Mourad, A. N., : Issues in the design of a storage server for video-on-demand. Multimedia Systems. 4(1996) 70-86

13 Ganger, G. R., Worthington, B. L., Hou, R. Y., Patt, Y. N., : Disk Arrays, High performance, High Reliability Storage Subsystem. IEEE Computer. (1998)

14 LI, V. O. K., Liao, W., : Distributed multimedia system. Proceeding of the IEEE. 85(1997) 1063-1108

15 Ozden, B., Rastogi, R., Silberschatz, A., : On the design of a low cost video-on-demand storage system. Multimedia System. 4(1996) 40-54

16 Schwetman, H., : CSIM18 – The Simulation Engine in Mesquite Software, Inc, Austin, TX. (1997)

17 Zipf, G. K., Human Behaviour and the Principle of Least Effort. Addison Wesley, Reading, MA. (1949)

18 Seagate Baracuda ALP family product specification. URL:http://www.seagate.com.

Object Carousel Simulator for Broadcast Applications

Christian Fuhrhop, Andreas Kraft, Ralf Kubis

Fuhrhop@fokus.gmd.de, Kraft@fokus.gmd.de, Kubis@fokus.gmd.de
GMD FOKUS
Research Institute for Open Communication Systems
Kaiserin-Augusta-Allee 31
10589 Berlin
Germany

Abstract. This paper describes an object carousel simulator developed for the testing of broadcast applications. It gives a short overview of the specific characteristics of a broadcast environment and describes tools developed to simulate them. Results and experiences from using a sample application, originally developed for end-user trials in the ACTS project IMMP, in the simulated broadcast environment conclude the paper.

Introduction

The Integrated Multimedia Project - IMMP - was part of the European Commission's research programme ACTS and primarily studied the integration of interactive multimedia services and system architectures addressing both residential and business environments with a focus on investigating and using IP/ATM connections. The project was extended to gather experiences with broadcast applications.

To achieve this, a set of tools for simulating the behaviour of applications in a broadcast environment were developed and a weather forecast application from the IMMP end-user trials was selected and adopted for broadcast use and tested with various configurations of the broadcast object carousel.

The following sections describe the specific characteristics of a broadcast environment and of an object carousel, the toolkit produced to experiment with different broadcast configurations and the measurements done with the weather forecast application.

Broadcast Environment

Providing applications for a broadcast environment requires more than taking existing web applications and to broadcast them. The characteristics typical for this environment, like bandwidth restrictions, delay, delay-jitter, limited available content, no upstream traffic (i.e. no return channel) and limited input devices must be taken into account when authoring new applications or converting existing ones for broadcast use.

The most obvious problem from the end-users point of view is the unpredictable order in which content arrives. In network based applications the content usually arrives roughly in the same order in which it is requested and when multiple connections are used in parallel it can be reasonably expected that smaller files will arrive before larger ones. If a page uses small navigational icons and if these are requested first, the icons will usually be visible before any other content of the page, allowing the end-user to navigate within the page or to other pages before other content like background images or decorative images is downloaded. Also, if a page contains only very small images, it can be assumed that the page and its content will be displayed quickly.

In a broadcast environment, files only become available when they are sent by the broadcaster, regardless of the size of the files. This means that even small icons, which would appear within seconds in a network application, remain unavailable for half a minute or longer. This forces the developers of broadcast applications to take this into account when designing applications and ensure that, for example, there is a text-based 'stand-in' for all graphical content.

It is also necessary to control the broadcast parameters to ensure optimum performance of the application. In the example mentioned above, sending the bitmaps for the navigational items shortly after sending the page description file (e.g. HTML, MHEG-5[1] or Java) would make it likely that the files will be available to the browser shortly after the browser requests them.

There are a number of additional characteristics that influence the behaviour of an application from the end-users point of view. Since it is not practical to test and optimise an application in an actual broadcasting environment, it is necessary to provide the developer with tools to experiment with these characteristics in a simulated broadcast environment.

To be able to simulate the parameters that influence the behaviour of an application correctly, it is first necessary to understand the operation of a broadcast object carousel (OC).

Object Carousel Characteristics

In a digital TV broadcast environment, files belonging to an application are usually stored and broadcast with a DSM-CC Object Carousel (OC). The OC consists of entries, which are either directories or files.

The main structuring mechanism in object carousels are OC modules. An OC module contains one or more entries. Each entry is part of exactly one OC module. The entries in an OC module are in sequential order, each entry preceded by a header containing a unique identifier for the entry and the length of the entry. To retrieve a file from the OC module, the client needs to parse the OC module until the requested entry is reached.

---

[1] Final form representation format according to ISO/IEC 13522-5 [1]

The size of an OC module is not limited in the DSM-CC standard, but specific profiles often define a maximum size for practical reasons. The UK DTT [2] profile, for example, limits the size of modules that contain multiple entries to 64 KB, larger modules are only allowed if they contain only one file.

From an application point of view, the main effect of a module is that receivers cache at least one module, so all files belonging to an OC module are directly available to the client.

During the broadcast, the object carousel usually sends the OC modules in sequential order, although this is not required and it is possible to interleave data blocks, mostly to keep large files from blocking the broadcast stream exclusively for a long time. Interleaving is also used in some application domains where clients can receive a data stream at full bandwidth only for a short period of time and need a pause to process the data before being able to receive the next block of data.

The priority of modules in the OC is handled by giving the modules different latency times. These determine how often a module gets repeated during one turn of the object carousel. Modules with short latency times will have a higher priority and be repeated more often than other modules [9].

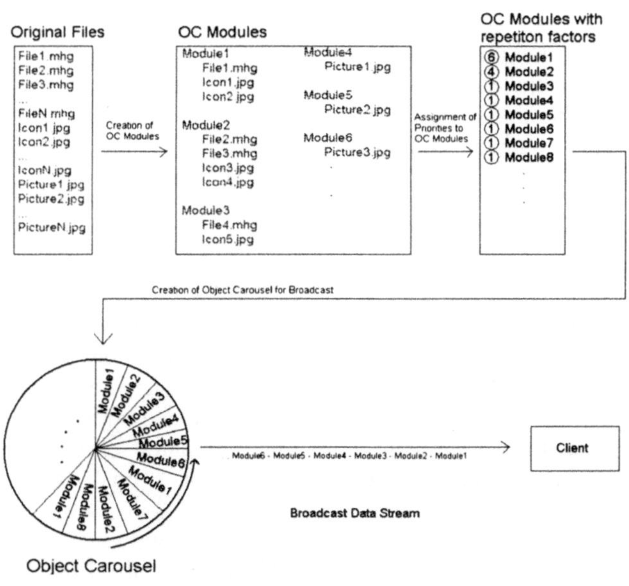

Fig. 1. Creation of Object Carousel from original application files

The main broadcast parameters that influence the behaviour of an application on the client side are therefore the grouping of files and directories in modules, the order of these modules and their priorities.

Broadcast Simulation Toolkit

Developing applications and testing them directly in an actual broadcast environment is usually neither feasible nor reasonable. This makes it necessary for the author of applications to use a simulated broadcast environment, for testing the applications and optimising the OC configuration. While methods to improve the delivery of applications in a broadcast environment exist [10], these are not application specific and will just increase the overall speed of the application. Further speed can be gained by tailoring the application to the broadcast environment, which is something only the application developer can do, and for which he needs support.

A set of tools has been developed in IMMP for this purpose. The toolkit consists of three components: a generic broadcast sender and two receivers, one for MHEG-5 applications and one for the testing of HTML and Java applications using HTTP, the transfer protocol typically used in the WWW. The special receiver for MHEG-5 applications was developed because GMD FOKUS has developed an MHEG-5 engine and it was considered convenient to integrate this function directly into the engine to simplify the testing of MHEG-5 applications and allow access to internal broadcast parameters to provide additional information for the developer. Since the MHEG-5 engine also supports the HTTP protocol, it would have been possible to use the HTTP broadcast client for this as well.

To simulate the behaviour of a broadcast application, usually only one sender and one client is used, although it is possible to use multiple sender and clients to simulate the use of multiple channels and the broadcast of mixed format applications (e.g. MHEG-5 and HTML) to different clients in one broadcast stream.

Structure of the Toolkit

The broadcast simulation uses UDP packets that are sent over a local network to transmit information to the client. This method has been chosen instead of a direct implementation of a DSM-CC OC because it allows a greater amount of low-level control while sharing a sufficient number of characteristics with real broadcast packets (i.e. connectionless transmissions, no guarantee of correct packet order, possibility of dropped packets, multicast capability), making a more realistic simulation of a broadcast environment possible.

The structure of the simulation environment is as follows: The broadcast sender reads the OC configuration file and fills the OC from the local file system according to the order, priority and module structure in the configuration file and starts to send the data from the OC as UDP packets. For MHEG-5 applications, the MHEG-5 engine can receive files from the data stream directly.

HTTP based browsers use a broadcast client that acts as a proxy. It accepts HTTP requests and retrieves the requested files from the broadcast stream and returns them to the browser. This client usually runs on the receiving system to simulate the behaviour of an HTTP browser on a set-top box.

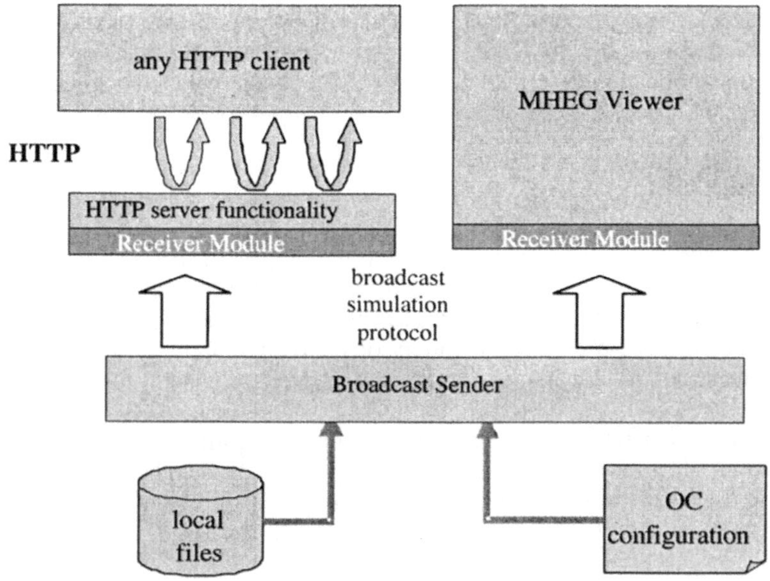

Fig. 2. Interaction of the toolkit elements

Broadcast Simulator Functionality

The sender tool is designed as an interactive application that allows the end-user to test the behaviour of an application under broadcast conditions and to optimise the performance by testing various configurations of the OC. To achieve this, the OC simulation must be easy to use and allow fast modifications of the configuration of the order, priority, and structure of modules. In addition, typical parameters of an broadcast environment, which can not be derived from the OC, like bandwidth and packet loss rate, have to be configurable.

The packet loss rate is one reason why the toolkit is not based on an actual DSM-CC data stream, which is designed to be reliable. Protocols that run over local networks rarely lose packets and DSM-CC implementations usually do not allow the artificial construction of an unreliable connection. In a broadcast environment however, lost packets have a noticeable effect, since the client has to wait for the next broadcast of the missed packet or potentially the whole file[2], causing a significant delay until the content can be presented to the end-user, making it necessary to allow their simulation.

In addition to allowing the modification of the parameters mentioned above, the sender tool shows information about the current OC configuration like the time needed for a complete turn of the OC or the actual order in which the modules are broadcast after taking initial order and priority into account. Furthermore, the format

[2] In some applications the content of the files may vary over time and may have changed until the next turn of the carousel, therefore requiring a new fetching of the whole file.

of the configuration file has been chosen to allow the simple creation of different broadcast configurations by external programs. For example, the test configurations used for the application described below have been generated from spreadsheet data.

Usage Examples of the Toolkit with a Real-Life Application

This section describes a sample application developed in the course of IMMP. The main objective of this ACTS funded project was to provide an integrated service platform that allows business and residential users to access the same interactive services. For the end-user trials, a variety of interactive applications from areas such as tele-education, advertising and commerce as well as general information services were developed.

The project was extended ior half a year in order to gather further experiences with broadcast applications andot be able to give recommendations and guidelines regarding the design of such applications. Because of this, one of the application used in the IMMP end-user trials was selected and adapted for broadcast use.

A Sample Application

The application chosen was a weather forecast application, giving a forecast for the European countries and selected cities in those countries for the next five days. The reasons for selecting this applications from the various applications developed for IMMP were that the content was scaleable, the application was considered to be of sufficient general interest to be broadcast, it requires no return channel and it is possible to simplify the interaction to be used with a remote control. In addition, weather forecasts are a typical part of existing teletext services, which led to the assumption that an enhanced weather application would be a typical part of an enhanced teletext [4] and the results from experimenting with this application would give insights that are applicable to other future interactive enhanced digital TV services.

The application is written in MHEG-5, because the aim of the application development in IMMP was not only to provide the applications for the trials but also to undertake experiments with regard to the design of MHEG-5 applications and evaluate the feasibility of this representation for interactive services.

MHEG is an ISO/IEC International Standard suite which specifies a coded representation of final-form multimedia/hypermedia information objects, for their interchange as units within or across systems, by any means of interchange, from storage devices to telecommunication and broadcast networks [1] [2] [5]. MHEG objects define the structure of multimedia/hypermedia presentations in a system-independent way. The objects describing the application look and feel and the behaviour are transmitted from a server to the client and executed by an MHEG engine.

With MHEG-5 as well as with other multimedia representations a similar functionality from the applications point of view can be provided in different ways which might differ with regard to the system performance, storage capacities needed, and navigation methods.

Fig. 3. Screenshot of the Weather Forecast Application

Experiment Description

After adapting the existing application for broadcast[3] , tests were performed with various configurations of the object carousel. The behaviour patterns of three end-users were defined and their actions repeated with the application broadcast under different OC configurations. The three simulated end-users were a 'local' user, looking up only the forecast for his home city, a 'surfer', looking up the wind conditions on coastal towns in his country and a 'traveller', looking up the weather in various countries for an upcoming journey. Care was taken that the influence of user reaction time and random starting point in the turn of the OC was minimised.

Result, Gained Experiences, and Guidelines

The results of the experiments are shown in figure 4. Detailed descriptions of the experiment and the configuration used can be found in IMMP deliverable D67 [7].

As a summary of results, the biggest improvement in speed, from configuration 1 and 2 to configuration 3 comes from the grouping of files belonging to one page in a module with the page description files. An additional improvement in speed, although

---

[3] A detailed description of the changes made to the original application to adopt it for digital television broadcast environment can be found in [6].

smaller and only noticeable for some end-users was achieved from configuration 3 to 6 to configuration 7 and 8 by grouping the city specific forecast files according to countries. This improved access for users selecting multiple city forecasts for one country.

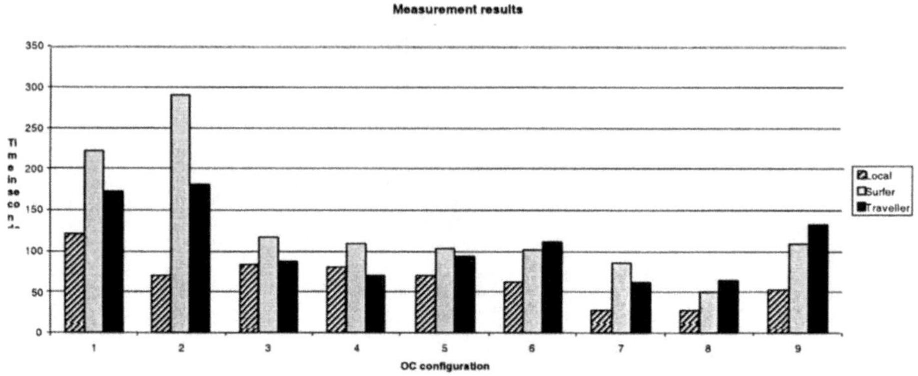

Fig. 4. Measurement results from experiments

The simplest way to speed up the retrieval of a specific page, is to send it more often by increasing its priority (i.e. lowering its latency time). In the experiments, modifying the priorities of files led to unexpected results. While it was assumed to be the easiest way to improve performance on the client side for specific end-users, the improvements were smaller than expected and the behaviour was often counterintuitive. This is mostly because increasing the priority of some files increases the amount of data that has to be sent before one turn of the OC is completed, increasing the wait time for all files with lower priorities. Unless an end-user accesses only files that have a high priority, the faster access to high priority files is often cancelled by the slow access to low priority files. OC configurations 3 to 6 use identical module structures and orders, and differ only in the prioritisation. While the priorities were selected in a way that was intended to benefit the local user, the actual improvement for this user was small. More significant however, even though the size and therefore the turn time of the OC varied by more than 350% for the configurations, the change in performance for the end-user was comparatively small.

Modifying the order of files can improve the performance if typical usage patterns are known. In the examples above, the order of files remained basically unchanged and the files are arranged in such a way that the city specific information is broadcast approximately 20 seconds after the country specific information, so if a user wants to see the forecast for a specific city and takes less than 20 seconds to select this city from the country page, as was the case in our experiments, the city forecast will appear without an inconvenient delay. Between configuration 8 and 9 the only change was the order of modules from the arrangement given above to a random order of modules, leading to a significant decrease of performance.

The most important guidelines that derive from this are:

- The most important content of a page should be displayed quickly. The best way to ensure this is to group it in one OC module together with the page description. Because the size of an OC module is often limited, it is necessary to keep the important content as small as possible or to provide low resolution versions of the content to include in the OC module.
- High priorities should only be given to small modules to avoid large increases to the amount of data broadcast per OC turn. The effects of modifying the priority are difficult to predict, leading to the need of experimentation.
- The files need to be arranged in the OC in such a way that is supportive to typical usage patterns, so that anticipated content requests can be fulfilled 'just in time". Technical restrictions of the client equipment, and the way in which page descriptions are parsed and executed, also influence the order in which the files need to be put in the OC.
- There are some interdependencies between the application design and the OC configuration. The most obvious is the need to access content in the same module as the file requesting the content before content in other modules, because otherwise data already retrieved may be needed to be retrieved again if the client cache only holds a small number of modules.

Conclusion and Outlook

Developing and experimenting with the broadcast simulation toolkit has shown that special care has to be taken when authoring or adopting applications for a broadcast environment. Not only have broadcast specific characteristics like limited bandwidth, asynchronous data availability and limited input devices to be taken into account when generating the application, but care also must be taken to adjust the parameters of the actual broadcast to ensure acceptable performance for the end-user.

Since the effect of changing the broadcast parameters is sometimes difficult to predict, the set of tools to allow interactive modification and simulation of broadcast parameters provides a needed and efficient way to improve the performance of applications in a broadcast environment.

Experiments have also shown that it is generally not sufficient to take a web based application and put it in a broadcast OC. In most non-trivial cases it is necessary to adopt the application specifically for broadcast needs and create an application specific OC configuration, unless serious performance degradation is acceptable.

Further work in the IMMP project included the development of a XML based version of the weather application and further broadcasts experiments with that version. In addition, mixed format configurations of the object carousel will be used, where the broadcast stream contains XML, MHEG-5 and Java implementations of the application, sharing the same content [8]. This will allow experimentation with broadcast applications in an environment with heterogeneous receivers.

References and Resources

This section comprises a list of references to important documents. A list of resources in the WWW with further information with relevance for the digital television concludes this paper.

References

[1] ISO/IEC IS 13522-5, Information technology — Coding of Multimedia and Hypermedia information — Part 5: MHEG Subset for Base Level Implementation.
[2] Digital Terrestrial Television MHEG-5 Specification, version 1.04
[3] EN 50221 Common Interface Specification for Conditional Access and other Digital Video Broadcasting Decoder Applications
[4] ETS 300 706, Enhanced Teletext Specification
[5] Klaus Hofrichter: MHEG 5 - Standardized Presentation Objects for the Set Top Unit Environment, in Proceedings of the European Workshop on Interactive Distributed Multimedia Systems and Services, Berlin, Germany, 4-6 March 1996, Springer Lecture Notes in Computer Science, 1996
[6] Klaus Hofrichter, Andreas Kraft: An Approach for Script-based Broadcast Application Production, ECMAST'99, 4th European Conference on Multimmedia applications, services and techniques, Spring 1999
[7] IMMP Deliverable D67 - Suitable IMMP applications in digital television broadcasting environment release, May 1999
[8] IMMP Deliverable D68 – Evaluation of forthcoming technologies for digital television broadcasting
[9] John F. Buford, Chetan Gopal - Latency Budgets for MHEG-5 Delivery in DAVIC Systems over ADSL Networks, in ACM Multimedia 97 - Electronic Proceedings, November 8-14, 1997, Seattle, USA
[10] Demet Aksoy, Michael Franklin – Scheduling for Large-Scale On_demand Data Broadcasting, in IEEE Infocom 1998, San Francisco, CA, USA

Resources

ATSC: Advanced Television Standards Committee: http://www.atsc.org
DAVIC: Digital Audio-Visual Council: http://www.davic.org
DVB: Digital Video Broadcast: http://www.dvb.org
IMMP: Integrated Multimedia Project: http://www-nrc.nokia.com/immp/
IMMP at GMD FOKUS: http://www.fokus.gmd.de/magic/projects/immp
MHEG-5 Users Group: http://www.fokus.gmd.de/ovma/mug
The MHEG Centre: http://www.fokus.gmd.de/magic/projects/ovma
W3C: World Wide Web consortium: http://www.w3.org/MarkUp/Activity.html
XML: http://www.xml.org

MMFramework - Distributed Environment for Control and Management of Multimedia Data

Krzysztof Zieliński, Łukasz Czekierda, Piotr Nawrocki, and Mariusz Michalski

Dept. of Computer Science, University of Mining & Metallurgy
Al. Mickiewicza 30, Cracow, Poland
tel:+48 (12) 617 39 82, fax:+48 (12) 617 39 66
{kz, luke, piter, cmich}@cs.agh.edu.pl
http://www.cs.agh.edu.pl

Abstract. This paper presents an open multimedia framework, called MMFramework. It may be used for dynamic creation of various multimedia applications. The proposed framework architecture consists of six layers. Its definition results from decomposition of the system into components with well-defined interfaces and internal implementation dedicated to the given hardware usage. Each layer represents a collection of components which are characterized by similar functionality. The system has been designed with support of existing CORBA Services and OMG specifications related to multimedia.

1 Introduction

The multimedia applications still represent important area of system research which addresses increasing demand for expanded functionality, higher quality, portability and flexibility. These requirements meet with common acceptance of new paradigms of distributed computer systems design and implementation built around distributed objects and thin clients dynamically loadable on demand. The distributed systems technology break-through appeared at great extent thanks to OMG efforts of CORBA standardization, and the spread of SUN-Soft Java. Both technologies despite theirs definition of general information processing architectures offer some support for multimedia. The OMG specification "Control and Management of Audio/Video Streams" (OMG A/V) [6, 7] defines a model for implementing an open distributed multimedia streaming framework while SUN-Soft supports JMF (Java Media Framework) [9] dedicated for multimedia GUI building. Neither of these proposals provides complete system support for implementation of distributed multimedia applications.

This paper presents an open multimedia framework, called MMFramework, which may be used for dynamic creation of various multimedia applications and which could be extended by new multimedia devices. The proposed framework architecture consists of six layers. Its definition results from decomposition of the system into components with well-defined interfaces and internal implementation dedicated to the given hardware usage or applied policy of the system control and management. Each layer represents a collection of components which are characterized by similar functionality. The system has been designed with existing CORBA Services and OMG specifications related to multimedia applications in mind.

The structure of the paper is as follows. In Section 2 the multilayer structure of the MMFramework will be presented. Section 3 concentrates on the Management and Access Control Layer functionality as the only layer of the defined framework directly visible by the user. Next in section 4 the communication mechanisms between components belonging to different layers have been analized in detail. Section 5 defines a procedure of attaching new devices to the system. Section 6 elaborates the example of GUI for dynamic construction of multimedia applications based on the functionality of the proposed architecture. The paper ends with conclusions.

2 MMFramework architecture

The proposed decomposition of the MMFramework into layers is depicted in Fig. 1. The detachment of the three bottom layers is straightforward. These layers provide full access to the multimedia devices configuration and usage. The complexity of the second and third layer is covered by layers four and five. These layers construct a uniform view of the system providing an easy to use abstraction of system components seen from the top application layer.

The first layer called **MMHardware and System Software Layer** deals with multimedia hardware and software provided by vendors. This layer is represented by a wide spectrum of devices such as: video cameras, computers, audio/video encoders/compressors (such as our NPoint device), media servers (for example Sun MediaCenter server), etc. These devices are usually equipped with proprietary control software. From the user's point of view, this layer looks like an inconsistent collection of different devices.

The second layer — **MMHardware CORBA Server Layer** packs up the vendor-provided software with CORBA interfaces. This layer introduces a uniform abstraction of the service provided by a given device from the lower layer. This abstraction is defined by an interface specified in IDL and standard communication mechanisms provided by the IIOP protocol. The IDL interfaces defined in this layer support all operations provided by the native software. The main goal of introducing this layer is to establish a common base for the system development. The choice of CORBA distributed objects model was one of the most significant decisions for the MMF architecture.

The third layer — **A/V Streams Control Layer** is dedicated to multimedia streams creation, control, and destruction. This layer implements the OMG specification [6, 7] and provides software objects which expose functionality of the lower layer CORBA servers in a standard form most suitable for audio and video streams control. It provides an abstraction of a stream encapsulated in the form of a CORBA object which represents its parameters and control opera-

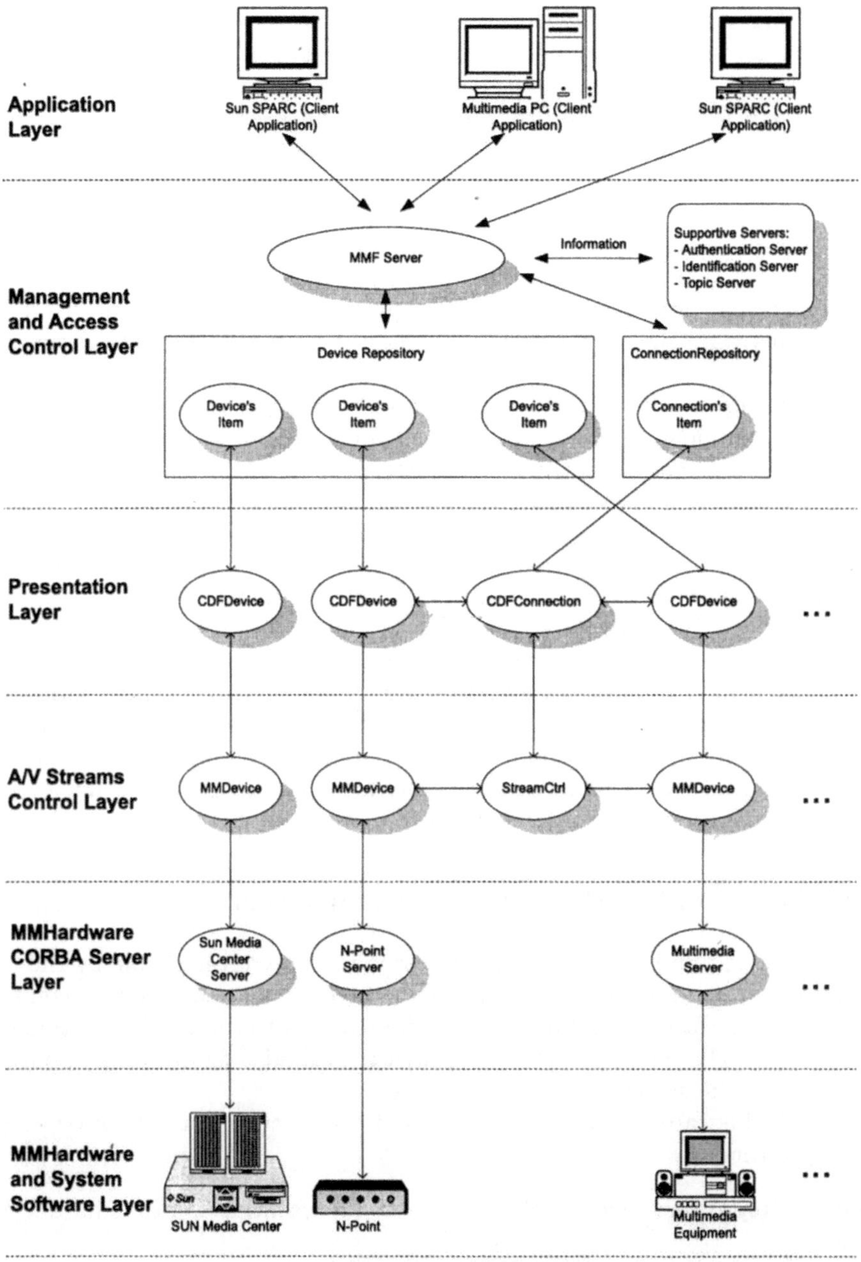

Fig. 1. Multilayer MMFramework architecture

tions. This layer deals not only with the streams control activity but also provides mechanisms for streams parameters negotiation between source and destination multimedia devices and provides streams addressing and QoS control.

The fourth layer — **Presentation Layer** resolves the problem of different types of data used for the parameters of multimedia devices and streams representation. The main goal of this layer is to translate the parameters types from their actual values to especially constructed CDF (Common Data Format). This format is used above the Presentation Layer to simplify presentation of the system's state and to provide a uniform view of the system components for control and visualization purposes. This layer supports users with a powerful mechanism of forms what makes the system configuration simple and less susceptible to errors.

The **Management and Access Control Layer** provides a uniform view of the MMF components' state and a set of functions for manipulating and accessing them. The most important design decision about the construction of this layer is the choice of a model for representation of the system's state components. The most natural representation of the system is a repository of observable objects. They are objects with their own interfaces and notification mechanism. There are two types of items: devices and connections.

A top layer of the MMF architecture is called **Application Layer**. The entities of this layer are collections of user interfaces that provide access to control and visualization of the system state in the most convenient form. The objects defined on this level act as observers of the system components and combine them in the given application scenario. They may also perform the MMF clients' role actively changing the system's state by operations invocations on the devices and connections abstraction provided by the lower layer.

3 Management and Access Control Layer

The Management and Access Control Layer is the only layer visible by the user applications. This influences the tasks of the layer. It has to deliver a compact and uniform interface for end users, that offers access to the whole functionality of the system. The next its task is to provide methods of informing about the actual state of the system (see next sections).

Figure 1 illustrates the key components of the layer. It consists of two types of the repositories:

- Device Repository, which collects objects representing multimedia devices, and
- Connection Repository, containing objects which describe and control the state of multimedia streams connections,

and so called Supportive Servers.

An item from the Device Repository is variously comprehended. This may be (i) 'real' multimedia device, e.g. video server or hardware MPEG coder, (ii) multimedia workstation with its hardware and software enabling sending/receiving audio and video streams, (iii) *mobile device*, which is ascribed to a system's user and associated at the given moment with one of the workstations. Despite this diversity, the items are treated uniformly from the Management Layer's point of view.

Items from the Connection Repository represent the state of the connection between two or more devices as well as allow performing operations on the streams, like `start` or `stop`.

The main objective during the Management Layer's design was to create one logically centralized object, MMFServer, having knowledge about the whole system. That makes it possible to efficiently organize (i) an access to the system functions, (ii) monitoring its state, and (iii) making this state available to users in case of their synchronous invocations. The client never has direct access to the repository item. The only object the client has access to is MMFServer. It is necessary to point out that notification information is sent to observers by each of repository items separately. The notification information is passed directly to the observers in the Application Layer, hence the MMFServer does not represent the centralized point of the system what could made a bottleneck.

As has been already mentioned, there is a number of so-called supportive servers also considered as a part of the Management and Access Control Layer. They are designed in such a way as to give an external support for items' management and creation and to provide to the Connection and Device Repositories some external services described below.

One of supportive servers is an Identification Server. Items are externally identified by theirs identifiers. The id parameter is translated by the Identification Server to the item's reference which is used for further operation processing.

External support is also needed for the access control function which is performed by an Authentication Server. Operations requiring authentication have an extra parameter — a user's key. The key is used by the Authentication Server to check user's permission to perform a given operation. Thus the repository items don't need to have knowledge about the users and their rights.

As can be seen, it is a role of the MMFServer to contact the Authentication Server and the Identification Server and then invoke an operation on the repository item.

The third supportive server — Topic Server is to handle topics used by OrbixTalk [2] — IONA's implementation of OMG's Event Service. These attributes concern the control of notification event channels' space. A number of such channels can be associated with each item. Using the channels the receivers can be precisely informed about actual state of the system taking advantage of the fact that each topic represents some aspect of the item's state. The used *push* model of information dissemination allows the receiver to implement the response to the notification message in the suitable way.

4 Information flow in MMFramework

Structuralisation of MMFramework in the form of observable objects' repository induces the following model of the information flow:

1. The changes of the device or connection settings are propagated from Application Layer to Management and Access Control Layer. Then the parameters in the CDF format are changed into hardware layer parameters such as QoS (by mechanisms of Presentation Layer).
2. All parameters are further propagated through layers (from the Presentation Layer to the MMHardware CORBA Layer) in form of QoS parameters and Properties (such as transmission parameters). These parameters are finally transformed into operation invocation(s) on CORBA servers from the MMHardware CORBA Server Layer. If the operation is possible to be executed, confirmation or the results are sent in response, if not — the negative answer is sent.
3. The results of the operations are propagated from hardware layer to the Presentation Layer. These results of the changes in the devices' or connections' states are transformed by the presentation server into the CDF form and reported to the device's item or the connection's item respectively.
4. The clients' objects may be registered as the observers of the change of the states of specific items from MaACL layer. All these observers are informed by the Event Channel mechanism about changes of devices' or connections' parameters. All observers are informed about positive results while only the client responsible for the action is informed about negative results.

It is easy to see that the information flow up the multi-layer hierarchy in MMF is provided by two mechanisms: (i) notifications, and (ii) responses to operation calls. The first mechanism corresponds to push monitoring model and the second is pull style of data collection. The flow down the hierarchy is performed only by the operation invocations.

The UML diagram in Fig. 2 shows a sequence of operations' invocations when a new connection is set. The main operations are *initConnection* which prepares connection's parameters and *setConnection* which invokes operations on objects in A/V Streams Control Layer. This UML diagram presents interaction between (from the left hand side) five objects (MMFServer, Authentication Server, Identification Server, Connection, TopisServer) which belong to Management and Access Control Layer and objects (CDFConnection, CDFDevice1, CDFDevice2) belonging to the Presentation Layer and the last three objects (StreamCtrl, MMDevice1, MMDevice2) which are contained in A/V Streams Control Layer. This illustrates the information flow (in the form of operations' invocations) between the layers of the MMFramework system.

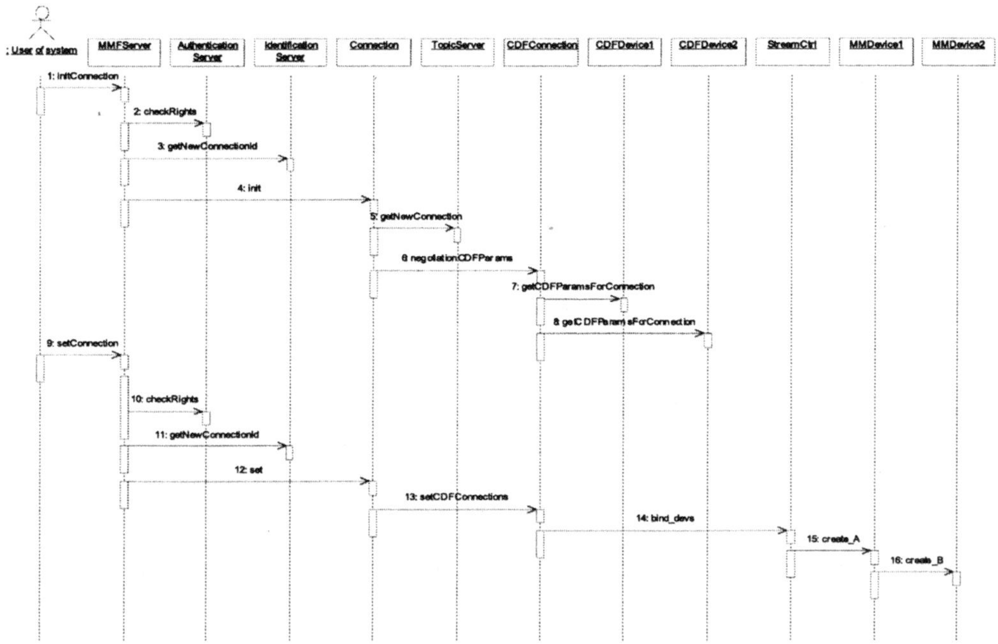

Fig. 2. UML sequence diagram describing how a new connection is established

5 Procedure of MMFramework extension with a new device

The MMFramework architecture makes it possible to easily add a new multimedia device. The procedure described below presents in four basic steps what to do to make a new network multimedia device accessible in the MMFramework system.

1. The functionality of that device should be accessed by CORBA interfaces. The role of the MMHardware CORBA Server Layer is to represent a multimedia device as CORBA object.
2. The next step is to create the MMDevice object. This component abstracts the behaviour of a multimedia device. The parameters of the object from the MMHardware CORBA Server Layer should be translated to QoS parameters which are understood by A/V Streams Control Layer. The QoS parameters give the uniform mechanisms for cooperation and negotiation of newly added device parameters' with existing components from the some layer.
3. For each multimedia device a CDFDevice object should be created. This component makes it possible to translate the parameters of the devices (such as QoS) to/from the Common Description Format (CDF). The parameters (in the CDF format) are passed by Management and Access Control Layer (MaACL). The programmer chooses which parameters of the multimedia device should be used by the MaACL and visualized by the client application.

4. The others components and items related to multimedia devices in the MaACL and the Application Layer are created dynamically by the system's administrator. All device's properties are passed to these two layers automatically, the programmer doesn't have to manually create any objects or components. These properties in a notification information form are sent from the MaACL to the Application Layer.

The last step of the described procedure, which is the creation of device's item in the Device Repository, is performed automatically by the system.

6 MMFramework client

This section describes the architecture of the MMFramework client. A graphic interface of client's program consists of two main types of components designed for it. The first component, called **NetChart**, represents a topology of the multimedia system i.e. devices and connections between them. The next components, called **Forms**, are used for presenting parameters and states of multimedia devices and connections, as it is shown in Fig. 3. For the communication of the client with the MaACL layer the programming environments such as OrbixWeb [3] and OrbixTalk [2] are used.

6.1 NetChart component

The main goal while creating the NetChart component was to achieve a compact graphic representation of the whole system, devices and connections what

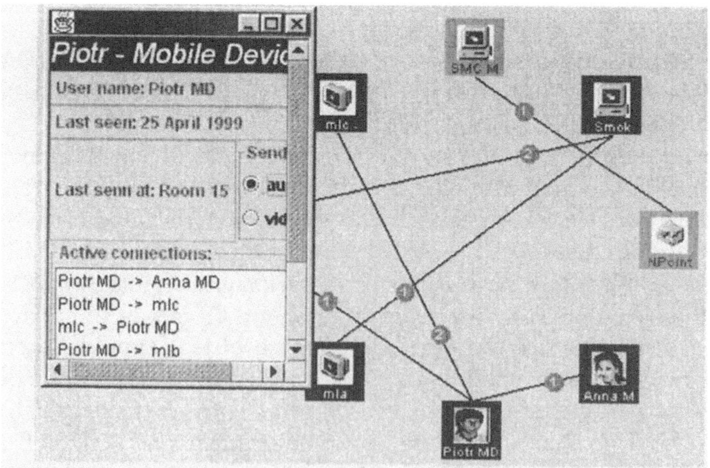

Fig. 3. NetChart component and Form component associated with Piotr MD device

provides access to their state and control functions. Thus, it allows users for a fast orientation in the system's state, making a control decisions and managing the system. Multimedia devices in this component are represented by rectangles placed on a circle as it is shown in Fig. 3. An appropriate icon and description of the device are placed inside each rectangle. Connections between devices are represented by lines drawn from one rectangle to another. Each line may indicate many connections between the same devices, therefore a label with the number of connections is plotted on each of them. This component also provides many options designed for customizing its appearance according to individual preferences. To each device and connection in the component is assigned a dedicated manager. The manager notifies them about the information changes.

6.2 Form component

The next component is a dynamically built GUI interface. It consists of simpler components called **Elems**, which are automatically laid out on the Form in the way best fitting its size. Each elem possesses the main component which is one of six graphic Swing components such as JList, JComboBox, JLabel, JTextField, JCheckBox group and JRadioButton group [10]. These Swing components are sufficient for good representation of all possible parameters of devices and connections. Each elem has additional title and border for good appearance and also possesses its manager which delivers events connected with the elem.

The Forms are used for presentation of the parameters of devices and connections or can be edited to introduce new values of parameters. These values are used for setting devices and connections parameters. The example of graphical representation of the Form is shown in Fig. 3.

6.3 Client communication mechanism

A communication from the client to the MMF Server is done using the IIOP protocol. General assumption is that the items from the MaACL layer communicate with the client using one-way multicast message propagation mechanism used by OrbixTalk. A communication from the server to the client is more sophisticated because there is no an appropriate OrbixTalk implementation for the Java platform. Therefore the client program has a sublayer in the form of a server written in C++ language, which receives multicast messages from the MMF Server and propagates them to the client using IIOP protocol. This is schematically presented in Fig. 4.

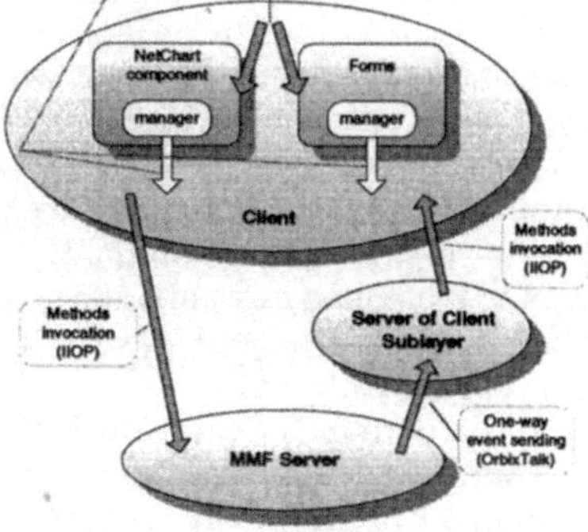

Fig.4. The communication mechanism

7 Evaluation of the system status

All layers of the architecture have been designed and successfully implemented. Of course, the system still needs further refinement, testing and validation; its basic functionality has been reached, however.

Even in such a small multimedia system as the one existing in the DCS at the UMM, it was purposeful to enrich its functionality with a scalable and efficient mechanism of notification about changes in the system's state allowing at the same time to monitor and archive events in the system.

One of the most important advantages of the MMFramework architecture is the implementation of the worked out CDF format. This powerful mechanism makes it possible to dynamically build applications. Taking advantage of CORBA architecture it has been possible to integrate different systems into one working framework.

8 Conclusions

MMFramework presents a novel approach to the multimedia applications design and implementation built around observable objects paradigm with event-based notification a principal communication mechanism. Based on the powerful OMG Control and Management A/V streams model, it unifies traditionally separate applications such as Video on demand, Videoconference and Live TV & video into one system. This is possible thanks to flexibility of the object oriented distributed programming provided by CORBA, which introduces clear conceptual model of the systems, mechanisms of dynamic binding and services. These features help to overcome inherent complexity of the multimedia systems control and management.

References

1. Continuous Media Toolkit, `http://bmrc.berkeley.edu/projects/cmt`
2. Iona Technologies Ltd., OrbixTalk White Paper, April 1996, `http://www.iona.com`
3. Iona Technologies Ltd., OrbixWeb Programmer's Guide `http://www.iona.com`
4. Multiparty Multimedia Session Control, `http://www.ietf.org/`
5. Notification Service, Joint Revised Submission by NEC System Laboratory et al., 1997.
6. Object Management Group, Control and Management of A/V Streams, OMG Document telecom/97-05-07 ed., October 1997.
7. Object Management Group, Control and Management of A/V Streams, Revised Submission, OMG Document telecom/98-10-05 ed., October 1998.
8. Object Management Group, CORBA Components, Joint Initial Submission by IONA Technologies et al., 1997, November, OMG Report.
9. SUN Microsystems, Java Media Framework, `http://www.sun.com/nab/java.framework.html`
10. Sun Microsystems Swing-1.0.1, `http://www.javasoft.com/`
11. Stream-oriented Information Flow based on CORBA Services in Large Distributed Systems, ESPRIT Project 20288-CRIT-2, March 1997
12. T. J.Mowbray and R. C.Malveau, CORBA Design Patterns, Willey, 1997.

Manipulating 3D character animation media objects

Daniela Giorgetti and Patrizia Palamidese

CNUCE Institute, CNR, Via S.Maria 36 - 56126 Pisa - Italy
{D.Giorgetti@guest., P.Palamidese@}cnuce.cnr.it

Abstract. Multimedia authoring tools enable the production of presentations that integrate text, video, audio, and images. To facilitate the creation of characters animation which include other media such as speech and sound, a new authoring system is defined that is able to generate a fully animated scene from a high level description supported by an extended version of the score paradigm. Introducing 3D animated data as a new kind of media object requires changes to both the timeline paradigm and to the traditional system architecture. Issues related to editing and to navigating inside the presentation are discussed.

1 Introduction

Multimedia authoring systems provide users with high level tools to create, compose, manipulate, and display multimedia contents. The aim of such systems is to simplify the inherently complex task of realizing an interactive multimedia application. Authoring systems vary widely depending on the type of multimedia application they are able to generate, the capabilities, and the ease of use.

In this paper we present an authoring and playback system which helps users to rapidly prototype integrated theatrical performances, where the main focus is on defining actor animations. Applications generated by this system are virtual 3D representations of scenes including digital animated actors, stages, props, lights, sounds, music, and speech. The composition and synchronization of the various elements in a scene is based on the musical score paradigm, where synchronous items are represented by boxes along horizontal parallel tracks, and where columns represent time marks. The score paradigm is integrated with the tape-recorder metaphor for a full control of navigation through the animation. The innovative aspect of this work is that the score paradigm, traditionally applied to text, still images, audio and video, is extended to include 3D character animation as a new media object. This type of data introduces new issues concerning both the score and the system architecture.

A research prototype CAST (Computer Aided STaging) is used to test and evaluate our approach. This prototype is not just a system to combine audio and animation, but is a kind of hyper-composer which performs both cross-media and intra-media composition. On the one hand, it synchronizes audio and animation, on the other hand its building block based architecture allows a dynamic composition of parameterized animation items for rendering. Issues considered are far from those addressed by traditional computer animation; for example the creation of Disney/Pixar's "A Bug's Life" was a time consuming process involving hundreds of artists and computer experts, where each frame took from 1 to 20 hours to be rendered, and its final result was remarkably photorealistic, but one-application oriented (i.e. not reusable). Our goal is to support real-time character animation on standard platforms, and the reusable building block approach that we rely upon aims to provide an environment for fast prototyping by non computer specialists of many different types of virtual 3D multimedia performances [1].

2 Background and Related Works

In this paper we consider two of the main factors concerning the design and implementation of a system for authoring multimedia digital animated scenes:

- ▹ issues related to the multimedia field, in particular to multimedia authoring;
- ▹ issues concerning the generation of animations of 3D human figures.

The multimedia authoring field deals with the design and implementation of tools that enable the production and presentation of complex inter-related objects [2]. Different layers can be identified in the multimedia authoring process. Data objects must be created (content layer), often using special-purpose tools (e.g. for motion capture), they must be integrated into a coherent presentation (design layer), usually requiring some form of media synchronization (control layer), and eventually they can be viewed (presentation display layer) [3].

Multimedia systems can be classified according to the (possibly multiple) paradigms they support [4]. The most common metaphors are the slide-show, the book, the time-line, and the icon. Other interesting and more unusual paradigms are Allen's interval scripts [5], on which Pinhanez at MIT built his story-based interactive system [6] to manage human interaction in immersive environments, and the Anecdote [7] model, which introduces the concept of a surrogate media and surrogate scene.

Commercial authoring systems often focus on low-level details rather than high-level structure, whereas research prototypes such as the CMIFed visual authoring environment support high level editing [2], and other environments support high-level scripting of complex interactive presentations [8]. There is a trade-off between the flexibility and complexity of an authoring system: the more a user is free to change data at the lowest level the more sophisticated, time-consuming and difficult to use the system is [9], [10], [11]. The learning curve of commercial products such as Maya, 3d Studio Max, MetaCreations Poser, and Macromedia Director increases slowly.

An important distinction in the human animation field is between virtual characters provided with a certain degree of autonomy and decisional power [12] (real time autonomous agents), and script-controlled actors. The state of the art for modeling and simulating real time digital humans is described in a recent

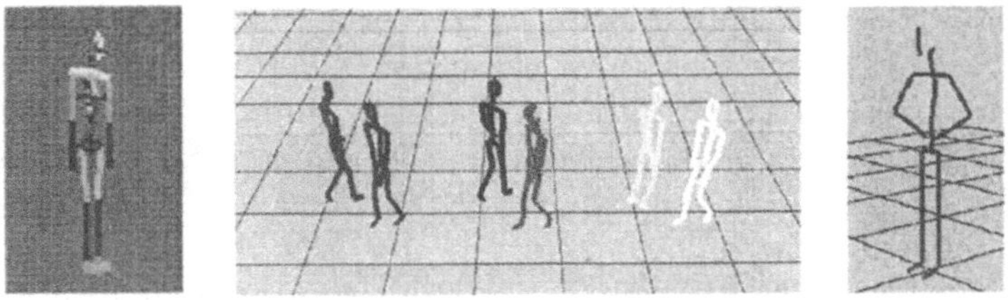

Fig. 1. 3D wire-frame human models

paper by Badler et al. [13]. Many research efforts concentrate on specializing human models along one of the possible dimensions (e.g. appearance, movement, autonomous action, etc.). A challenge is to build virtual humans that are suitable for different application areas.

The OZ project at CMU (Carnegie Mellon University) led by Bates [14] is aimed at the construction of Believable Agents using AI concepts, and the description of a computational theory of interactive drama. The Virtual Theater project, part of the Adaptive Intelligent Systems - AIS project at Stanford University, led by Hayes-Roth [15] studies the creation of intelligent, automated characters that can act either in well-defined stories or in improvisational environments. ALIVE (Artificial Life Interactive Video Environment) is a joint project between the Vision and Modeling Group and the Autonomous Agents Group at the MIT Media Lab [16]. The system uses a magic mirror idiom to create an enhanced world for the user on the other side of the looking glass. Jack is a software package (running on SGI workstations) developed at the Center for Human Modeling and Simulation at the University of Pennsylvania. It features a detailed human model and includes realistic behavioral controls (e.g. anthropometric scaling, automatic reach and grasp). The Improv system developed at NYU by Perlin's group [17], [18] enables users to create real time behaviour-based animated actors that respond to users and to each other in real-time.

However sophisticated a motion generator is, it doesn't automatically solve the problem of how to control the animation. How the user specifies complex animated scenes, the need for an intuitive conceptual action model, and the need for an easy interface, still are the main issues in character animation. To support these aspects we have developed a score-based animation model, where primitive animation items are treated as media objects. It is easy for the user to combine elements on the score to create a complex presentation of 3D articulated models (Fig. 1) and play real-time animations on standard PCs.

3 Authoring a Theatrical Performance

Our primary goal is to develop an environment for the real time simulation of a play and an authoring tool for manipulating data at a high level of abstraction to easily produce content-rich and complex scenarios for a wide range of theatrical performances. Moreover, we believe that the framework developed for theatre representations can be reused (with suitable changes and extensions) in other fields such as cinema and television. The system helps directors to quickly set up a computer preview of a multimedia performance, and this can be useful in a pre-production phase as a virtual rehearsal and for educational purposes as well. A theatrical performance can be planned, scene by scene, by setting up the camera, the stage, the lights, the sounds, the actors and their behavior (motions, speech, interactions). The whole structure can be modeled in a hierarchical way (Fig. 2). The authoring process begins with the definition of a new scene belonging to a

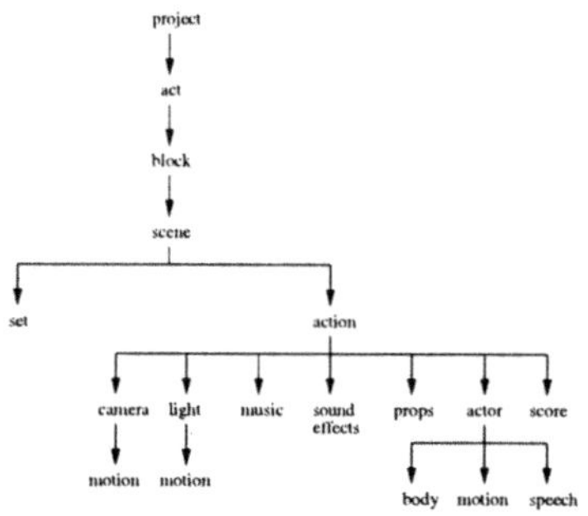

Fig. 2. Object hierarchy: the father-child relationship is 1:m, except for set and body

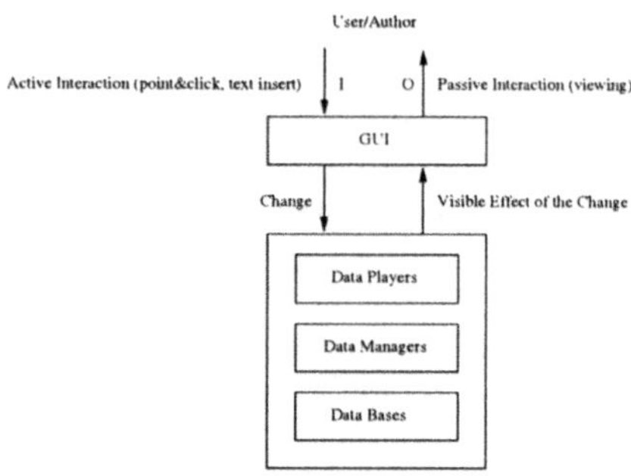

Fig. 3. The system basic architecture

particular block in a project. A scene is characterized by a name, a temporal length, a virtual stage that can be loaded from a library (VRML or iv format), lights (spot, directional and point), a camera which can be interactively created and adjusted, and actors which can be loaded from a library (VRML format) and can be assigned many different kinds of motions chosen from a library (internal format). The system is able to adapt pre-recorded animation items to the spatial and temporal conditions determined by the application, and to generate locomotion (e.g. walk, run, go up/down stairs) along specified paths.The scene's audio components are music, sound effects, and lines belonging to actors, which often have to be synchronized with their motions. The outcome of the authoring process is a computer animated script, which can replace the traditional hand written script, and whose simulation can be displayed in the system viewing window (Fig. 4). On this basis users can go on refining and modifying some elements in the scene until they reach a good synthesis.

The theatrical score includes in a single graphical window both the hierarchy structure and the temporal structure of a scene (Fig. 4). The temporal structure is represented by a timeline, which allows the sequential and parallel composition of atomic objects. Atomic objects can be both 3D graphical objects (e.g. an actor's body) and abstract objects such as a motion or a speech line, which are usually related to a 3D object (e.g. actor). All objects are dynamic and time dependent: i.e. they are characterized by a moment when they are created (start time) and a moment when they complete their life-cycle (implicitly defining the object duration). Moreover, the graphical objects are displayable on the rendering window via a scene graph data structure (an Open Inventor hierarchical node tree) which provides a snapshot of the scene at a given time. By using prefabricated components that can be easily manipulated, combined and rearranged users can create a variety of virtual performances.

4 Architecture of the Animation System

We begin describing the system architecture with a basic diagram (Fig. 3) representing the author high level interaction through the GUI, which affects the underlying data structures, and eventually causes visible changes in the GUI. In describing the user interactions through the GUI we will make a distinction between the two possible kinds of interaction:

- ▷ *runtime*: the system is in simulation mode (viewing the animation);
- ▷ *off line*: the system is in authoring mode (interactive editing).

4.1 The GUI

The CAST GUI (Fig. 4) can be split up into:

- ▷ A *rendering window* (spatial editing, display) (*presentation display layer*). In its off line input role it allows spatial changes in the scene such as a change in position/orientation/selection of the current object and it can allow indirect access (via mouse) to the specific object interface window. At run time it allows the user to change just the position/orientation of the camera viewing the scene. In its output role it gives a snapshot representing the graphical and spatial aspects of the scene at time t (in fact the scene is rendered on a frame basis);
- ▷ A *score window* (temporal editing) (*design layer*). In its input role it allows the composition/synchronization of the elements in the scene and hence temporal editing (change in start time and duration of an element). It can give indirect access to the specific object interface window. In its output role it gives a hierarchical view of the temporal structure of the whole scene.
- ▷ A *simulation control window* (run time control) (*control layer*). It has just a run time input role, which provides the user with a mechanism to run the simulation from a temporal point of view (play/stop/pause etc). The simulation control acts as the clock of the animation system.
- ▷ *Object interface windows* (*editing layer*). This kind of interface allows users to edit all the spatial and temporal parameters related to a specific object (actor's body, actor's motion, actor's speech, stage, lights etc) belonging to the scene.
- ▷ *Library windows* (*content layer*). The CAST system provides building blocks of the different components of the scene that the user can directly select from extensible libraries. In the current implementation the main ones are

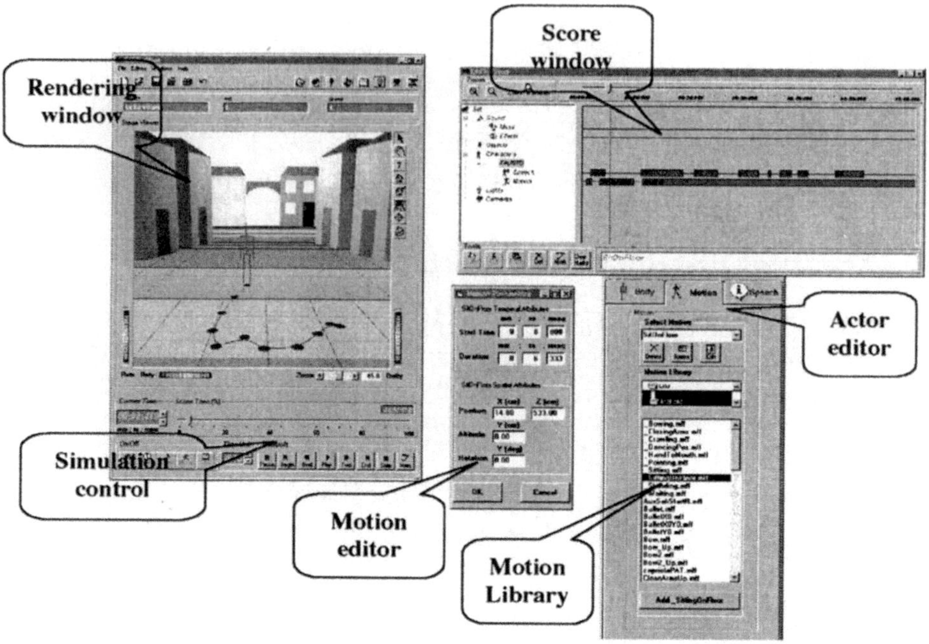

Fig. 4. The rendering window and the other GUI elements

an actor's body library, a motion library, an audio library (including speech, music, and sound effects sub-libraries), and a stage library.

4.2 The Realization Layer

In this section we describe the system generated space and time constraints. The creation of the scene is a *realization layer* task; this layer works at a data structure level following both the author's commands given through the GUI and some system-added automatic procedures. The layer underlying the GUI includes atomic objects (stored in different databases), and mechanisms to relate objects of the same type (e.g. motion) or to relate objects of different type (e.g. motion and speech).

Digital actors are currently represented by stick models embedding a hierarchical rotational joint structure described in VRML format. The system is based on re-using and adapting existing key framed animations that are stored in a movement library. Key frames may have been generated by any of the techniques available such as motion capture, an interactive animation tool, or an off-line algorithm, and then included in the animation library. When a user selects a motion from the library and assigns it to an actor, the system performs some actions to integrate the new motion in the actor motion chain:

▷ the current scene time is assumed as the start time for the motion;

- ▷ the new motion starts in the same position on the stage where the actor is;
- ▷ if the motion is recognized as a procedural motion (cyclic motion) (e.g. walk, run, go up/down the stairs) it also has to be generated from the primitive step data and adapted to a user-given path;
- ▷ the duration of the motion is inferred from the motion template in the library for non-cyclic motions, and is calculated on a path basis if the motion is cyclic (given the constant velocity of the motion and the length of the trajectory).

There are many issues here on how the system should interpret user wishes. Some solutions are illustrated in 5.1. At the lowest level, the system finally produces a set of time dependent interpolation coefficients, which are accessed during the simulation by the Data Player to determine the exact position of all the actors' joints.

5 User Defined Space and Time Constraints

We use the timeline paradigm to control the time flow among media objects, but for 3D animated objects the timeline is not enough, and a method to control the flow in the 3D space is also needed. The user can place objects in the 3D space of the stage using the mouse or set up the position parameters in the object interface window. Moreover, it is possible to draw trajectories in the display window that give a track for the movements of the actors. Every single actor motion can be assigned an arbitrary start position and orientation, but if the user doesn't specify them, the system computes a position and orientation relying on the previous motion in the chain.

The following two subsections describe how the user can deal with time aspects of the scene when the system is in editing mode or in simulation mode.

5.1 Score Based Synchronization and Composition of Scene Elements

A typical design problem in a multimedia dynamic system is how to express time dependencies of animated objects when the animation is not running. The traditional solution is to separate the individual parts of the problem, where a timeline window shows the time relationships and a graphic window displays the motion path of the objects and the motion itself at runtime. Other approaches [19] have tried to integrate into a single visual representation the relations between motion, time and distance, but the risk is a rapid cluttering of the display window due to the overlapping of graphical elements that increase with the number of motions.

The score paradigm is appropriate to describe theatrical scenes because characters animations are inherently made up of parallel, time-based events. In CAST the score provides both the hierarchical view and the timeline view of the scene (Fig. 4). The hierarchy view allows the user to structure the scene by defining all the media items top-down. The leaf nodes of this hierarchy are the media played during the simulation. Typical timelines support text, image, video, and music objects. We have extended the timeline capabilities to support animation as a new kind of media object. Animation is a procedural object, which requires some caution when being adapted to the general timeline philosophy. There are some issues related to the timeline-based approach which have been identified for traditional authoring systems [2] and which have a particular impact on 3D data. We will consider below object editing and presentation navigation. The score allows a user to select, add, delete, edit an element, drag an animation item along the timeline to change its start time, shrink or enlarge its length to change its duration, and manipulate groups of elements. The synchronization of audio and animation is obtained by considering audio as the primary media, i.e. the user can change the animation time by stretching or shrinking its duration, while the audio duration is left unchanged. Another way to achieve a good synchronization without changing the motion speed is by using graphical time marks, which give the tempo that both audio and animation must keep to. The granularity of the score can be scaled and the maximum detail is obtained with a time unit of one millisecond, which coincides with the internal precision of the animation system. The timeline provides a very compact description of a scene, as it shows the order of events, not only with respect to one actor, but also to the actors as a whole.

Object Editing. The main problem with object editing is establishing which side effects condition other animation items when the start time or the duration of a particular animation have changed. It is not just a matter of shifting subsequent items when a new item is inserted inbetween, but changes to the semantics of the scene have to be considered, in particular changes to its temporal and spatial constraints have to be dealt with. Since the start position of an animation usually coincides with the end position of the animation which precedes it on the timeline, changing the order in a list of motions usually creates a spatial inconsistency. For example (Fig. 5), the ordered list of movements [A1, A2, A3] may create the wrong effect if it is substituted by the list [A1, A3, A2]. This aspect is difficult to handle automatically because it very much depends on the user's wishes. We thus decided to allow the user to freely define whether A3 and A2 have to change their start positions according to the new order on the timeline or not. While spatial constraints affect the movements of one actor, temporal constraints can affect the movements of all the other actors as well. For example, if the item A2' is inserted in a new position to form the list [A1, A2, A2', A3], the system wonders whether it has to shift only the items that follow A2 on the same track or also the items on other tracks This problem is solved through the grouping concept. When the start time of A3 is changed, the same change is automatically extended to all the members of the group.

Presentation Navigation. Presentation navigation is the possibility to move to a specific part of a presentation by adjusting a time pointer. When applied to 3D animation, this concept entails visualizing the frame corresponding to the selected time and running the other data player (music, speech) if

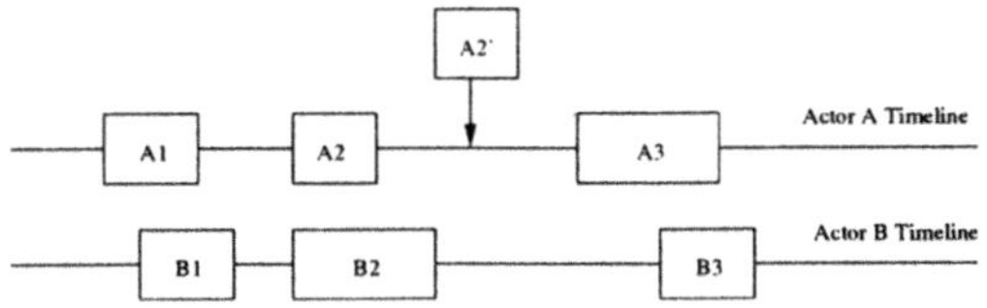

Fig. 5. Does A2' affect only actor A or also actor B?

possible. The animation player makes a real-time frame interpolation when this time is set.

Transition effects such as fading are considered as timeline properties in some systems. Applying a similar mechanism to animation data requires specific interpolation mechanisms (weighted interpolation [20]) between a few ending frames of a motion and a few starting frames of the motion next to it on the timeline.

5.2 Simulation Control

The user interface to control animation is based on the familiar tape-recorder paradigm; it includes play/stop/pause/fast forward and rewind functions whose frame rate can be adjusted by the user (Fig. 4).

Time is continuously displayed also in other formats on all the windows to allow the user to keep full control on which part of the scene is being displayed. A numeric display shows the value of time in minutes/seconds/milliseconds, and a percentage scale allows the user a rough positioning within the scene (e.g. move towards the end of the scene or towards the middle of the scene). The internal mechanism used to achieve real time animation and interaction is multi-threading.

6 Conclusions and Future Developments

Authoring animation through the score paradigm considerably facilitates and speeds up the creation of complex scenes, above all when many actors have to be designed. On the other hand, this approach supports a discrete model of the animation, made up of a list of separate actions (e.g. go there, sit down, raise the arms) which may not reproduce the details and the nuances of the real actions.

To improve the automatic generation of a great variety of scenes by simply manipulating and modifying existing primitives, aspects related to adaptive animation items can be further extended and enhanced. It is well known that creating animation data from scratch is very costly, time-consuming, and requires highly specialized people. Reusing and adapting media data is a topic common to all authoring systems, but animation data require particularly sophisticated methods, which are still being researched into. Advanced techniques include creating a new character movement by composing primitive movements (e.g. walk and hand wave), or introducing noises on a movement signal to change its characteristics (e.g. emotional effects).

References

1. P. Palamidese: Computer Aided Staging. The Journal of Visualization and Computer Animation, Vol. 10, 3–14, 1999.
2. D. C. A. Bulterman and L. Hardman: Multimedia Authoring Tools: State of the Art and Research Challenges. Lecture Notes in Computer Science, Vol. 1000, Springer-Verlag, Berlin Heidelberg New York, 575–591, 1995.
3. M. Bordegoni, G. Faconti, S. Feiner, M. T. Maybury, T. Rist, S. Ruggieri, P. Trahanias, M. Wilson: A Standard Reference Model for Intelligent Multimedia Presentation Systems. Computer Standards and Interfaces: International Journal on the Development and Application of Standards for Computers, Vol. 18, 477–496, 1997.
4. J. Siglar: Multimedia Authoring Systems FAQ. Version 2.23, 4 April 1999 http://www.tiac.net/users/jasiglar/MMASFAQ.HTML.
5. J. F. Allen: Towards a General Theory of Action and Time. Artificial Intelligence, Vol. 23, 123–154, 1984.
6. C. S. Pinhanez, K. Mase, A. Bobick: Interval Scripts: a Design Paradigm for Story-Based Interactive System. ACM CHI97 Conference Proceedings, Atlanta, GA, 1997.
7. K. Harada, E. Tanaka, R. Ogawa, Y. Hara: Anecdote: A Multimedia Storyboarding System with Seamless Authoring Support. ACM Multimedia 96, 1996.
8. S. Agamanolis: High-Level Scripting Environments for Interactive Multimedia Systems. MIT Master Thesis, Cambridge, MA, 1996.
9. D. J. Wiley, J. K. Hahn: Interpolation Synthesis of Articulated Figure Motion. IEEE CG&A., Vol. 17(6), 39–45, 1997.
10. T. Calvert, A. Bruderlin, J. Dill, T. Schiphorst, C. Welman: Desktop Animation of Multiple Human Figures. IEEE CG&A, Vol. 13(3), 18–22, 1993.
11. T. W. Calvert, S. H. Mah: Choreographers as Animators: Systems to Support Composition of Dance. In: N. Magnenat-Thalmann, D. Thalmann, (eds): Interactive Computer Animation, 100–126, Prentice-Hall, 1996.
12. C. W. Reynolds: Steering Behaviors For Autonomous Characters. Proceedings of the 1999 Game Developers Conference, San Jose, CA, March 1999.
13. N. Badler, R. Bindiganavale, J. Bourne, J. Allbeck, J. Shi, M. Palmer: Real time Virtual Humans. International Conference on Digital Media Futures, UK, 1999.
14. A. B. Loyall, J. Bates: Personality-Rich Believable Agents that Use Language. Proceedings of the First International Conference on Autonomous Agents, 106–113, Marina del Rey, California, February 5–8, 1997.
15. B. Hayes-Roth, L. Brownston, R. v. Gent: Multiagent Collaboration in Directed Improvisation. Proceedings of the First International Conference On Multi-Agent Systems (ICMAS-95), 148–154, Menlo Park, California, June 1995.
16. P. Maes, T. Darrell, B. Blumberg: The ALIVE System: Full Body Interaction with Autonomous Agents. Computer Animation 95 Conference, Geneva, Switzerland, IEEE Press, 11–18, April 19–21,1995.
17. K. Perlin, A. Goldberg: Improv: a System for Scripting Interactive Actors in Virtual Worlds. IEEE Computer Graphics, Vol. 29 (3), 205–215, 1996.
18. K. Perlin, A. Goldberg: Improvisational Animation White Paper. http://www.mrl.nyu.edu/improv/whitepaper/index.html, 1998.
19. M. Pell: Overlaying Motion, Time and Distance in 3-Space. ACM CHI 97 Electronic Publications, 1997.
20. A. Bruderlin, L. Williams: Motion Signal Processing. Proceedings of the ACM SIGGRAPH'95, 97–104, August 1995.

Realization of an Extensible Multimedia Document Model

Jürgen Hauser

Institute of Parallel and Distributed High-Performance Systems (IPVR),
University of Stuttgart, Breitwiesenstr. 20-22, D-70565 Stuttgart, Germany,
hauser@informatik.uni-stuttgart.de

Abstract. Most multimedia systems or standards provide one fixed concept for the temporal and spatial specification of documents. But different application areas - like computer based training or multimedia games - require different (application specific) concepts to support and simplify authoring. It is a very complex or even impossible task to specify documents for different application areas based on the same document model. This paper presents a document model, an approach to simplify authoring of documents in different application areas and a framework that supports the realization of the introduced concepts. The framework uses an event based approach and a scheduling graph to realize the semantics of an application concept.

1 Introduction

Nowadays, multimedia documents become more interactive and include even application (specific) functionality. For example, computer-based training becomes more effective if the learner experiences the content of the lesson. Multimedia games are another example for highly interactive presentations. This existence of a multitude of application areas leads to the requirement that a presentation system and its document model have to support presentation and creation of documents in different and new application areas.

Simple multimedia games can be taken as example for a new application area. A multimedia game consists of several temporal and spatial relations between entities of a game, and hence, can also be considered as multimedia document. In practice however, not all types of multimedia games can be realized as multimedia documents because of performance problems (3D graphics) or complexity of the specification. The following example bases on a maze wherein the player moves a figure. A *follow* relation describes that an opponent's figure follows (and tries to reach) the player's figure. Here, the author would like to use directly the *follow* relation. Hence, the multimedia system has to be extensible for new application areas to support authoring and presentation of multimedia games.

The following scenario describes another advantage of an extensible multimedia system. There are a lot of different concepts for the specification of the temporal relations between media items. A comparison of various models can be found in [7]. Different concepts have different advantages (e.g. expressiveness or simple to learn).

Hence, an author wants to use a concept that best fits authoring requirements and therefore a multimedia system has to be extensible to support integration of different concepts.

Each application area has particular concepts to define the course of the presentation (e.g. spatial layout, temporal layout and interaction possibilities). An extensible multimedia presentation system has to support the integration of new application specific concepts. Once, a new concept is integrated it can be reused by other authors.

During the presentation, the semantics of each concept have to be implemented by the presentation system. There are two possibilities to implement the semantics of application concepts. The first one is to use a scripting language and the second one is an extensible document language (e.g. a DTD (document type definition) based approach like HyTime [3] or XML applications [6]).

The scripting language approach has three disadvantages: (1) most scripting languages are insufficient (e.g. functionality or performance), (2) missing support for reuse of script programs (the script is included in the document) and (3) missing support for the semantically definition of relations and their integration into the document model. Besides, it is not very useful to implement a new document model in the scripting language of another document model because this leads to two coexisting models. And finally, the original document model probably remains unused. From the author's point of view this approach provides more programming than authoring. And hence, requires an author to be also familiar with programming.

An extensible document language permits the definition of new tags that can be used by the author. From the author's point of view this concept seems to satisfy all needs. But before tags can be used, their semantics have to be defined. There are two possible ways to specify the semantics of new tags: (1) mapping of the operators on existing tags and (2) the semantics have to be realized in a presentation system.

The semantically realization of the *follow* operator for the maze example has to compute the directions in which the opponent's figure has to move to reach the player's figure. Hence, to realize the follow-relation the expressiveness of a programming language (e.g. a control flow) is required, and therefore a simple mapping on existing operators is not sufficient.

Because mapping on existing operators is insufficient, the presented approach takes the second possibility. The approach uses an extensible document model and an extensible presentation system. The extensible document model allows to integrated new concepts. And the extensible presentation system permits the implementation of the semantics of the new concepts. The presentation systems supports and simplifies the implementation of the semantics by offering APIs (application programming interfaces) to the developer.

Instead of using tags, the approach of MAVA (*M*ultimedi*a* document *v*ersatile *a*rchitecture) describes relations between media items with operators. The semantics of operators are implemented in manager components (for short managers) - that are programmed in Java using the MAVA framework. The framework uses an event management for the communication between the media items and managers and a scheduling graph to achieve temporal synchronization. The extensibility of MAVA is the possibility to add new operators with their managers and new types of media items.

MAVA documents will be authored with a visual editor. The author uses operators to specify the relations between media items. If the required application concept is not available, a new operator set and an appropriate manager have to be developed. This is not a disadvantage because the normal temporal and spatial relations are available. Programming skills are only required where they were required anyway to do the script programming. But once, the operators are developed they can be easily reused by other authors.

MAVA is developed in a German Research Foundation (DFG) funded project in the research initiative "Distributed Processing and Exchange of Digital Documents (V3D2)". Further information on that initiative can be found in [4].

The remainder of this paper is organized as follows. The next section introduces the document model and the architecture of the MAVA presentation system. In section 3 the realization of the managers and the semantics of operators is discussed (i.e. the integration of a new concept). Section 4 presents related work. Finally, section 5 contains a summary.

2 MAVA Framework

The MAVA framework consists of two parts: The document model and a presentation system. The document model describes the structure of documents and the architecture describes the software architecture of the presentation system and included concepts that simplify the development of managers.

2.1 Document Model

The document model of MAVA uses an operator approach. An operator defines a relation or an interdependence between operands. For the document model, the operands of an operator are media items. Media items represent the information units of the presentation, for example audio or video sequences or simple text. In the example *audio while video*, *while* is the operator and *audio* and *video* are the operands. Additionally, an operator can be parameterized like *audio while(3,5) video*.

For the description of the document model itself the actual media data is not needed. Only the attributes (e.g. type, location of the media data,...) of the media items are to be considered. Hence, only the attributes are used in the document model. The attributes of a media item are contained in a media object.

Documents are structured into logical units with the usage of so-called containers. A container includes a set of media objects and operators. To build recursive structures a media object can also be a container. The root container of a container hierarchy is the document itself. A container has no certain semantics besides the ability to build recursive structures because all semantics are specified with operators.

A container can be used to store parts of the document for later reuse. Containers can also be used to build templates. A template defines the structure (e.g. operator usage) of a part of the document. The concrete media objects are added later by the author. Templates can be used to achieve a similar layout or to simplify authoring of recurring parts of a document.

2.2 Document Example

The elements of the MAVA document model (i.e. media objects, operators and containers) are visualized as shown in figure 1. Media objects are represented as rectangles with rounded edges. Inside the rectangle the type or a symbolic name is given for better readability. Operators are represented as rectangles. Inside the rectangle the type of the relation is given. A container is represented by a rectangle with a shadow.

Figure 1 shows one (root) container (i.e. the document) including two media objects and one operator. The first media object is an image and the second media object is an audio sequence. The operator is a *while* operator. The intention of the author was that during the presentation of the image the user will hear the audio. This semantics of the relation is expressed with the *while(3,5)* operator (i.e. a temporal interval operator, they are discussed in [14]). The parameters of the *while* operator specify delays between the beginning and ending of the two media items in seconds.

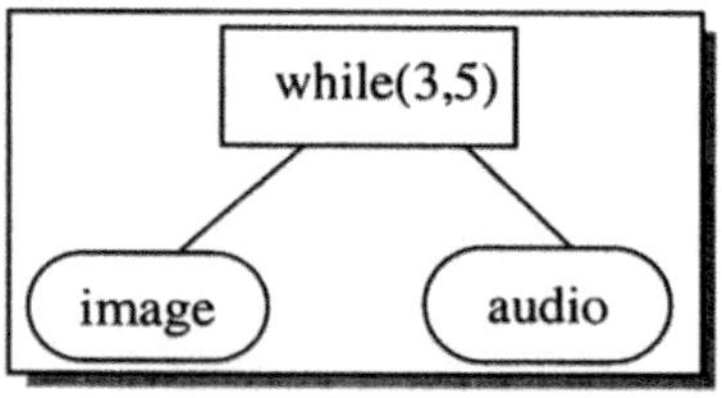

Fig. 1. MAVA Document.

2.3 MAVA Architecture

During the presentation the semantics of the used operators have to be implemented by managers. The MAVA framework provides an event management, the MAVA engine and further support (discussed in section 3) that are used by managers. Hence, the framework simplifies the development (e.g. programming in Java) of managers.

2.4 Managers

There are different classes of managers, for example spatial, temporal oder interaction managers. A manager for a temporal concept requires two classes of events: The notification events (including a *started* and *stopped* event) and the control events (including a *start* and *stop* event). If a temporal manager receives a *started* event it will send control events to other media items to realize the semantics of the operators used in a document. Hence, for MAVA a concept consists of a set of operators, two event sets and a manager. The event model used between managers and media items is shown in figure 2. This approach will be extended in the next section.

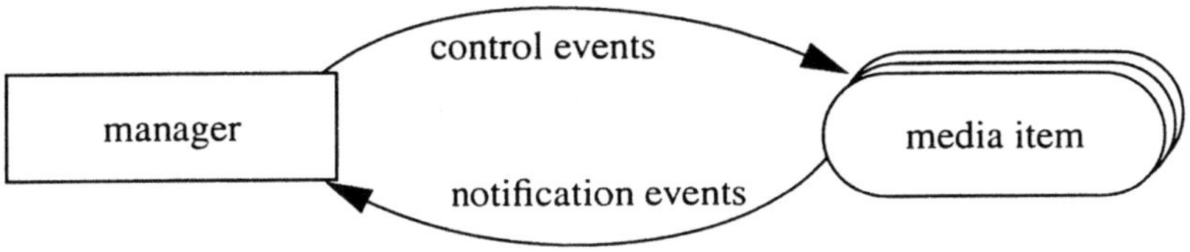

Fig. 2. Communication between a manager and a media item.

The example shows a constraint for media items that have to be used with a particular operator set respectively manager. A media item can only be used within a particular concept if it supports both event sets of the according manager.

Operators are used during the authoring process to specify the relations between media items. During presentation time managers and media items communicate via events to ensure the semantics of the operators. The task of a manager mainly consists of the processing of incoming events. After receiving an event the manager generates new events or sends the same event to other media items. Thereby, the processing depends on all operators used in the document.

2.5 MAVA Engine

Basis of the MAVA framework is the MAVA engine. It has two task: The first task is to build an environment for the presentation of a document and the second one is to support the managers during presentation time and their development.

The MAVA engine provides the base functionality for the MAVA presentation system. The MAVA engine loads documents and contains a class loader to load required classes of media items and managers from the local disc or network. Additionally, it provides the loading and management of media data.

The MAVA engine is used to simplify the event management and cooperation between managers with a scheduling graph. This is presented in details in the next section.

2.6 Final Architecture

After the description of all components of the MAVA system the final architecture of the framework is presented in figure 3. The basis of the architecture is the MAVA engine. For the presentation of a document the MAVA engine is extended with managers according to the operators used in the document. The framework is extensible with media items, operators and managers that realize the semantics of the operators.

3 Scheduling of MAVA Documents

The MAVA approach takes a graph as basis for the scheduling, which is similar to event nets [12], timed petri nets [1] and the scheduling graph of TIEMPO [5]. The MAVA

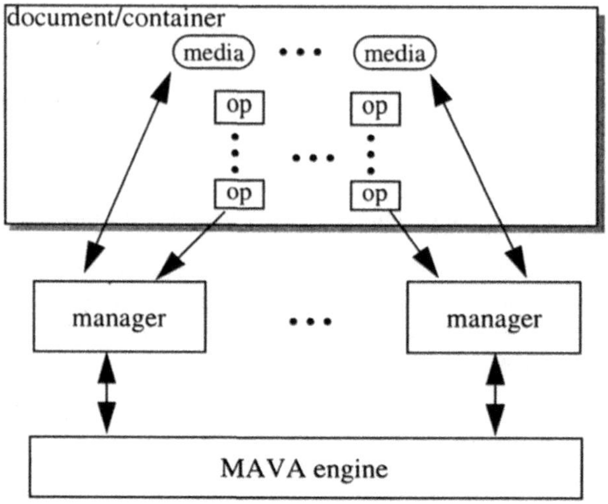

Fig. 3. MAVA architecture.

framework supports the temporal synchronization by an API for the construction of the temporal scheduling graph. The scheduling graph is used by all managers that are realizing the semantics of operators with temporal properties. During the presentation this graph is used to achieve the temporal layout of the presentation.

3.1 The Temporal Scheduling Graph

The temporal scheduling graph is a directed graph which represents the temporal course of the presentation. The elements of a graph (figure 5) are vertices, representing a particular event and edges. Edges are associated with a delay d.

All vertices are associated with a media item which will receive the event when the scheduling algorithm reaches the vertex. There are two classes of vertices:

1. Media begin vertices (BV): This vertex indicates the beginning of the presentation of a media item.
2. Media end vertices (EV): This vertex indicates the end of the presentation of a media item.

Instances of the three vertices are connected with edges. These edges determine the delay between the events of a vertices. Finally, the presentation of a document can be divided into 6 phases.

1. Building the initial scheduling graph structure (begin vertices, end vertices and all edges for known durations (delays) of media items)
2. Each manager completes the graph according to the operators used in the document
3. Computation of unspecified delays in the graph
4. Each manager registers itself for certain types of events at the media items
5. "Execution" of the scheduling algorithm for the presentation
6. According to the received events a manager alters the scheduling graph or sends

events directly to other media items.

The registering for arbitrary event types and the direct sending of events to media items are used to realize non-temporal concepts. For example, the result of a question in a computer based training lesson can be sent directly to an evaluation media item. But in this paper only the temporal aspects are covered for simplification.

3.2 The Scheduling Algorithm

Each document has a root vertex (RV in figure 5). This vertex has no events and no media item associated with it. It is used to specify all delays relative to the beginning of the container.

The algorithm simulates the delays associated with the edges of the scheduling graph. The delay set used by the algorithm is a set of delays (with their corresponding edges) that all are currently active. After a vertex has sent its event all outgoing edges become active and therefore they are added to the delay set.

Initially, the algorithm starts with the root vertex. Because the root vertex has no event all edges are added to the delay set. The algorithm takes the shortest delay of the delay set, waits the corresponding time and then subtracts the passed time from all other delays contained in the delay set. Then the event of the vertex is sent to the corresponding media item. If the vertex has outgoing delays edges they are added to the delay set. If the delay set is empty the algorithm will terminate and the document is completely presented.

The following algorithm is used to realize the scheduling:

```
method schedule(rootvertex)
  delayset = all edges from rootvertex;
  while delayset not empty
    sleep ( shortest delay of delayset);
    current vertex = vertex with shortest delay;
    remove shortest delay;
    subtract shortest delay from all delays in delayset;
    execute current vertex; // send event(s)
    add all outgoing edges of current vertex to delayset;
  end while;
end schedule;
```

3.3 Example: Temporal Synchronization

After the theoretical introduction of the scheduling graph, the scheduling of the sample document shown in figure 4 will be discussed. The sample document consists of two media items, an image and an audio sequence (with an implicit duration of 15000 milliseconds). Milliseconds are used because they permit a higher resolution of the temporal relations than seconds. Additionally there are two operators, which specify the temporal layout of the document. The first operator *start-at 1500* is from the concept of a time line. It means the presentation of the media item has to start 1500 milliseconds after the beginning of the document. The second operator *while(3000,5000)* is from the concept of temporal interval operators. This example shows that different concepts can be used alternatively or even in conjunction.

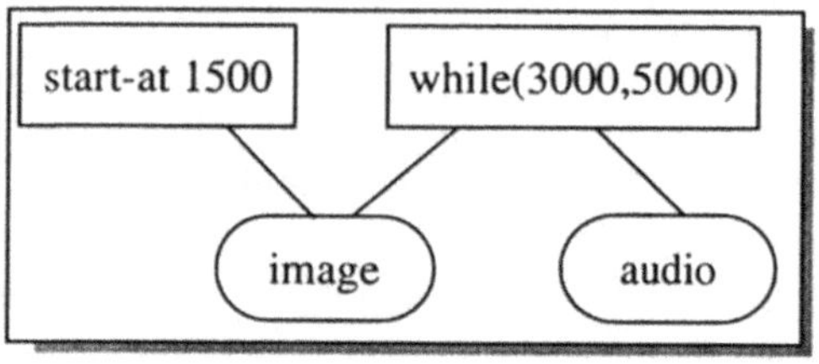

Fig. 4. A sample document with two different concepts.

For the presentation of the sample document (figure 4) the scheduling graph will be constructed. The first phase will build the initial graph structure which is marked with a grey background in figure 5. Then the managers of the two used concepts will com-

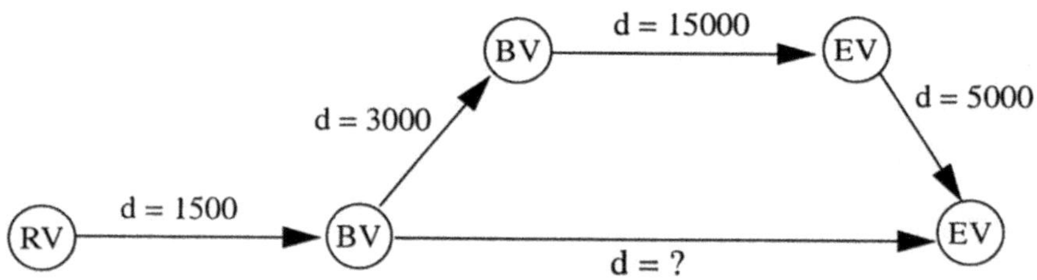

Fig. 5. Scheduling graph for the sample document (figure 8).

plete the graph. As first one the manager for the time line model, will insert an edge from the root vertex to the begin vertex of the image media item. The delay of that edge is set to 1500 milliseconds. It can be easily seen that this corresponds to the semantics of the *start-at 1500* operator. After that, the manager for the temporal interval operator will add two edges. The first edge is added between the two begin vertices of the two media items. According to the operators parameters the delay of the edge is set to 3000 milliseconds. The second edge is established between the two end vertices with a delay of 5000 milliseconds.

The final graph describes the semantics of the temporal relations between the media items. The presentation algorithm is now able to present the document. To handle the unknown delay (i.e. the duration of the presentation of the image) either the algorithm has to be extended or an additional phase that computes unknown delays has to be added. In the example, the unknown duration can be computed to 23000 milliseconds (i.e. the sum of the delays of the second path form the BV to the EV of the image). Another extension is the verification of the scheduling graph for consistency.

4 Related Work

There are a lot of document models that use an object hierarchy for media items, for example [7, 9, 11]. Most of the approaches deal with the realization of the scheduling for one particular temporal concept. These concepts are in most cases the temporal interval operators of Allen [14] or variants of it, for example [7, 9]. MAVA does not want to develop new temporal or spatial operators. MAVA provides a framework wherein different (existing and new) concepts can be integrated as managers. To integrate an existing approach for each concept (e.g. temporal, spatial) of the approach an adequate manager has to be developed.

Additionally, MAVA permits the integration of application specific operators (like the *follow* operator). This integration is the programming of a manager and its operators what is not very different compared to script programming. But managers and their operators can be reused by other authors and thus simplifying authoring of application specific multimedia documents. Naturally, this can be also done in all approaches that permit script programming. But MAVA avoids the problems of script programming that are mentioned in the introduction of this paper.

All DTD based approaches (e.g. SMIL [10] or HyTime) need to specify the semantic of their tags. If authors are allowed to define new tags the semantics have to be realized in the presentation systems. The *follow* operator example of the introduction showed that mapping on existing operators is not sufficient for all operators. Hence, a new presentation system or an extensible presentation system (i.e. the ability to add executable code) like MAVA are required to implement the semantics of new tags.

5 Summary

Because of its extensibility, the MAVA presentation system is able to present documents from different application areas like information providing, computer-based training or even small multimedia games and from new application areas that are actually not considered. Another aspect of the extensibility is to support both the authoring of documents and the implementation of the semantics of concepts of new application areas.

The MAVA prototype and the applicability of the concepts have been tested with following sample scenario to show their validity. The sample document consisted of several media items with temporal relations between them. The temporal relations were chosen from three different models for temporal synchronization: The first one has been a time line (start at, stop at), the second one the temporal interval relations (while, equals etc.) and the third one Weiss relations [13] (seq, par-min and par-max).

The presented approach has been implemented using Java. This leads to a platform independent realization which permits the integration into the Internet. Time dependent media items have been realized with the Java Media Framework (JMF) [8]. The provided media players are used to realize viewer components (i.e. classes responsible for the visualization of media items).

A DTD based approach and the MAVA approach do not exclude each other. The extensibility of the DTD approach requires also an extensible presentation system to achieve the semantics of the extensions.

This paper presented the results of the first research and development phase of MAVA. In a second phase a visual document editor and the improved storage format basing on XML will be realized. Additionally the Internet integration will be extended by a class loader. The class loader permits the loading and presentation of documents if the classes for the managers and media items or not locally available.

References

1. Senac, P., Diaz, M., Leger, A., De Saqui-Sannes, P. " Modeling Logical and Temporal Synchronizations in Hypermedia Systems. IEEE Journal on Selected Areas in Communications, Vol 14, num 1, 1/1996.
2. Wahl, T,; Rothermel, K. "Representing Time in Multimedia Systems". In Proceedings of the IEEE International Conference on Multimedia Computing and Systems". 1994.
3. Buford, J. F., "Evaluation HyTime: An Examination and Implementation Experience". In Proceedings of the 7th ACM Conference on HyperText. 1996.
4. German Research Foundation (DFG). "Distributed Processing and Exchange of Digital Documents". URL: http://www.cg.cs.tu-bs.de/dfgspp.VVVDD.
5. Wirag, S. "Adaptive Scheduling of Multimedia Documents". In Proceedings of Kommunikation in Verteilten Systemen (KiVS). 3/1999.
6. Bray, T., Paoli J. Sperberg-McQueen, C.M. ."Extensible Mark-up Language (XML) 1.0" Working Recommendation. W3C. 1998.
7. Pérez-Luque, M.J.; Little, T.D.C. "A temporal Reference Framework for Multimedia Synchronization". IEEE Journal on Selected Areas in Communication, 14 (1996).
8. "Java Media Framework". URL: http://java.sun.com/products/java-media/jmf/ index.html.
9. Jourdan, M., Layaida N., Roisin, C., Sabry-ismail, L., Tardif, L. "Madeus, An Authoring Environment for Interactive Multimedia Documents". In Proceedings of the ACM Multimedia 98. 1998.
10. Hoschka, P. (Ed.), "Synchronized Multimedia Integration Language (SMIL) 1.0 Specification". W3C Proposed Recommendation. W3C. 4/1998.
11. Geyer L. et al. "MHEG in Java -- Integrating a Multimedia Standard into the Web". In Poster Proceedings 6th International World-Wide Web Conference. 4/1997.
12. Buchanan, M.C., Zellwenger, P.T. " Scheduling Multimedia Documents Using Temporal Constraints". In Proceedings of the International Workshop on Network and Operating System Support fir Digital Audio and Video. 1992.
13. Weiss, R., Duda, A., Gifford, D.K., "Composition and search with a video Algebra". IEEE Multimedia, vol 1 num. 2. 2/1995.
14. Allen, J.F. "Maintaining Knowledge about Temporal Intervals". Communication of the ACM, Vol 26, Num 11. 11/1983.

Object Coherence in Distributed Interaction

Colin Allison, Feng Huang†, Mike Livesey

Division of Computer Science, University of St Andrews,
St Andrews, UK.
{ca,fh,mjl}@dcs.st-andrews.ac.uk

Abstract. Realtime distributed groupware (RDG) systems use computers and networks to support geographically separated users in their work on a common task at the same time. An RDG session typically consists of two types of interaction – that which involves one or more shared objects, and the use of audio-visual conferencing. It is important for users of such systems that the responsiveness of their interaction with shared objects has the same immediacy as their audio-visual communications. At the same time shared objects must have their integrity guarded in the face of multiple concurrent readers and writers. These coherence and responsiveness requirements often pull implementations in opposing directions. The concept of interactive atoms is introduced to address this problem. The successful construction of a distributed shared multi-user spreadsheet using multicast-based interactive atoms and multicast-based audio-visual channels is described.

1 Introduction

Computer supported collaborative work (CSCW) refers to methodologies that allow multiple users to collaborate on shared tasks. Groupware refers to tangible, usable applications that implement CSCW methodologies. Groupware that specifically supports simultaneous interactions between geographically separated users may be termed *realtime distributed groupware* (RDG), and typically exploits networked computers to support common group-oriented interfaces [1]. RDG is of special interest as its functionality subsumes that required by other modes of interaction, and interoperability between different interaction modes has been identified by Englebart as a key groupware requirement [2]. Ellis and Gibbs [3] have listed some other requirements of RDG systems as follows:

- response times must be short
- participants are not required to be connected to the same machine
- participants are free to come and go at any time
- participants are not required to follow a pre-planned script
- there is the possibility of a high degree of access conflict
- participants can communicate with each other via an audio-visual channel

The RDG application described in section 4 – a distributed, shared, multi-user spreadsheet – meets all of the above requirements. This paper focuses on the issues surrounding concurrency control and the use of *interactive atoms* to maintain shared

† Feng Huang now works for Citrix Systems (Cambridge) Ltd.

object integrity in groupware systems. Concurrency control in groupware demands more co-operation than competition: the users are aware of each other and intend to cooperate, in contrast to the conventional database approach which creates the feel of a private and isolated session.

Warp [5,6] is a coherence mechanism for general wide area distributed computing which provides a simple but powerful API based on *atoms* – a flexible and enhanced type of transaction. One of the key features of atoms is that they enjoy the correctness of serialisable behaviour. This paper describes their use in support of RDG. What makes the success of the approach interesting is that serialisability has often been rejected [3,4] as being unsuitable in RDG concurrency control. The next section discusses these issues.

2 Concurrency Control Issues in RDG

The discussion of concurrency control in the groupware context centres around the issue of ergonomics – the operational "feel" that a particular protocol gives to the user through the groupware "console". Moreover, much of the discussion is concerned with showing that concurrency control techniques based on serialisability are inherently unergonomic.

2.1 Serialisability

Greenberg and Marwood [4] present two scenarios as serialisability counter-examples. In the first, two users of a shared drawing package get into a tug-of-war over the position of a circle. Such a scenario can certainly arise, but Greenberg and Marwood attribute it to the system's attempts to serialise the moves of the two users. But if this were the case, then *removing* serialisation should solve the problem, or at least alleviate it. But of course, it does not – it could even exacerbate it, by allowing the circle to adopt an arbitrary sequence of intermediate positions. In fact, serialisation is orthogonal to the problem, which arises through lack of co-operation at the user level.

Greenberg and Marwood's second scenario concerns simultaneous update of a sentence in a shared editor. User Saul attempts to delete the sentence, say: "Now is the time for all men to come to the aid of the party", while user Dave attempts to insert the word "good" before "men". However, three actions get serialised:

- the delete;
- typing "go"; and
- typing "od".

If these are the atomic actions that the system identifies, then it is hardly surprising that serialising them can lead to undesirable behaviour. In the example, they are serialised in the order (2), (1), (3), leaving the state of the sentence as "od". There are two distinct problems here. The first is that the non-existent word "od" can appear in a text; the second is that any insertion at all is allowed to take place in an already deleted sentence. As regards the first problem, *not* serialising the actions can only make matters worse, by allowing even finer interleaving and therefore a greater variety of unwanted effects. The problem is not a consequence of serialisation – it is logically prior to serialisation and results from an inappropriate choice of temporal granularity – the subdivision of an operation into the atomic actions that get serialised. In the example, there should be only two such actions: the delete, and typing "good".

In contrast, the second problem does directly concern serialisability. A variant of it is also identified by Ellis and Gibbs [3]. In their scenario, two users each simultaneously issue serialisable transactions to "delete the third letter of a shared text string *S*". Here the unwanted effect is the clearly unintended deletion of the third and fourth letters of *S*. We claim that this apparent paradox arises not from *forcing* serialisation, but on the contrary from a *failure* of serialisation. This is because (in the context of the Ellis and Gibbs version) the second delete is actually not atomic – the state in which it is performed is different from that in which it was perceived to be necessary. The non-atomicity is caused by a misrepresentation of the semantic structure of the transactions involved. They are not of the form "delete the third letter of the *S* value read by the transaction", but "delete the third letter of *this S* value which I (the user) am looking at as I launch the transaction". We call such a transaction *dependent*, and it should do nothing to any other value of *S*. The real source of the paradox is attempting to use pre-programmed transactions in an interactive system. The Warp solution, which is described in sections 3 & 4 is to provide *interactive atoms* which encapsulate not only the actions on the data but also the user's decisions and choices about those actions. In the example under discussion one of the deletions will be unsuccessful and get backtracked. Its user will see that the new situation renders the delete obsolete, and can proceed accordingly along a different course.

2.2 Pessimism vs. optimism

When Kung & Robinson [7] described their original optimistic transaction mechanism, they claimed that it would outperform locking under low conflict. This notion became folklore, but Agrawal [8] has shown it to be largely a myth. Nevertheless, even if the choice between pessimism and optimism has no performance implications, it certainly has an impact on the ergonomics of a groupware system. Broadly, a pessimistic mechanism will give good progress but poor immediacy, because it must wait for every lock. For example, the Argus system [9] integrated database techniques into a programming language intended for use in application construction but an attempt to build a shared document editor, CES, frustrated researchers: "..in our initial experiments with the editor, response time was slow enough for the editor to be unusable in realistic testing...."[10]. Conversely, an optimistic mechanism will give poor progress (because uncommittable actions are allowed) but good immediacy. In an interactive system, particularly one liable to generate long transactions, it can be counter-productive if optimism frequently proves unfounded and large amounts of work are invalidated through conflict. The choice is a compromise.

3 The Warp Coherence Mechanism

The Warp coherence mechanism has been implemented in prototype centralised and distributed versions [15,16]. In the distributed implementation, objects reside at their creation sites and are managed by associated object managers (OM). A brief overview of the Warp coherence protocol is now given. A more detailed description of the protocol and the proof of its correctness can be found in [12].

Warp provides serialisable atomic actions (called *atoms*) across widely distributed objects. These objects are passive data items accessed by globally unique location independent names (OIDs). The Warp application programming interface (API) is shown in Table 1.

Table 1. The Warp API

Call	Description
`atom_begin`	Start an atom
`atom_end`	Try to commit the current atom
`atom_abort`	Abort the current atom
`atom_anchor`	Detect whether the current atom owns all the objects it has touched and then indicate not to touch any new objects

Warp atoms are different from conventional transactions in two important ways. First, in contrast to most transaction systems, a Warp atom always commits. Abort can only result from failure or an explicit invocation of `atom_abort`. In this setting, user abort appears as a backtrack to the start of the atom followed by immediate commitment. The second difference concerns the optimistic nature of atoms. The basic Warp mechanism is optimistic, but it can be controlled by the user in such a way as to support a variety of both optimistic and pessimistic concurrency control policies – this is *varimism*. To our knowledge, Warp is the only coherence mechanism that combines all the following properties:

- serialisability
- freedom from deadlock
- liveness
- responsiveness
- varimism

3.1 Serialisability

Serialisability is the primary remit of the Warp mechanism. Each atom operates on private shadow copies of the objects it accesses. The first access to an object is referred to as the atom's touch of the object. The state of the host process immediately prior to the touch is checkpointed. Atoms proceed optimistically, but must ultimately acquire locks on their objects (called *owning* the objects in Warp) in order to commit.

3.2 Distributing the Conflict Table

All the information relating to conflict between atoms is held in a logical data structure called the *conflict table* (CT). The rows of the CT represent atoms and its columns represent objects. Each CT entry therefore corresponds to a particular atom-object pair (A,x), and holds the information about the access of x by A. Distribution of the Warp system is then achieved simply by distributing the CT in a suitable manner. The communication layer supports a distributed shared memory system specific to the distributed CT. Table 2 shows how Warp operations are mapped onto the CT rows and columns which in turn are mapped onto multicast group communication channels. Messages cast to a row are seen by all objects involved in an atom, messages to a column are seen by all atoms involved with an object. When an atom completes its row disappears.

Table 2. Operations on CT rows and columns

Operation	CT Dimension
initial touch	row
backtrack	column
backoff & commit	row

IP multicast [22] is used to enhance scalability in two respects. Unreliable multicast is used in support of audio-visual channels and tools [17]. A multicast-based variant of RPC-2 [21] developed by the Warp project is used for reliable row/column group communications. Scalable reliable multicast can make significant demands on network infrastructure. It is therefore important to note the required *degree of scalability*. If a multimedia editing session is unlikely to ever consist of more than, say twenty, participants, then scalability beyond that dimension is of no great interest in that context.

3.3 Conflict Resolution

Conflict between two atoms is resolved by backtracking one of the atoms to the last checkpoint preceding its touches of all the conflicted objects in combination with releasing locks. A curfew on lock holding by an atom that is unable to commit ensures freedom from deadlock. Timeout values are set to reflect the type of application and its operating context. An RDG application will typically use values of less than one second. In contrast to conventional transaction systems, backtrack is graceful – an atom is backtracked just as far as is required to resolve the conflict. Moreover, even should an atom be backtracked to its start, this is not the same as conventional transaction restart. The atom retains the same identity, so its rerun is distinct from a new atom just entering the system.

3.4 Liveness

Atom identity ensures liveness. When an atom releases a lock, it passes to the atom with the smallest atom ID (AID) amongst those waiting for that lock. AIDs are numbers assigned as atom "birth dates", thereby giving priority by longevity. Because an atom retains its AID until commitment, regardless of intervening backtracks, it is guaranteed commitment when it eventually becomes the oldest extant atom in the system. However, the AID ordering is not an enforced serialisation order, because an atom can commit whenever it has all its locks. This can easily occur before all older atoms have committed.

3.5 Responsiveness

AID generation underpins the responsiveness of interactive atoms. Although liveness ensures eventual progress, it carries no bound on waiting time. AID generation from a local realtime clock could give a permanent priority advantage to a slow clock. Warp uses a method based on Lamport's clock algorithm [13] for maintaining a form of equity across distributed AIDs in order to avoid this problem.

3.6 Varimism

Varimism [14] provides a sliding scale of optimism. This is achieved by allowing the locking to occur more eagerly. An atom can *anchor* itself once it has acquired all the locks it needs. Provided that it guarantees not to attempt to acquire any new locks, it is immune from backtrack even though its computation may still be in progress and it is not ready to commit. This varimism allows a groupware system to be tuned to provide an application-specific optimal trade-off between pessimism and optimism. At the most pessimistic end of the spectrum, an atom must anchor before doing any computation.[1] This models a "checking in/out" regime, where anchoring corresponds to checking out the objects, and commitment to checking them in again. This mode of operation would particularly benefit atoms representing long transactions. At the most optimistic end of the spectrum, an atom can checkpoint once at the start and make no attempt to anchor until its computation is complete, risking a complete rerun in the event of a backtrack. This is similar to Kung & Robinson's original notion of optimism [7], with anchoring corresponding to their transaction validation.

4 Case Study: A shared spreadsheet

The spreadsheet executes on the distributed version of Warp and appears as shown in Figure 1. Its development was carried out using inter–desktop communications between participants at five locations on the Fife and Tayside Metropolitan Area Network, using multicast-based protocols for both the shared object and the Mbone audio-visual conferencing tools [17].

[1] It requires that it can predict the objects it is going to need.

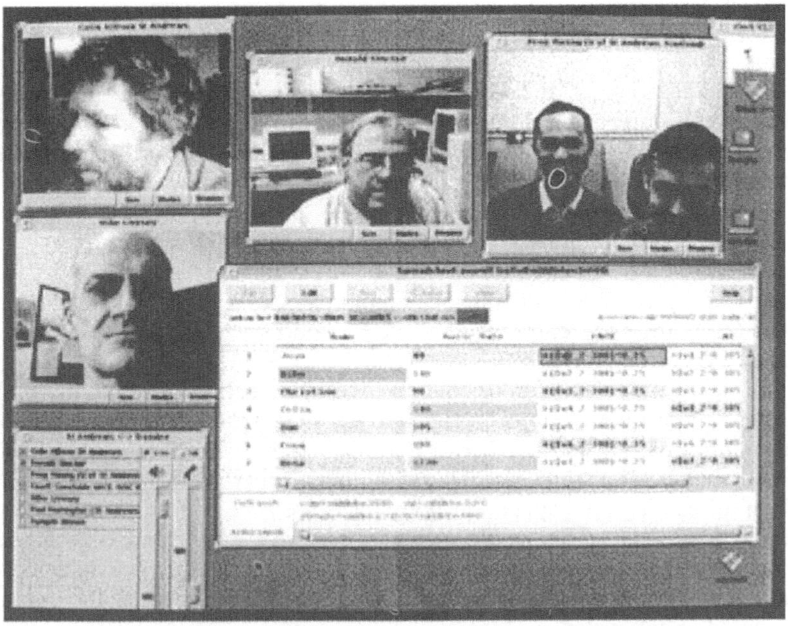

Fig. 1. A shared spreadsheet development session

4.1 Group awareness features

Each execution of the shared spreadsheet program is identified by a unique EID consisting of the user name, the host name and the port number. The title bar shows the name of the currently loaded spreadsheet and the EID. The graphic interface starts with a menu bar that enables the user to control the program. It is followed by a description of the colour code: *white* indicates that the object is untouched; *blue* shows that the object has been touched by someone else; *green* indicates that the user is the only one touching the object; *yellow* means that the user is the owner of the object but there are other users touching the object; and *red* shows that the user is in conflict with the owner of the object. Clicking on a cell/region which is potentially being modified by more than one user will display details of the other participants involved. It is then possible to use audio-video channels to discuss the situation with these other participants.

The overall status of an editing session is also displayed when a user starts editing a spreadsheet. A list of the participants in the collaboration is displayed below the spreadsheet. Clicking on a participant will reveal their personal information. Clicking on the "Active Sheets" button will expand the window to show all currently active spreadsheets. Clicking on a spreadsheet name will give a list of users who are currently accessing that spreadsheet.

4.2 The shared context

A shared context is a set of objects where the objects and the actions performed on them are visible to a set of users. In the shared spreadsheet case, the shared context consists of cell objects and a root object. All these objects are Warp objects. A cell object represents a cell in the spreadsheet. The root object holds the following information:

- the number of rows
- the number of columns
- the OID of the version number object
- the OID of the object storing the column names
- the OID of the object storing the column widths
- the OIDs of cell objects

Insertion or deletion of a row or column involves creating or removing multiple cell objects and modifying all objects related to the sheet structure e.g. the root object, the list of column names and the list of column widths. In these cases all objects are bundled together for a single checkpoint to improve performance.

When refreshing the display, the Warp OMs are accessed to get an up-to-date copy of the shared context. This would normally involve a lot of context switches and data copying. In order to reduce these overheads, a version number is associated with each spreadsheet. When an atom commits, the version number of the spreadsheet is incremented. Each instance of the application caches a version number. When it tries to refresh its display, it compares the cached version number with the version number in the OM. The application gets the up-to-date shared context from the OMs when its cached version number is smaller.

4.3 WYSIWIS issues in the shared spreadsheet

Group interfaces differ from single-user interfaces in that they depict group activity and are controlled by multiple users rather than a single user. What You See Is What I See, *WYSIWIS*, is a well known approach. In strict WYSIWIS everyone sees exactly the same image of the shared context but in practice this can prove too inflexible [18]. Alternative user-centric approaches have been made such as flexible user interface coupling [19] and window-level sharing [20]. The shared spreadsheet also opts for a more user-centric display and relaxes strict WYSIWIS in the following ways:

- Only the local cursor is displayed as multiple cursors are distracting.
- Uncommitted modifications are not automatically visible to other participants. This relaxation is quite natural in that a user would not normally want to make a modification visible until it was complete and committed, in a similar fashion to pressing the `enter` key to send a command from a terminal
- Committed modifications are propagated to other participants lazily. It is easy to identify key points where a display update is essential: firstly when a user starts a modification, and secondly when a user requests an updated view. When a user commits an atom the committed results are not propagated to another user until that user next accesses the Warp coherence mechanism or initiates an operation that involves a display refresh. In addition, the display is automatically refreshed every ten seconds.

- User-centric colour codes are used to communicate the relative status of regions of potential conflict.

4.4 Editing Sessions

An *editing session* is the interactive view of an atom provided by the user interface. A user must explicitly start, end or abort an editing session. During an editing session, a click on a unit of the shared context, results in a *touch* on the object representing that unit. All of the objects touched in an atom form the *touch set* of that atom. They are guarded by the atom and are subject to backtrack. As described earlier, one of the novel features of Warp is atom anchoring. The interface therefore allows a user to anchor an editing session explicitly, on the understanding that if the session subsequently touches any new objects the anchor is forfeit. It is reasonable to assume that, in the absence of backtrack, a non-interactive atom will terminate. In contrast, an interactive application comes with no such guarantees. A user might start an atom and acquire the ownership of some objects, then go for lunch or go on holiday! This would block other user atoms and prevent them from committing. To avoid such blocking, a *time-out abort* policy is adopted – if an atom receives no user input for more than a certain time, it is automatically aborted. At present no warning is given to the user, but a simple enhancement could consist of a countdown display.

5 Conclusions

The provision of appropriate concurrency control mechanisms in distributed interaction has been identified as a difficult but essential task. This paper has examined current thinking about the problem in the context of Realtime Distributed Groupware and explored the use of the Warp distributed coherence mechanism to address this problem. Experience with interactive atoms has shown that the only reason serialisability gives undesirable behaviour is through misuse, not through an intrinsic flaw in the model. The atom provides a very flexible interface which enables a variety of concurrency control flavours to be obtained and gives fine control over the interactive ergonomics of the system. It is the responsibility of the application designer to use serialisability correctly by choosing the appropriate temporal granularity, and the Warp model is powerful enough to enable them to do so.

An example groupware application, a shared spreadsheet, has been constructed, and is being used outside the research environment in multi-user business games in Finance and Management education contexts. Both the application data and audio-visual components are supported by IP multicast-based protocols. Experience has shown that the group interface and the interactive performance are acceptable for the required numbers of concurrent users.

References

1. ELLIS, C. A, GIBBS, S.J. & REIN G. L, Groupware -- Some Issues and Experiences, *CACM* 34,1, pp 39-58, Jan. 1991.
2. ENGELBART, D.C. Knowledge-domain interoperability and an open hyperdocument system, *Proc. of the Conference on Computer-Supported Cooperative Work,* ACM, pp 143-156 Oct. 1990.
3. ELLIS, C.A., and GIBBS, S.J., Concurrency Control in Groupware Systems, *Proc. of the ACM SIGMOD '89 Conference on the Management of Data* (June 1989) 399-407.
4. GREENBERG S& MARWOOD D, Real Time Groupware as a Distributed System: Concurrency Control and its Effect on the Interface, *Proc. of the Fourth ACM Conference on Computer Supported Cooperative Work*, pp 207 - 217 (Oct. 1994).
5. LIVESEY M.J & ALLISON C., Coherence in distributed persistent object systems, in *A.Albano & R.Morrison (eds.) Persistent Object Systems*, Proc. 5th Intern. Workshop on Persistent Object Systems, Springer-Verlag, pp 186-197 (Sept.1992).
6. ALLISON C, HARRINGTON P, HUANG F. & LIVESEY M, A Global Atomicity Primitive *in IWOOOS'96*, IEEE Press, Oct. 1996.
7. KUNG H.T & ROBINSON J. T, On Optimistic Methods for Concurrency Control, *ACM Transactions on Database Systems* 6,2, pp 213 - 226, June 1981.
8. AGRAWAL R & AND DEWITT D. J, Integrated Concurrency Control and Recovery Mechanisms: Design and Performance Evaluation, *ACM Transactions on Database Systems,**10*,4, pp 529-564, Dec. 1985.
9. LISKOV B., Distributed programming in Argus, *CACM* 32, *3*, pp 300–312, March 1988.
10. GRIEF I, SELIGER, R., AND WEIHL, W, Atomic Data Abstractions in a Distributed Collaborative Editing System, *Proc. of the 13 Annual Symposium on Principles of Programming Languages*, 160-172, 1986.
12. ALLISON C., HARRINGTON P, HUANG F. & LIVESEY M.,, The Warp Distributed Coherence Protocol and its proof of Correctness, *Technical Report W2/96*, Div. of Computer Science, Univ. of St Andrews. 1996.
13. LAMPORT L., Time, clocks, and the ordering of events in a distributed system, *CACM* 21,7 pp 558–565, July 1978.
14. LIVESEY M.J., Distributed varimistic concurrency control in a persistent object store **in** *Implementing Persistent Object Bases: Principles and Practice*, Morgan-Kaufmann pp 293-304, 1991.
15. ALLISON C, HARRINGTON P, HUANG F. & LIVESEY M,Warp 2.1.2 Release Notes and User's Guide, Tech. Report W3-95, Div. of Computer Science, Univ. of St Andrews. 1995.
16. ALLISON C, HARRINGTON P, HUANG F. & LIVESEY M., A Distributed Implementation of Warp, Tech. Report *W13-95*, Div. of Computer Science, Univ. of St Andrews. 1995.
17. MCCANNE S, Scalable Multimedia Communication - Using IP Multicast and Lightweight Sessions, IEEE Internet Computing, 3,2, pp33-45, March 1999.
18. STEFIK M, BOBROW D G, FOSTER G, LANNING S, & TATAR D, WYSIWIS Revised: Early Experiences with Multiuser Interfaces *ACM Transactions on Office Information Systems* 5,2, pp 147 - 167, Apr. 1987.
19. DEWAN P. & CHOUDHARY R. Coupling the User Interfaces of a Multiuser Program *ACM Transactions on Computer Human Interaction* **2**,1, pp 1- 39, March 1995.
20. PRAKASH A. & SHIM H. S, DistView: Support for Building Efficient Collaborative Applications using Replicated Objects, **in** *Proc. of the Conference on Computer-Supported Cooperative Work,* ACM pp 153-164, Oct.1994.
21. SATYANARAYANAN M, RPC2 User Guide and Reference Manual, School of Computer Science, Carnegie Mellon University, Aug. 1995.
22. DEERING S, Host extensions for IP multicasting, *ARPA RFC 1112*, 1989.

Integration of structured video in a multimedia authoring system

Cécile Roisin, Tien Tran_Thuong, Lionel Villard

OPERA project, INRIA Rhône-Alpes.
655 avenue de l'Europe, 38330 Montbonnot, France.
{Firstname.Lastname}@inrialpes.fr
http://www.inrialpes.fr/opera

Abstract. In this paper, we integrate some results on automatic structuration of video in a multimedia authoring system. For that purpose, we identify the specific video structuration requirements of this kind of application and we propose an XML syntax for the description of the structure, the temporal and spatial organization of video. Finally we describe a prototype application that takes advantage of this structured video format.

1 Introduction

Multimedia applications have to handle heterogeneous objects such as text, video and picture. Among these applications, we can identify applications for *multimedia documents* when the objective is the organization and the management of collections of different media. In multimedia documents, media objects are organized in both spatial and temporal dimensions according to their intrinsic basic attributes (duration of video, size of picture, etc.) and the *composition rules* given by the author.

Until now, applications consider media objects as atomic objects. But new needs appear, such video annotation, video indexing, or more generally multimedia document indexing with more elaborate synchronization scheme, etc. Media objects are not just atomic, but more complex and structured with additional information than their pure data coding. Emerging problems are therefore how to extract, to represent this information and to use it in multimedia applications.

Numerous works exist in the area of image analysis and in video analysis [18], [12]. As an example, the Movi project at Inria [3] contributes to the description of audiovisual objects, mainly on video structuration. Based on image analysis, several algorithms have been developed in order to group images in shots and to detect objects or events in shots.

There is also an important activity in the domain of specification and development of multimedia applications [4], [16]. In our project we have experimented multimedia composition through *Madeus*, an constraint-based authoring and presentation system [10].

In this paper, we propose to integrate some results on structuration of video (presented in section 4) in a multimedia authoring system (see section 5). We show in section 3 that specific needs of multimedia authoring imply to consider not only the structure of the video but also its temporal and spatial organization.

2 Existing video formats

Digital video information is encoded in different formats in order to meet various application processing needs. Video formats can be classified by their abstraction level:

- At the lower level, formats encode "only" the visual content of video. Formats such as Mpeg2 [14], Quicktime3 and AVI are adapted for storage (thanks to compression features), rendering or videoconference.
- At a medium level, we find formats for basic annotation and video editing. With these formats, tools can manage a video as a set of continuous frames on which annotations can be added. It is even possible to access a subset of frames in order to compose them with other types of media such as text or image [1]. The encoding of additional data is generally stored in a proprietary format. Recent formats, such as Quicktime4 and Mpeg4 [14], provide new facilities for inserting more structured information and for simplifying the edition process.
- At the highest level we find formats which store semantics data of videos (not just frames). This is useful for more sophisticated annotation services, for indexing in query systems and for access-by-content applications. Works on these formats are still in progress (such as the future standard Mpeg7[14]).

All the previous formats are video-centered. On the opposite we have formats which homogeneously integrate different kinds of media. They are mainly used in multimedia systems. Except Smil [17] and Mheg [13] which are standards, these formats are completely dependent to the tool in which they have been specified: Macromedia Director [11], CMIFed [16] or Madeus [10]. Moreover, all of them consider each type of media as an atomic piece used for temporal and/or spatial composition.

Our objective is to extend multimedia formats in order to integrate semantics data of video in a similar way than high level video-centered formats.

3 Requirements for structured video format

Multimedia documents are collections of heterogenous objects (such as video, audio, text, picture) organized in both the spatial and the temporal dimensions. Designing such documents is known to be a complex and error prone task, specially because they have to deal with complex temporal information (tasks synchronizations and objects durations).

The composition of an heterogenous set of media (text, video, sound, etc.) can be processed by placing spatial and temporal relations between objects. For instance, specifying that two objects play in sequence is expressed by a *meets* relation between them [10]. In the same way, for spatial dimension, specifying that two objects are left aligned can be done by placing the *left_align* relation.

Until now, we have considered that video (and audio) media were atomic media. But for many applications it is not enough accurate to manage and synchronize such coarse objects. Consider for example the slide show in Fig. 1: on the right of the screen, there is the video of the show and on the left appears the currently presented slide. It is difficult to synchronize these two objects in such way that during the presentation each slide is synchronized with the corresponding video excerpt. If we decompose and structure the video, we will be able to compose *video elements* such as shots or scenes with other media of the document. In the previous example, the temporal composition will express that each slide must be played at the same time that its corresponding scene in the video. This need is slightly different than video annotation [5] or video editing

Fig. 1. Slide show multimedia document

such as with the Adobe premiere tool. In fact, a multimedia presentation requires to manage dynamic behaviors due to user interactions and indeterminism due to unstable rendition conditions (load processor and network bandwidth).

Before presenting the format that we have defined for the video, we identify the requirements that such a format must meet in order to allow its use in a multimedia authoring and presentation system. First of all we need to point out and access suitable chunks of video, as provided by its logical organization;

second we want to set temporal relations on these chunks with other media objects of the document, so we need to model temporal and spatial information between video elements in order to ensure global consitensy during composition; finally all these actions must be available through simple and rapid actions.

4 Video structured format

4.1 Basic choices

The choices taken in our video model are mainly motivated by the requirements of the first application we want to realize: we want to compose in space and time fragments of video (the appearance of a character, the beginning of a scene or shot) together with other media objects (text, picture, sound,...) of the multimedia document. Therefore the definition of the video structure must specify the video decomposition in terms of elements together with space and time relations among these video elements.

We choose the markup language XML (eXtensible Markup Language) because it is a language suited to describe structured information and their properties. Moreover, in order to easily integrate video structures in multimedia systems, we choose XML because it is yet used as a description language for multimedia documents such as in Smil [17] and Madeus [10] (on which our prototype has been built, see section 5.2). Even the Expert Group that specifies Mpeg4 envisions the use of XML for Mpeg4 definition [14].

The complete DTD (Document Type Definition) of our video definition can be found in the web site of our project [15].

4.2 High level structuration

Basically, a video is a series of continuous images, which can be organized in a hierarchical structure. Therefore our description format for video will express that organization in terms of the elements that reflect that structure and the relationships among these elements.

Basic entities and relations. In a video structure (Fig. 2), we can identify two categories of elements: temporal elements (Sequence, Scene, Shot, Occurrence, Event,...) and non-temporal elements that identify characters or objects that appear in the video (called Class). The set of time relations used in our video model is a subset of Allen's relations [2]: meets, starts, equal, during, finishes.

As an example, Fig. 4 gives an excerpt of the XML source file of the structuration for the video `Allocine.mpeg`. Notice that the current element is designated by the character "." in the temporal relations. Three types of spatial relations are used in our model: topological relations (Near, At), projective relations (Right, Left, Above, Below, In_front_of, Behind, Beside) and the relation Between. This set could be extended such as in [7].

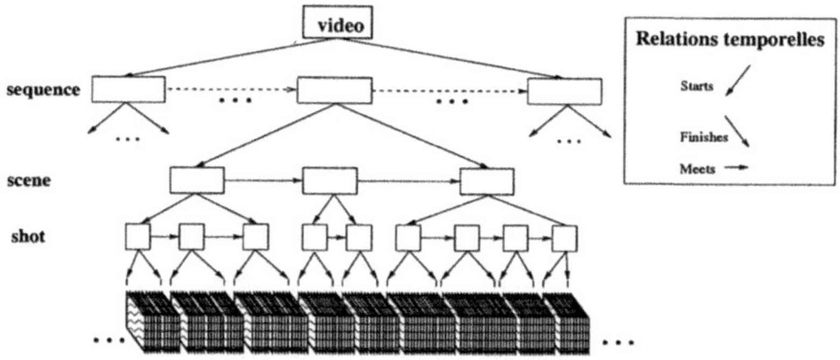

Fig. 2. Basic structure of video

```
<!-Elements of structure video --!>
<!ELEMENT Video (Sequence+,Class*, Rel_Temporal)>
<!ELEMENT Sequence (Scene+,Rel_Temporal)>
<!ELEMENT Class (Instance+)>
<!ELEMENT Scene (Shot+, Rel_Temporal)>
<!-Relations -->
<!ELEMENT Rel_Temporal (Equal | Meets | Finishes | Starts |  During)+>
```

Fig. 3. DTD part of high level video entities

```
<Video Name="allocine'' FileName="allocine.mpg" NumberImage="902" ...>
   <Sequence  Name="Seq" FirstImage="1" LastImage="902" ...>
     <Scene Name="Scene1"  FirstImage="1"  LastImage="120"  .../>
     <Scene Name="Scene2" FirstImage="121" LastImage="768" ...>
        <Shot Name="Shot4" FirstImage="121" LastImage="173" .../>
        <Shot Name="Shot5" FirstImage="174" LastImage="433" .../>
        <Shot Name="Shot6"  FirstImage="433" LastImage="510"  .../>
        <Rel_Temporal>
          <Starts Interval1 ="."  Interval2 = "Shot4" />
          <Finishes Interval1 ="." Interval2 ="Shot11"  />
          <Meets Intervals = "Shot4 Shot5 Shot6"/>
        </Rel_Temporal>
      </Scene>  ...
   </Sequence>
   <Rel_Temporal> <Equals Interval1="." Interval2="Seq" /> ... </Rel_Temporal>
</Video>
```

Fig. 4. XML structure of the allocine video

Hierarchical structure of video. The basic structure of video consists of three kinds of components, from the smallest to the biggest: shot, scene, and narrative sequence [6]. A *shot* is defined as a series of images, from the moment the camera begins to run to the moment it stops, usually a few seconds. A *scene* is a dramatic unit composed of a series of shots strung together, showing action in one place and at one specific time. A *sequence* is the highest dramatic unit of video, composed of several scenes, all linked together by their emotional and narrative momentum [6].

These elements are organized in the hierarchical structure as follows: a video element contains sequence element; a sequence is composed of scene elements; and a scene includes shot elements. The temporal relations among these elements are defined as follows (see the corresponding XML syntax in Fig. 3):

- sequential relation (*meets*): between two continuous shots of a scene, two continuous scenes of a sequence and two continuous sequences of a video.
- parallel *starts* (resp. *finishes*) relation: between the first (resp. last) shot of a scene and that scene (i.e. its parent in the structure), between the first (resp. last) scene of a sequence and that sequence, between the first (resp. last) sequence and the video.
- parallel *equal* relation: when a shot, scene or sequence is the unique component of a scene, sequence or video.

4.3 Low level structuration: shot description

The description of the former basic components allows to synchronize coarse elements (shots, scenes or sequences) of video in multimedia documents. It can be useful to allow a more fine grained synchronization and for that purpose it is necessary to be able to describe the content of shots such as the occurrence of characters or objects, the transition between shots, etc.

We have defined three types of components in shots: transitions, occurrences of characters or objects and events:

- A *transition* element describes the passage from one shot to the next one. A transition can be: a fade-in, a fade-out, a dissolution or a wipe [6]. As we have chosen to include transitions into shots, we can have meets relations between shots, scenes and sequences (see 4.2).
- An *occurrence* element describes a person or an object that appears in the shot. It refers to the *class* element that corresponds to that person or object. The structure of class elements is defined in section 4.4.
- An *event* element describes a particular situation in the video that is considered as a relevant part such as a motor explosion, a plane taking off, a demonstration, a storm, etc. The event element can also describe a period in a shot in which a spatial property among persons or objects is valid.

These three types of elements are components of shots in the hierarchical structure of the video (see Fig. 6). Events may also belong to a scene when they are spread through several shots. A transition only appears when its shot begins, hence, it is located in time by a relation *starts* with that shot. An occurrence or an event can appear at anytime in the shot in which they are included. Therefore, we use the *during* relation between these elements and that shot. The corresponding part of this description in the DTD is given in Fig. 5.

```
<!ELEMENT Scene (Shot+,Event*,Rel_Temporal?)>
<!ELEMENT Shot (Transition?, Occurrence*, Event*, Rel_Temporal?)>
<!ELEMENT Rel_Temporal (Equals | Meets | Finishes | Starts |  During)+>
```

Fig. 5. DTD part for shot description

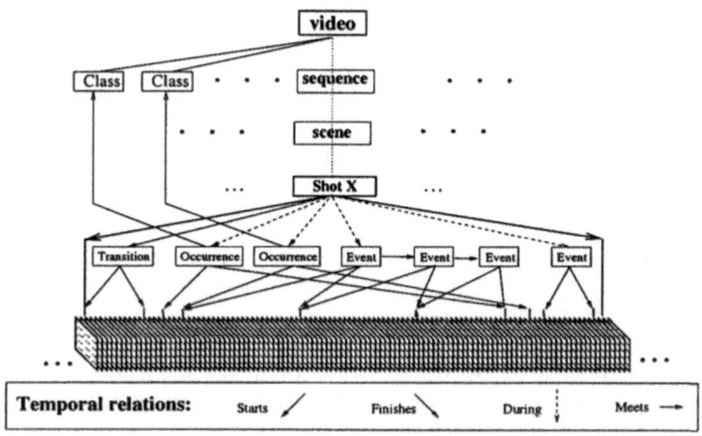

Fig. 6. Structuration of a shot

Spatial relation is a way to define events in shots. It is defined among characters or things that appear at the same time in a shot, such as A stays behind B, A walks on the left side of B, etc. Notice that due to the intrinsic dynamic behavior of the video, spatial relations can change with time. For instance, in the fifth shot of video Allocine.mpeg, there is a Taunus car that follows a Volvo; when the Taunus approaches the Volvo, the Taunus overpasses the Volvo by the left side and then goes ahead the Volvo. To describe these changes, we have to define many periods in the shot corresponding to the different spatial relations among the occurrences. In the former example, we can separate that part of the shot in several periods connected together with a *meets* relation (see Fig. 7).

4.4 Non-temporal elements of video

In order to describe characters or objects in video, we use the *class* element whose content is a list of *instance* elements. The *instances* of a class identify different

```
<Shot Name="Shot5" FirstImage="174" LastImage="433" ...>
  <Transition Name="Trans" Type="Fade-in" FirstImage="174" LastImage="193" ...  />
  <Occurrence Name="Taunus runs" FirstImage="194" LastImage="420" .../>
  <Occurrence Name="Volvo runs" FirstImage="234" LastImage="400" ... />
  <Event Name="Position1" FirstImage="234" LastImage="294" ...>
    <In_front_of-Behind Interval1="Volvo runs" Interval2="Taunus runs"/>  </Event>
  <Event Name="Position2" FirstImage="295" LastImage="332" ...>
    <Near Interval1="Volvo runs" Interval2="Taunus runs"/>    </Event> ...
  <Rel_Temporal>
    <Start Interval1="." Interval2="Trans"/>
    <During Interval1="." Interval2="Position1" Delay="60"/>
    <Meets Intervals="Position1 Position2 ... "/> ...
  </Rel_Temporal>
</Shot>
```

Fig. 7. XML Description of a shot of allocine

occurrences of that class that will appear in shots: each *instance* element points to the corresponding *occurrence* element in the shot. *Class* elements are located at the highest level in the video structure (see Fig. 6). Notice that *class* elements are the only elements in our video structure that are not directly related to time.

5 Implementation

We describe in this section how the video structuration that we have defined in the above section can be used in our multimedia authoring environment Madeus.

5.1 Madeus: a multimedia authoring tool

Madeus is an authoring environment for multimedia documents which meets the following requirements: a high level of expressiveness for both spatial and temporal dimensions; a user-friendly interactive interface; and portability. It differs from other multimedia environments mainly by its constraint-based approach and the tight coupling of presentation services with editing services. Indeed, the authoring services provided in Madeus are based on multiple views [9]: the **presentation view**, the **timeline view** and the **hierarchical view**. The views are strongly linked: any operation performed in a view is passed on the other views in order to ensure data consistency.

5.2 Integration of video structured media

The composition of video entities with other media in a multimedia document is realized in three stages:

- the analysis of the video in order to extract video elements,

- the generation of this resulting information into the XML exchange format as described in section 4,
- and finally the integration of structured video elements in Madeus thanks to editing facilities provided through synchronized views.

The analysis and structuration of the video are processed using a tool named *Videoprep* [3]. This application uses semi-automatic processes to give any video a complete structure. This structuring is obtained in 3 steps: shot cut-out, zone extraction and class definition. For each step, the automatic process can be followed by a checking of the results and by manual editing, using a video player and specific graphic tools. This application uses a proprietary format for storing the video elements that have been detected and structured.

The generation of a XML document is straightforward from the Videoprep format. First, Videoprep data, such as basic components (scenes, shots, ...), numbers of shot frames and spatial positions of occurrences, are directly converted into the XML format. Second, the implicit temporal relations are generated with respect to the rules taken in section 4.

The final step is the composition of video elements with other document elements. This is provided through a new view added in the authoring tool. This view, called the ***structured video view***, contains four main parts:

- (1) is the rendering of the selected video element.
- (2) is the description area of the selected video element; for instance, the images that characterize a shot in the selected scene.
- (3) is the visualization of video elements in a hierarchical structure.
- (4) displays quantitative information of the selected video element.

6 Conclusion

In this paper, we have presented a solution for integrating structured video in multimedia authoring tools. We have specified a format that not only describes the logical organization of video elements but also their temporal composition.

The current state of our prototype allows to write a multimedia document that contains video media defined in the format of section 4. It is possible to compose elements of video with other media objects in a time consistent way and to play the resulting document. The structured video view is fully implemented and provides basic functionalities as described in this paper.

Future works evolve towards the modeling of other features of video. One important direction is the spatial organization and the motion of video objects. This work will allow the user to align other media objects (a text for instance) with the position of a video object (for instance a character in a video scene), even if that object moves inside the video. For that purpose, it is necessary to determine spatial relations among video objects thanks to the automatic analysis provided by Videoprep. However the problem is complex because (1) the set of useful spatial relations is user dependent and (2) these relations evolve during time due to moving objects and camera movements. It is clear that manual specification is also required.

Another direction of work is to develop the specification of class elements in the video. In this paper, classes are described as a flat structure (every class element is placed as a child of the root in the XML video structure). However it could be useful to specify a more structured set of classes (with subclasses) that will reflect object classification.

References

1. Adobe,"Premiere",*http://www.adobe.com/products/premiere/*, 1999.
2. J. F. Allen, "Maintaining Knowledge about Temporal intervals", *CACM,* vol. 26, num. 11, pp. 832-843, 1983.
3. Bertolino P., Mohr R., Schmid C., Bouthemy P., Gelgon M., Spindler F., Benayoun S., Bernard H., *Structuring Video Documents for Advanced Interfaces,* INRIA, http://www.inria.fr, to be published, 1999.
4. Buchanam C., Zellweger P.T., "Specifying Temporal Behavior in Hypermedia Documents", *Proc. of the ACM Conf. on Hypertext,* pp. 262-271, December 1992.
5. Carrive J. Pachet F., Ronfard R., "Using Description Logics for indexing Audio-visual Documents", *Int. Workshop on description Logics,* pp. 116-120, 1998.
6. Chandler D., "The 'Grammar' of Television and Film", *UWA,* vol. 1994, http://www.aber.ac.uk/~dgc/gramtv.html.
7. Gapp K.P.,"From Vision to Language: A Cognitive Approach to the Computation of Spatial Relations in 3D Space", *Cognitive Science Program,* vol. Dept. of Computer Science, Universitat des Saarlandes, D-66041 Saarbrucken, Germany.
8. Hammoud R., Chen L., Fontaine D., "An Extensible Spatial-Temporal Model for Semantic Video Segmentation", *First International Forum on Multimedia and Image Processing,* Anchorage, Alaska, May 1998.
9. Jourdan M., Roisin C., Tardif L.,"Multiviews Interfaces for Multimedia Authoring Environments", *Proc. of the 5th Conference on Multimedia Modelling,* Lausanne, 1998.
10. Jourdan M., Layaïda N., Roisin C., Sabry-Ismail L., Tardif L., "Madeus, an Authoring Environment for Interactive Multimedia Documents", *6th ACM Multimedia'98,* Bristol, 12-16 September 1998.
11. Macromedia,"Director", *http://www.macromedia.com/software/director/,* 1999.
12. Meng J.., Chang S.F., "CVEPS - A Compressed Video Editing and Parsing System", *ACM Multimedia'96,* pp. 15-24, ACM Press, Boston, 1996.
13. Meyer-Boudnik T., Effelsberg W.,"MHEG Explained", *IEEE Multimedia Magazine,* vol. 2, num. 1, pp. 26-38, Spring 1995.
14. The MPEG Home Page,*http://drogo.cselt.stet.it/mpeg/.*
15. Opera,*DTD for video,* Inria, http://www.inrialpes.fr/opera/dtdvideo.txt, 1999.
16. Rossum G., Jansen J., Mullender K., Bulterman D., "CMIFed : A presentation Environment for Portable Hypermedia Documents", *Proc. of the ACM Multimedia Conf.,* California, 1993.
17. W3C Recommendation,"Synchronized Multimedia Integration Language (SMIL) 1.0 Specification", *http://www.w3.org/TR/REC-smil,* 15 june 1998.
18. Zhang H. J., Low C. Y., Smoliar S. W., Wu J. H., "Video Parsing, Retrieval and Browsong: An Integrated and Content-Based Solution",*ACM Multimedia'95,* pp. 15-24, ACM Press, San Francisco, 1995.

Head-Tracked Light Field Movies: A New Multimedia Data Type

Gavin S. P. Miller, Steven M. Rubin, Philip M. Hubbard, Jenny Dana, and John Woodfill

Interval Research Corporation, 1801 Page Mill Road, Building C, Palo Alto, California 94304
{Miller, Strubin, Hubbard, Jdana, Woodfill}@Interval.com

Abstract. This paper presents a new multimedia data type based on time-varying light fields. Such a light field movie may be precomputed using computer graphics, or photographically captured from real objects as they change over time. Such movies allow a user to experience motion parallax in response to head motion in addition to motion cues within the scene as well as stereo vision cues. Important elements to make such media practical include light field movie capture devices, effective compression schemes with real-time playback, and accurate head tracking. This paper addresses these areas and presents results from the current system as well as directions for future work.

1 Introduction

As the area of multimedia matures, desktop video has become a well-supported data type with both hardware support (such as MPEG2) and efficient software-based algorithms such as vector quantization [1]. However, even the best video systems (analogue or digital) do not create a flawless illusion of looking through a window at a real object. This is due to the absence of certain visual cues, two of the most important of which are stereo disparity (derived from a different image at each eye) and motion parallax in response to head motion. As the power of personal computers continues to advance it is appropriate to consider multimedia data types that accommodate these cues. We start by examining prior work.

"Fish tank" virtual reality [2] (and its horizontal counterpart a "visual workbench" [3]) has been presented as a way to create the illusion of a 3-D world using a conventional flat display. In such a system, a user's head is tracked, and 3-D graphics is used to render the appropriate image to be presented to each eye, using stereo glasses. While such systems can create a convincing effect they have two severe limitations: the images must be rendered with small enough latency for the perceived world to remain spatially stable as the user moves his or her head, and the scenes need be represented using 3-D models. The rendering capability of the hardware places a constraint on the maximum visible scene complexity and it is very hard to create convincing models of real-world scenes and people.

These constraints may be overcome using image-based rendering such as light fields [4] or lumigraphs [5]. (These, in turn, can be seen as generalizations of QuickTimeVR object movies [6], with sufficiently dense sampling of orientation space to allow interpolation of views by blending.) By combining light field rendering with head-tracking and stereo display we can achieve a form of virtual holography, in which a user's head position determines the view presented to each eye. This paper describes such a system for light fields. By extending light fields to be time varying, we create "light field movies".

An ideal light-field movie system would consist of a camera that can observe an object or a scene, and then create the illusion of viewing that scene remotely, either live or from a recording medium. (Such scenes could also be rendered synthetically.) The scene, when viewed, would provide a convincing illusion of depth. To see behind an object, a user would move to one side to gain a different point of view. Specular materials would glint and sparkle in response to head motion and both eyes would fuse their views to allow the perception of a flawless 3-D world.

1.1 Capturing Light Field Movies

A capture device for such a system is illustrated in Fig. 1. A linear array of cameras is directed towards a target object (the heart) centered on the object plane. The cameras would be separate physical devices, for a live video system. However, when the scene is static or only changes slowly, a single camera may be used in combination with a positioning table. Such an arrangement is shown in Fig. 2 and Video 1 [17]. The camera is translated by a linear table and rotated, to track the center of the object.

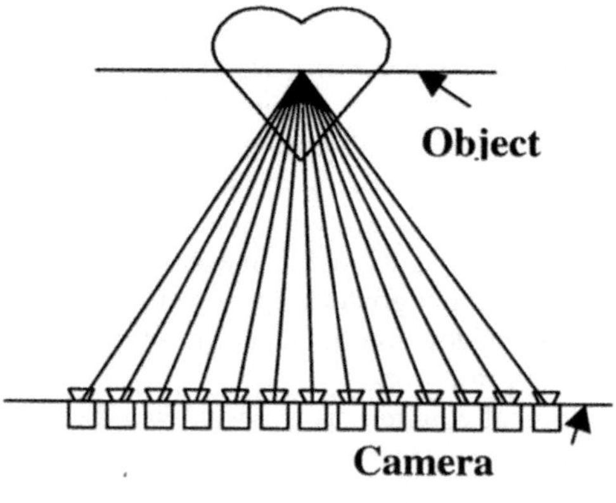

Fig. 1. Light field capture geometry

Fig. 2. Linear light field gantry filming "Icarus"

During image capture, the camera translates laterally. Since the camera also tracks the object, a re-mapping must be used to compute the image as if projected back onto the object plane.

1.2 Displaying Light Field Movies

To view light field movies requires a display that shows an image to each eye that has been reconstructed from the appropriate slices of camera data. This can be done in one of two ways. The display can project light in a view-dependent fashion so that the current eye position selects the appropriate slices (like a conventional hologram), or we can track the user's eye positions and display to each eye an image dependent on that eye's location. The optical modulation scheme has the advantage that the user does not need to wear special glasses, and there can be more than one viewer. However, special optical elements are required [7][8] and the entire light field video stream must be decompressed to modulate the display. This leads to prohibitive bandwidth requirements, equivalent to hundreds of channels of uncompressed video. The tracking-based approach only requires the rendering of two images per time step. To implement such a system requires an appropriate display, a head-tracking device and a graphics system fast enough to refresh the images with imperceptible lag. We will consider each piece in turn.

Stereo display can be achieved using a conventional cathode ray tube in combination with stereo glasses. If the use of glasses is considered undesirable, then an autostereoscopic display [9] may be employed, although effective systems are not currently available commercially. The rendering subsystem would compute the appropriate image for each eye with minimal latency and high frame rate. A software-based motion-light-field renderer is on the edge of being practical for such a task. An algorithm for this is described in Sections 2 and 3. This opens up the prospects of supporting light field stills and movies as first class multimedia data types, once an acceptable tracking system is perfected. Recent research suggests that the perceptible lag for such a system may need to be as low as 10 to 15 ms [10], which implies the need for hardware rendering support to achieve imperceptible latency. A high accuracy, low latency head-tracking system is described in Section 4.

2 Light Field Geometry and Sampling

This section describes the geometry and generation of the light fields for this paper.

2.1 Light Field Geometry

Levoy and Hanrahan [4], and Gortler et al. [5] described a way to render light fields using rays indexed by their intersection with two planes. We place one of the two planes of the light field to be coincident with the screen pixels. (This is identical to the geometry required to generate a slit hologram [11].) Illustrated in Fig. 3.

Given a new viewing location L, we project a ray from a screen pixel through L back onto the capture plane. This gives us the P, Q parameters for the captured image for which the corresponding X, Y pixel holds the correct view of the scene. By similar triangles P and Q can be seen to vary linearly with screen location X and Y.

A light field with only horizontal motion parallax may be captured by moving the capture camera along a linear trajectory parallel to the imaging plane. Such images may be rendered or captured using a gantry such as that in Fig. 2. Moving off this trajectory in depth (towards and away from the screen) will only lead to mild projection errors. Moving up and down leads to more pronounced artifacts, but this happens less readily, when the user is sitting in front of a monitor on a chair.

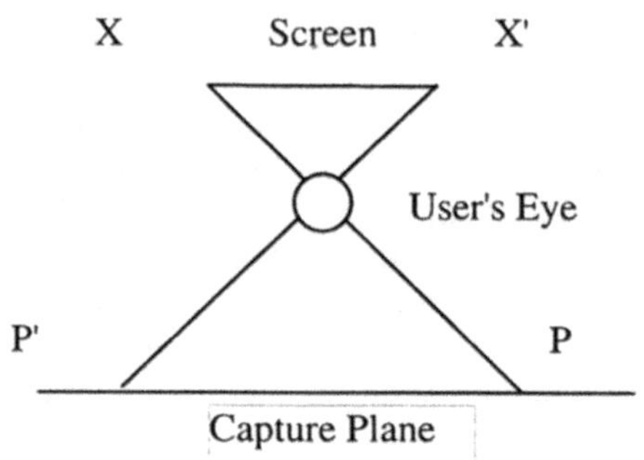

Fig. 3. Plan view of capture camera versus view location

2.2 Motion Light Field Generation

Motion light fields may be rendered or captured photographically. Plates 1 and 2 show stills from computer generated light field movies (Videos 2 and 3 [17]). We also wanted to capture motion-light fields of real objects. Our approach was to move the objects slowly enough to be captured by the gantry. Stop frame animation was achieved using a mechanical automaton (Icarus) under stepper motor control. A full sweep was made of the gantry, for each stepper motor position. Each sweep involved 100 images (in P) with 6 sub-steps averaged for depth of field filtering. The animation can be seen in Video 4 [17]. Plate 3a illustrates the center view, and the view constructed from the far right-hand camera position, after a corrective projective mapping. Plate 3b and Video 5[17] illustrates melting ice to generate motion. A longer-term goal is the construction of a light-field movie camera.

3 A Software Renderer for Motion Light Fields

We are interested in implementing light field movie playback on current personal computers. To achieve this requires both efficient resampling of the light field data (based on the current viewing location) and efficient decompression schemes.

3.1 Constant Background Optimization

To take advantage of regions of unchanging background, we constructed a "foreground map" which represented all pixels that were not background for at least one of the orientations. Plate 1 shows views of a time-varying ornament along with its foreground map. During display, any pixels not tagged by this map will not change from the background color. Such regions do not require light-field samples, nor do they require resampling during rendering. Using this optimization, rendering performance for the decorative ornament was doubled compared to light fields that updated all of the screen pixels. Plate 2a represents a motion light field for which the foreground optimization is ineffective. The shark, during its motion, touches almost all of the foreground pixels.

3.2 Coherence for Efficient Resampling

Given the screen-aligned parameterization of Section 2.1, the question arises of the most efficient way to resample the light field. For a one-degree-of-freedom light field (i.e. those with only horizontal motion parallax) a single interpolation is required rather than the bilinear interpolation required for 2 degrees of freedom. It is worth noting for efficiency, that computational gains are possible by computing a column of pixels at a time. Since P changes linearly with X, P is constant for a given column of pixels. By arranging X, Y images to be contiguous in Y, it is possible to achieve good memory caching performance along a column. Additional savings may be achieved by using cheaper forms of blending such as 1-bit interpolation, where two values are averaged, if the blend value is more than one half, otherwise the first value is copied. This leads, on average, to a reduction in rendering time of one third. Plate 4 shows a comparison of blending with 1-bit interpolation.

The current implementation generates an off-screen buffer and then copies that buffer to the screen. The maximum frame rate for the pixel copy was approximately 78 frames per second, which significantly degraded the performance of our algorithms. All timing for light fields in this paper correspond to gray-scale stereo images (since we used red-green stereo for display) and are for a Xeon-based personal computer running at 400 MHz.

3.3 Light Field Movie Compression

For a light field movie of some duration, the data sizes can be very large. Our Icarus sequence is 10,000 images (3 GB uncompressed) for 3 seconds of motion. The shark sequence was 256 images in orientation by 230 time steps or 17.25 GB of uncompressed data for 7.5 seconds of motion. A naïve light field movie channel might require up to hundreds of video channels of a conventional cable system.

These requirements can be alleviated somewhat by the same tricks used with video clips on CDROMS. Short sequences can be interspersed with less expensive media, movie loops can show a cyclical or brief event, and compression may be used to reduce the cost of data transmission and storage provided that decompression may be done in real time. Just as vector quantization was used to enable software-based video codecs, VQ has been applied successfully to light fields [4]. However, in the scheme presented, a fixed compression ratio of 24 to 1 was all that was possible on the fly. To gain lossless compression of the VQ indices required an off-line decompression step of the entire set of indices for a given time step. A preferable scheme would allow decompression of just the set of indices to be viewed.

3.4 Vector Quantization Compression

As a starting point for our compression schemes, we employed the vector quantization scheme of Hanrahan and Levoy, although our scheme used 16 pixel blocks to represent the two spatial dimensions, one orientation, and time. Table 1 shows the compression ratios obtained using VQ coding with run-length elimination of constant backgrounds. Frames per second (FPS) is shown for one and two processor machines. As expected, the shark and ornament compress well. Since these scenes are grayscale, we would expect a ratio of about eight-to-one without run length encoding,

Table 1. Compression ratios for run length VQ

Sequence	Ratio	FPS 1 Proc.	FPS 2 Proc.
Ornament	43.4	46.7	60.2
Shark	43.05	23.8	35.0
Snake	7.83	23.4	35.8
Icarus	7.88	22.0	32.6

3.5 Codebook Minimization

We generated VQ codebooks with 16384 sample blocks. To gain further compression, and to speed encoding, we combined codebook entries together by iteratively merging the two closest codebook entries. This was continued until the mean-squared difference of the closest pair was above a given threshold. (For the examples in this paper, this threshold was set to 2.0, where intensity values range from 0 to 255. The mean squared error of our compressed image sequences was approximately 1.5 levels out of 256.) The entries in the codebook were, in turn, used to compress the images leading to an array of block indices. Further compression was then possible using various lossless schemes for these indices.

In the special case of light fields with 1 DOF, we can use coherence in a column of pixels (or indices) to use various forms of lossless encoding on the fly. Before each column of pixels is resampled, we decode its corresponding column of indices.

3.6 Optimum Word-Size Encoding

Fixed table Huffman coding may be used to compress the indices. Table 2 shows the playback and compression rates for the different movie sequences. Huffman decoding is slow, but it acts as a good method to compare with the performance of other, less computationally expensive algorithms. Given the large number of similar images to be compressed, we were able to store large conditional probability tables to aid with lossless compression. In one scheme we used the conditional frequency distribution for a given index, we determined the optimal number of bits to represent the most frequent 2^N entries of that distribution.

In the bit stream, each index was encoded with a leading bit, which determined whether the subsequent bits represented a short code, or a full sized code. The meaning of the short code was determined by the previously decoded index. This scheme outperformed Huffman coding in both compression ratio and speed. However, it more than halved the performance of the renderer.

Table 2. Huffman Coding performance

Sequence	Rel. Ratio	FPS 1 Proc.	FPS 2 Proc.
Ornament	1.22	12.9	21.2
Shark	1.66	12.6	17.8
Snake	2.36	4.4	8.1
Icarus	1.71	3.5	6.2

Table 3. Conditional Word-Size performance

Sequence	Rel. Ratio	FPS 1 Proc.	FPS 2 Proc.
Ornament	1.43	25.7	33.0
Shark	2.10	18.8	26.5
Snake	3.74	10.7	12.1
Icarus	2.56	9.1	10.9

Table 4. Index Pair-Quad Coding performance

Sequence	Rel. Ratio	FPS 1 Proc.	FPS 2 Proc.
Ornament	1.08	35.7	50.8
Shark	1.81	22.7	33.8
Snake	2.80	20.7	31.5
Icarus	1.89	18.9	29.8

3.7 Word Aligned Lossless Encoding

Given the basic cost of unpacking bit streams, we decided to explore using encoding schemes that were word aligned. Since our codebook sizes were restricted to a maximum of 14 bits, we could employ the additional two bits in a two byte word for additional compression information. A conditional frequency table was used to come up with a list of the N most frequent index pairs. N was limited to a maximum of 2^{14}. The table was not grown beyond the point at which the frequency of a given pair was less than two. In practice all 14 bits worth of table were always used. A second table was generated for successive pairs of indices into the first. This index-pair conditional frequency table was used to generate a quad index table that stored the M most common pairs of index pairs. M was limited to a maximum of 2^{15}, or less if the next most common pair of index pairs had a frequency of less than 4.

The list of indices for an image was encoded as follows. If the four indices matched an entry in the quad index table, then the most significant bit was set and the address in that table was stored in the other 15 bits. If not, then each pair of indices would be tested to see if they were in the index pair table. If so, the second most significant bit was set, and the address in that table was entered into the remaining 14 bits of the code. Finally, if neither was true, the original code index was stored in the code word. This allowed for very efficient decoding as is evident from Table 4. The compression ratios obtained were somewhat lower than the conditional word size scheme. However, rendering performance nearly matched the light field renderer with only run length encoding, and is the preferred method for our system. This compression algorithm can be seen as a form of variable block size VQ coding.

3.8 Temporal Coherence

To exploit temporal coherence, our implementation kept the uncompressed indices of light field 0. The run length encoding scheme kept the indices for subsequent light fields where they were not identical to those for light field 0. Two blocks were considered "identical" if their mean squared difference was less than a threshold (in this case 2.0). As the indices were decompressed, the zero runs were filled in with the corresponding indices from light field 0. Rendering performance was unaffected relative to the non-frame-differenced scheme. Table 5 shows the results of using index differencing. The relative ratios are with respect to the size of the VQ compressed image.

Table 5. Compression ratio with index differencing

Scheme	Snake	Icarus
None	5.77	1.93
Huffman	9.02	2.81
Cond. Word	11.49	3.9
Pair-Quad	8.66	2.75

4 Tracking

As described in Section 1.2, one approach to the display of light field movies requires tracking of the user's eyes. This section summarizes the requirements of tracking and some techniques for meeting these requirements.

4.1 Requirements and Existing Techniques

The tracking system must be able to determine the eyes' positions in three dimensions, including depth. The ideal system would track the eyes directly, but in practice, the system may track the head and infer the eye positions. The tracker must provide real-time performance, the most important aspect of which is low latency. Ideally, latency should be below 10 to 15 ms [10]. The tracker must provide high accuracy, with freedom from jitter and drift being most important. Finally, the tracker must be convenient for the user. Convenience is reduced if the user must wear special equipment, or if the user must manually initialize the tracker.

Tracking can be accomplished by a variety of means: mechanical arms like the Immersion MicroScribe, electromagnetic systems like the Polhemus FASTRAK, active vision-based systems like the LED-based Northern Digital OptoTrak and the infrared technique of Morimoto et al. [12], and passive vision-based techniques like color-histogram algorithms of Bradski [13] and Birchfield [14].

4.2 A Multi-Modal Vision-Based Algorithm

For our tracking system, we wanted the convenience of a passive vision-based technique, with the further convenience of no user initialization. Our algorithm was inspired by the success of previous multi-modal algorithms [15].

The first technique in our algorithm uses traditional ideas for matching templates in an intensity image by minimizing the sum of squared differences (SSD). The other technique uses a depth image computed by real-time stereo hardware [16], searching this image for a *face-blob*, a region with a depth profile similar to a human face. The algorithm uses the face-blob's position to initialize the intensity template and to correct for drift in the template matching process.

The face-blob finder searches the depth image for the shallowest pixel (closest to the stereo cameras). In regions around this pixel, it performs a sequence of tests to count the pixels within a specified depth interval from the shallowest pixel. If a face-blob was found at the current frame but not the previous one, then a face has entered the scene and the tracking algorithm grabs a new intensity template at the face-blob's position. The algorithm also uses a vector from the template match position to the face-blob's position to slightly adjust the overall tracked position, thus reducing drift.

Plate 5a shows a user in front of the two cameras used by our stereo hardware. We have added a modest texture to the user's red-blue glasses, as texture helps both algorithm techniques. Some results of our algorithm appear in Plate 5b and Video 7 [17].

The algorithm reliably finds users' heads and begins tracking without user initialization. It comes close to meeting our requirements for real-time performance. Given the depth image, it takes 15-16 ms to update the tracked position using a 300 MHz Pentium II. Our current version of the stereo hardware introduces two frames (66 ms) of latency to produce the depth image, but a future version should eliminate much of this latency. The algorithm's accuracy also comes close to meeting our requirements, but there is still some jitter.

5 Conclusions and Future Work

We presented a novel software-based light field renderer that can run at from 30 to 60 frames per second with two to four times higher compression ratios than previous techniques, both for precomputed animations and captured images.

The system originally used a mechanically-based tracker. By combining real-time stereo with template-based correlation, we developed a passive vision-based tracker, although work remains to be done in terms of robustness, jitter and latency.

Our work to date has shown that light field movies can provide a vivid illusion of viewing a moving 3-D scene. However, a number of problems remain. The most pressing of which is the large data size of the files even after compression. It seems likely that static light fields could be downloaded over the web given next generation modems. However, downloading entire light field movies would be tedious.

Plate 1. Three views of an animated ornament with its foreground pixel map

Plate 2. Two images from a) shark light field movie and b) snake light field movie

Plate 3. Images from a) the Icarus automaton light field and b) the melting ice time lapse light field

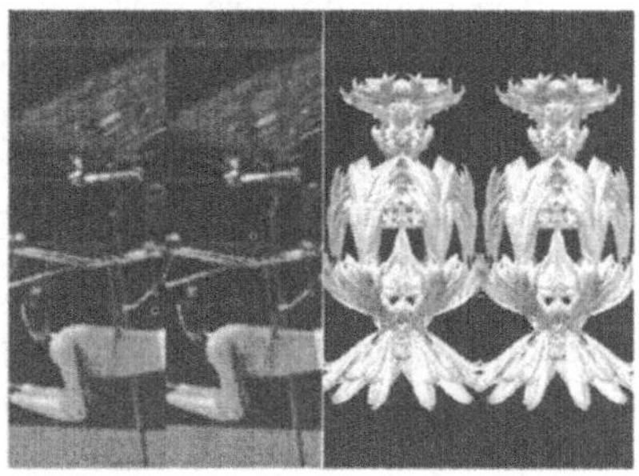

Plate 4. Two comparisons of 1-bit interpolation (on left) versus linear blending (on the right)

Plate 5. The vision based tracker a) seen in use and b) with the tracking result as seen by the cameras.

Similarly, broadcasting light field movies would require large amounts of bandwidth, probably on the order of tens of video channels given better compression techniques.

A likely near-term application of light fields would be e-commerce, allowing users to preview photographically captured static objects. Short light field movie clips may also be added to DVDROM titles, such as encyclopaedias, where they would be well suited to showing cyclical mechanisms, plants growing etc. They could also be used for any 3-D scientific visualization too slow to render in real time, such as time-dependent volumetric scanned medical data or weather simulations.

References

1. Gersho, A., Gray, R.M.: Vector Quantization and Signal Compression. Kluwer Academic Publishers, Dordrecht (1992)
2. Deering, M.F: High Resolution Virtual Reality. Computer Graphics Proceedings, Annual Conference Series, ACM SIGGRAPH, New York (1992) 195—202
3. Cutler, L.D., Frolich, B., Hanrahan, P.: Two-Handed Direct Manipulation on the Responsive Workbench. 1997 Symposium on Interactive 3D Graphics, ACM (1997) 107—114
4. Levoy, M., Hanrahan, P.: Light Field Rendering. Computer Graphics Proceedings, Annual Conference Series, ACM SIGGRAPH, New York (1996) 31—42
5. Gortler, S.J., Grzeszczuk, R., Szeliski, R., Cohen, M.F.: The Lumigraph. Computer Graphics Proceedings, Annual Conference Series, ACM SIGGRAPH, New York (1996) 43—54
6. Chen, S.E.: QuickTime VR–An Image-Based Approach to Virtual Environment Navigation. Computer Graphics Proceedings, Annual Conference Series, ACM SIGGRAPH, New York (1995) 29—38.
7. Lucente, M., St-Hilaire, P., Benton, S.A., Arias, D.L., Watlington, J.A.: New Approaches to Holographic Video. SPIE Proceedings #1732, Holographics International (1992) 377—386
8. Kajiki, Y., Yoshikawa, H., Honda, T.: Three-dimensional Display with Focused Light Array. SPIE Proceedings #2652, Practical Holography X (1996), 106—116
9. Shiwa, S., Tersutani, N., Akiyama, K., Ichinose, S.,. Komatsu, T.: Development of Direct-View 3D Display for Video-phones Using 15 inch LCD and Lenticular Sheet, IEICE Trans. Inf. and Syst. Vol E77-D, No. 9, Sept. 1994.
10. Regan, M., Miller, G.S.P., Rubin, S.M., Kogelnik, C.: A Real-Time Low-Latency Hardware Light-Field Renderer. To appear Computer Graphics Proceedings, Annual Conference Series, ACM SIGGRAPH, New York (1999)
11. Halle, M.: Holographic Stereograms as Discrete Imaging Systems. SPIE Proceedings #2176, Practical Holography VIII (1994) 73—84
12. Morimoto. C., Koons, D., Amir, A., Flickner, M.: Pupil Detection and Tracking Using Multiple Light Sources. IBM Research Report, 1998, available from the WWW site: domino.watson.ibm.com/library/cyberdig.nsf/Home.
13. Bradski, G.R.: Computer Vision Face Tracking for Use in a Perceptual User Interface. Intel Technology Journal, Q2 1998, http://developer.intel.com/technology/itj/q21998.
14. Birchfield, S., Elliptical Head Tracking Using Intensity Gradients and Color Histograms. Proceedings IEEE Computer Society Conference on Computer Vision and Pattern Recognition (1998) 232—237
15. Darrell, T., Gordon, G., Harville, M., Woodfill, J.: Integrated Person Tracking Using Stereo, Color, and Pattern Detection. Proceedings IEEE Computer Society Conference on Computer Vision and Pattern Recognition (1998) 601—609
16. Woodfill, J., Von Herzen, B.: Real-Time Stereo Vision on the PARTS Reconfigurable Computer. Proceedings IEEE Symposium on Field-Programmable Custom Computing Machines (1997) 242—250
17. Video Clips 1-7 http://web.interval.com/papers/1999-076

Visually Critiquing Web Pages

Pete Faraday

Microsoft Corp,
Redmond, WA, USA 98058
Petefar@microsoft.com

Abstract. This paper explores how visual information is organized in a web page. A cognitive framework is outlined for how web pages are processed into a visual hierarchy. The guidelines derived are implemented as rules in a critiquing system and embedded in a web editing tool, allowing the user to spot potential design problems. The paper concludes with a critique of two well known web pages.

1 Introduction

What makes some web pages easy to understand, whilst others appear as a complex jumble ? Several writers have pin-pointed the design of the page as being of key importance. Yale's style guide [14] suggests 'Overuse of graphic emphasis leads to a 'clown's pants' effect where everything is garish and nothing is really emphasized' Meads [16] agrees that 'web pages that dazzle the user can also be distracting and can hide important information... they can make text unreadable and turn off a viewer.' Fleming [9] admits that 'rather than being seen as a solution to some of the web's usability problems, graphic design is often regarded as their source... churning out useless visual distractions that glitter and sparkle on the screen.'

The first question is, how can we develop a framework to explain effective web page design ? Bernstein [3] suggests problems with applying subjective ratings of sites : 'critical judgements are inevitably open to censure as arising from personal affection, idiosyncrasy, affinity or poor judgement'. However, Bernstein also concludes that usability tests are not in themselves the answer : 'usability testing can reveal flaws in poorly designed pages.. but can not prove that the pages are well executed'.

We argue that the process of viewing a web page is a cognitive one, and that in order to understand 'good design', we must first understand these cognitive processes. Web pages are made up of a complex combination of perceptual elements: static and animated media, text and image; in different sizes, different colors, font styles, groupings and spatial layouts. This paper reviews cognitive studies to explore how these variables can be used to guide the viewer through the web page, providing them with an ordered 'visual hierarchy' of information. We claim that the ordering of this hierarchy should match the content being communicated. Tufte [21] suggests that 'contrasts of elements will tend to produce a visual hierarchy, with layers of inactive background, against notable content. When everything is emphasized, nothing is emphasised; the design will be noisy, cluttered and informationally flat'.

The first section of the paper presents our framework, with each section discussed in terms of relevant studies and our derived guidelines, and their predications compared to existing web page design heuristics. A case study example of a company home page is used to motivate our guidelines. The second section uses the framework as the basis for a critiquing system. This provides the designer with a web page layout and editing tool that attempts to predict the viewing order of the page using a set of rules.

2 Case Study Example

The paper is illustrated by an example for a company home page. This is shown in figure 1 (the new.gif image is shown animating when the page loads).

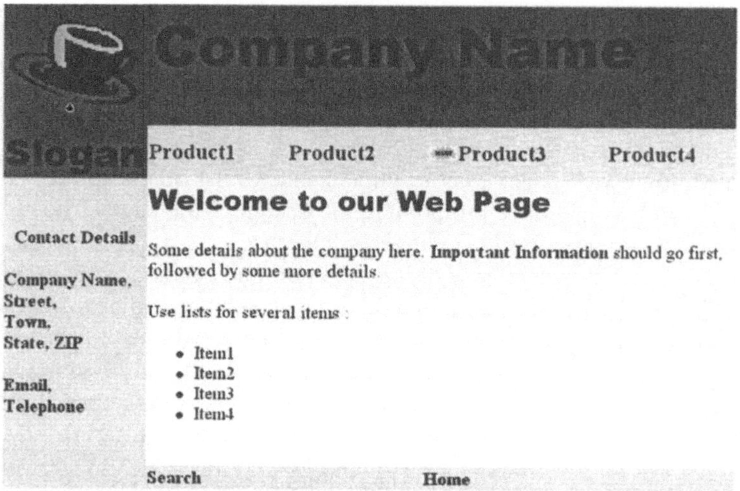

Figure 1 Company home page. The 'new' .gif is shown animating. Try squinting at it to see it as a set of perceptual elements.

This web page has a number of levels of information, such as the company identity, a welcome message, links to its products, and contact details. The designer may intend certain information to be more important eg a new product is more important than the old; or the companies name is more important than their telephone number. The role of the example in this paper is not to typify good design, but to illustrate our guidelines.

3 Cognitive Framework

We suggest the visual processing of web pages forms a distinct visual hierarchy in which certain perceptual elements have priority. We divide the process of reading a web page into two phases : the first phase is termed 'search', the second is 'scanning'. The search phase takes place when the viewer attempts to find a salient entry point into the page. Once an entry point is found, the scanning phase is then used to extract the information.

3.1 Search

The first search phase decides where attention should enter the page. The guidelines that we have identified for the search phase are ordered as follows:

3.1.1 Motion :

The most important variable in the search phase is motion. Triesman [20] suggests that motion is detected within the region fixated upon by the eye by low level receptors. She notes that motion detection is automatic, causing the object in motion to 'pop out' of the display.

Several web page design heuristics note motion as being a strong cue. Fleming [9] suggests that 'movement draws our attention; used judiciously and with purpose, animation can be an exciting and effective way to communicate information' However, Yale [14] cautions 'animation should be meaningful, not distracting. Ideally, it should add something to the content of your page'.

In the case study example shown in figure 1, the animated 'new' .gif would dominate over the rest of the page, drawing attention to it before any other elements.

3.1.2 Size :

The second place variable in our hierarchy is size. Bertin [4] provides a list of 'retinal variables', suggesting that size is most important. Support for this claim can be found in Arnheim [2], who notes that larger objects will be focused on in preference to smaller. Empirical evidence for the importance of size is given by eye tracking studies undertaken by Yarbus [24]. He showed that larger objects had primacy in pictorial items, and that the user would fixate on them first, and for longer than smaller displays.

Our guideline here is that larger elements will be attended to over smaller elements. Two sets of web page heuristics support this. Ameritech [1] note 'in general, the larger an item is, the greater its perceive visual importance and likelihood of attracting attention. Make sure that items of greatest importance are easy to see'. Fleming [9] agrees, suggesting that 'larger items will generally draw attention first and be seen as the more important elements on the screen; when these clues are not available, sorting through the information can be an overwhelming experience'.

In the case of figure 1, the size of the 'Company name' text and the company logo image would make them equally dominant over other static items in the page, since they are the same height.

3.1.3 Images :

The third variable is the use of images. Stone & Glock [25] performed an eye tracking study of subjects reading a set of instructions. They found that subjects first looked at the illustration for 1-2 seconds, then the text caption. Brandt [5] provides some empirical evidence that graphics and images are attended to in preference to text. He performed a number of eye tracking studies of newspaper pages. He concludes that 'pictures and figures have an exceedingly high attentional value; reading copy is only a last resort in many cases.'

Our guideline here is that images will be attended to in preference to text. Yale's web page guidelines [14] note that viewers 'begin to pick out specific information, first from graphics, and only afterward do they start parsing the 'harder' medium of text'. [22] proposes that 'graphics should be used to attract attention to the target area'.

In figure 1, company logo .gif would dominate over the company name text. This means that attention will search into the image prior to the text.

3.1.4 Color :

Where several elements have a similar size, color can be used to discriminate which element is most important. Arnheim [2] suggests that parts of images which are more brightly colored will gain focus : 'Bright colors are heavier than dark ones'. Triesman [20] concludes that differences in surface characteristics such as color and brightness can provide cues for visual search.

Our guidelines here is that brighter colored elements will dominate over darker. Fleming's guidelines [9] agree that 'color and contrast also show relationships between items and establish importance, a highlight color on a page tends to draw the eye'.

3.1.5 Text style :

The fifth place variable concerns text styles, such as font and type format. Glynn et al [10]; Lewis & Walker [6] propose that physical typeface information may be attended to. Glynn et al note that certain type styles, such as type face, weight or font size, italics, underlining become part of meaning of the text, or provide a 'typeface personality' upon the text: 'typographical cueing systems are nonverbal devices for attracting and focusing the readers attention.'

Web page guidelines also suggest text style as being useful to draw attention to important words. Nielsen [17] offers that 'hypertext links serve as one kind of highlighting ; typeface variations and colors are another'. Yale [14] agrees that 'Editorial landmarks like titles and headers are the fundamental human interface issue in web pages'.

3.1.6 Position :

Finally we use position to arbitrate an entry point if the size, type, color and style can not make a distinction. [15] suggest that a page of text is viewed at a number of granularities, with a top-left bias in selecting where reading should begin. However, [2] notes that in non text displays, the center will be dominant; and that if a number of images are shown, factors such as symmetry will displace the center.

For simplicity, our guidelines favor elements at the top and left of the page, based on reading order. Fleming [9] concurs 'items placed to the left and top of centre tend to be noticed first and are considered more important'. C-NET [7] notes that 'in page layout, the top of the page is always more dominant.'

3.2 Scanning

Having located an entry point into the page during the search phase, the second phase now produces scanning of the area which contains the entry point :

3.2.1 Area :

Wertheimer [22] argues that elements are grouped according to Figure and Ground relationships, forming a 'Gestalt'. Figure elements are 'completely enclosed' by other ground elements, which cause them to grouped, and separated from other figure objects. Arnheim [2] notes that 'Area establishes a hierarchy by creating distinction. A scale of importance leads through intervening steps, from foreground to background.'

The web page guidelines also suggest that grouping is important. Fleming [9] proposes that 'grouping or placing elements in proximity provides information about there relationship' C-NET[7] notes that 'colored backgrounds and table cells can lead the readers eye down the page'. Ameritech [1] agrees that 'Items which share the same color will typically be seen as relating to each other'

In figure 1, we would predict that the animated 'new' gif would attract attention into the upper product name area; scanning would then proceed in this area until the elements enclosed within it had been viewed. Thus the product names are likely to be viewed before the name of the company, or the welcome text.

3.2.2 Proximity & Reading Order :

Wertheimer [22] defines that 'proximity describes the tendency of individual elements to be associated more strongly with nearby elements than those which are farther away.' Our guideline here is that elements which are in close proximity will be grouped together; and that grouping will follow a reading order, moving from left to right, and top to bottom.

Several web page heuristics acknowledge reading order as being useful. Fleming [9] notes 'placement or position can suggest the relative importance or sequence in which we are meant to digest them'. Yale [14] suggests that 'readers of English read from left to right and from the top of the page to the bottom... this fundamental axis dominates most design decisions'

In figure 1, the animated 'new' gif will set an entry point into the image, with the order then being set from left to right and top to bottom with elements in proximity of the product name area.

5. Web Page Critiquing Tool

A significant difficulty with design or evaluation using our visual hierarchy guidelines is the time it takes to perform the analysis. Authors of web pages are used to being able to rapidly change a page : eg re-format and move elements around the page. Predicting a problem leads to the need to change the web page, and thus requires further iterations of evaluation and design improvement. The time and effort consumed makes paper based guidelines unwieldy for real world use.

Our answer to these problems has been to embed the guidelines within a tool, enabling the generation of the visual hierarchy to be automated. The notion of a 'critic' is similar to Fischer [8] who defined critic based advisors that do not automate design, but attempt to spot and alert users to design problems which they can then fix.

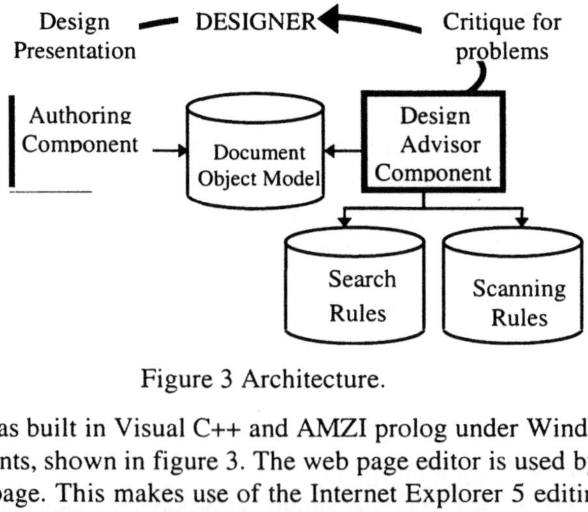

Figure 3 Architecture.

A prototype tool was built in Visual C++ and AMZI prolog under Windows 98. It has two main components, shown in figure 3. The web page editor is used by the designer to manipulate the page. This makes use of the Internet Explorer 5 editing component to provide WYSIWYG page manipulation. The visual hierarchy is produced using a set of rules which search the document object model in a priority order, based on the search guidelines.

6. Rule Implementation

The critic components were built in prolog. The rules used to produce the visual hierarchy and to critique it will now be described in more detail :

a) Initialize : The first set of rules are used to initialize the visual hierarchy search. Rules are defined to parse out the HTML tags into visual elements, and to combine tags which refer to the same visual element. The result is a set of facts which refer to visual elements by screen location, color, size, media type, and style.

b) Search phase : The next set of rules search through the elements, seeking components which could potentially be in focus. A particular element is selected based on the following rules

i) Dynamic media : the rules first search for any animated images on the page. These rules recognize that animation have a very high attentional value and will gain focus as soon as the page is shown. If several animated .gifs are found then rules ii)-v) are used to arbitrate. In figure 2, the entry point is set as the animated 'new' .gif by these rules.

ii) Size : the next rules use height as a surrogate for area to determine which element is the largest. This is because it is difficult to accurately find an average screen area of a word in a line of text. If several candidate elements are the same height, then rules iii)-v) are used. In figure 2, the rules determine that the 'Welcome..' text is an entry point in the lower area over 'Contact details' because of the larger height of the font.

iii) Images : these rules are used to search for images over text. If several text elements are found then rules iv) and v) are applied. If several image elements are found of the same size, then rule vi) is applied. In figure 2, the coffee cup .gif is used as an entry point in the top area because these rules favor images.

iv) Color : the rules favor brighter colored text over darker, or the default black text. Our current implementation does not extract an average color value from images, so we are unable to compare image color in the critique.

v) Text style : The rules ignore the default paragraph style, searching for areas of importance in the text. They favor hyperlinks, then bold, then italic and underline.

vi) Position : the rules favor the top of the screen and left of the screen, over the bottom and right. This is based on the reading order of the page, and provides a default entry point into the page if all of the elements do not differ across any of the rules in i) to v).

c) *Scanning phase :* Having found an element to enter the page upon, the critique now prioritizes the elements which are grouped as follows:

i) Area : rules search for any areas of color which completely enclose the element found in the search phase. This set of rules constrains scanning within this area, so that elements are grouped. The rules attempt to expand the enclosing area until either another color area is found, or blank space is encountered. In figure 2, once the animated new. gif sets the entry point in the middle area, these rules confine scanning to that area, moving from left to right from the entry point to 'Product 3' and 'Product 4'.

ii) Proximity & Order : Within any area found, the rules now simulate a reading order from left to right and top to bottom, starting from the entry point. This is based on the reading order for english, and assumes that once an entry point is found by the search phase, ordered scanning will then take place. These rules treat an image as a single whole, and ignore any text which is not formatted using color or text style or formatting to draw attention.

iii) Recurse into Search Phase: When the bottom-right of the current area is reached, the rules recurse back into the search phase to find another element to act as an entry point. A separate set of rules biases search toward areas of color which are the same as the last area which the viewer scanned eg if the Area rules finds that an element is enclosed in a red area, then red areas will gain priority in the next search phase. This allows areas of color to specify paths, which will be searched in preference to other areas. In figure 2, the recursive search causes areas of similar background color to that found enclosing the animated new.gif to be searched. This is why 'Product 1' is found as an entry point over the larger text and images elsewhere on the page.

7. Examples

Several examples of how the rules critique the company home page are described in figure 2-3. The arrows and numbers on the page show the output of the critique, giving the predicted viewing order.

In figure 2, the animated new.gif provides an entry point during the search phase within the product name area; the scanning rules then expand into the product name area, and the reading order causes 'Product 3' and 'Product 4' to be read. Recursion then takes search back to 'Product 1', since it shares a background color with 'Product 3' The next phase of search moves to the company logo area because of the image, with the image dominating over the text. Reading goes left to the 'Company Name', then down to the slogan. Search then enters at the 'Welcome' message because its font is larger than the that of 'Contact Details'. The highlighted text and bullet points are then searched; the non formatted text is ignored. Finally 'Contact details' is found. Since all of 'Contact Details' text is the same size and formatted in bold, search defaults to entering at the top-left of the area.

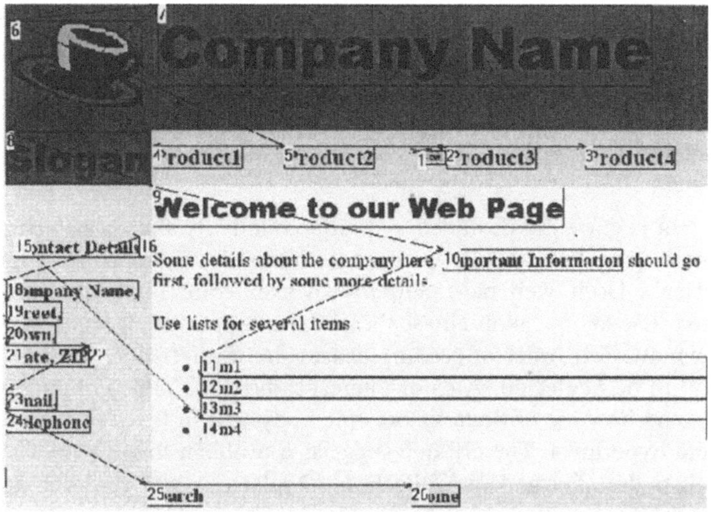

Figure 2 Critique of the web page shown in figure 1.The numbers and arrows show the critiquer's predicted viewing

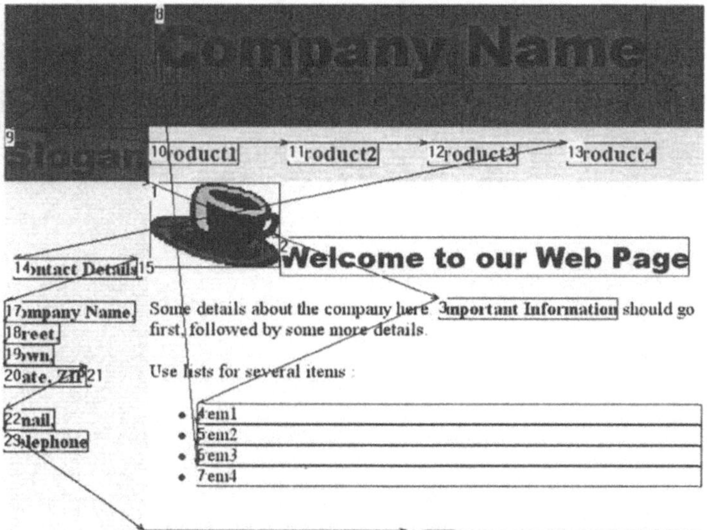

Figure 3 Edited page : the company logo .gif is moved and animated new.gif is deleted

Because the critiquing rules directly access the document object model, they can monitor changes made when the user edits the web page. In figure 3, the user deletes the animated gif and moves the cup image down next to the welcome message changes the reading order considerably. The search phase finds the cup image is now dominant over the other static text elements. This causes search to enter the 'Welcome' area. The scanning rules then run through the welcome text; only the formatted or bullet pointed text are picked out. The next phase of search then enters the company name area because the 'Company Name' is in a larger font than any of the other text on the page. 'Contact Details' are found last.

8. Real world examples

Whilst the tool is currently designed to critique relatively simple web pages, we have begun to scale up the rules to allow it cope with more complex pages. Figure 6 shows Jakob Nielsen's Useit web page, http://www.useit.com. First, note how Nielsen's large colored 'useit.com Jakob Nielsen's Website' upper title acts as the entry point, but the down and left order of reading causes the top-left title 'Usable Information Technology' to be neglected. Also of interest is how the table columns separate out the content, and how the critique ignores the body text in favor of scanning the lists, bold text and hyperlinks. The critique suggests a problem that the 'News' title is less dominant than the 'Permanent Collection'. Nielsen might consider swapping the ordering on the page, making the 'News' title bigger or colored, or using a graphic to guide attention to the new content.

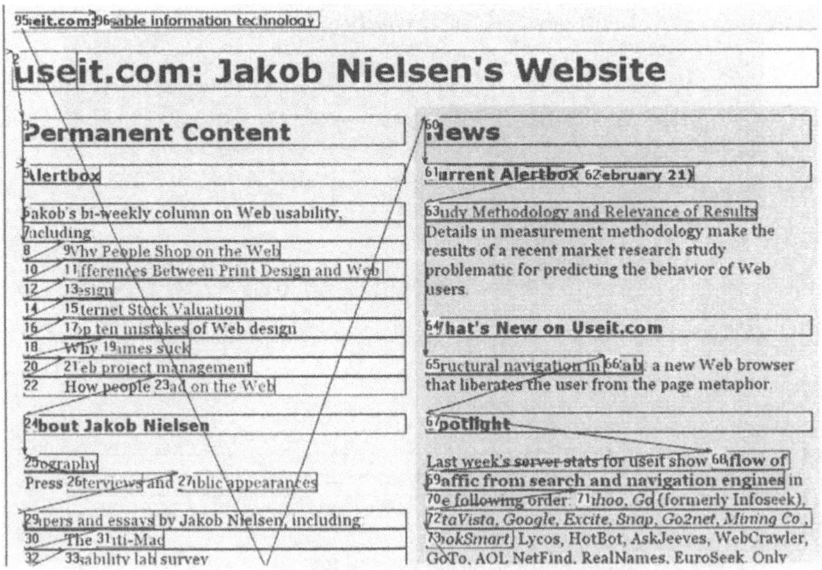

Figure 6 Critique of Jakob Nielsen's Useit.com

Figure 7 shows an example critique of the SIGCHI CHI 99 home page, http://www.acm.org/sigchi. Note in this case the effect of the larger SIGCHI logo on the far right. This acts as an entry point, causing reading to then have to move back in an unnatural right to left order to get to the smaller icons. Next, search moves to the right hand side table, because of its larger red label for 'SIGCHI news'. Examining the critique suggests a problem in the complete neglect of the explanatory paragraph

'ACM SIGCHI brings together…' below the title area. The lack of any formatting to make this stand out over the busy means the information about the purpose of SIGCHI is likely to be missed.

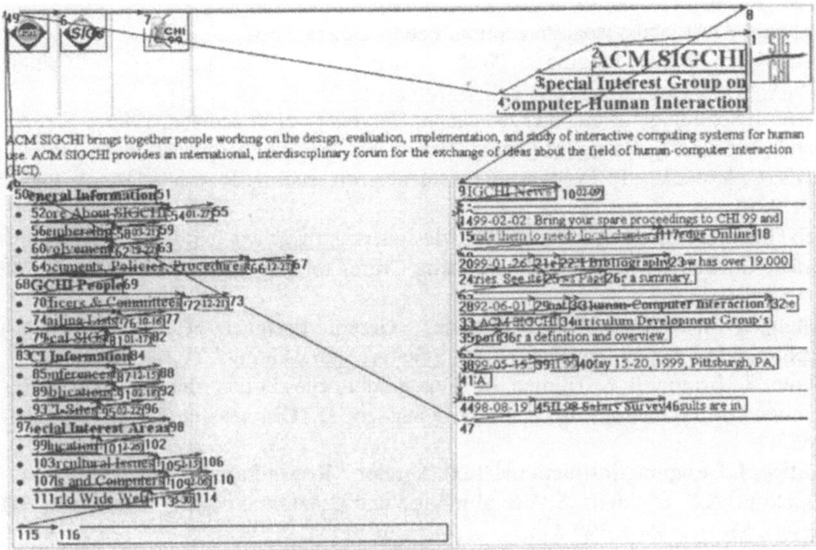

Figure 7 CHI 99 home page.

9. Current Work & Conclusions

We believe that our tool provides considerable value in its visual critique of web pages, particularly for novice designers. By automating this process via our visual hierarchy rules, we can gain a greater understanding of what 'good web page design' means.

The tool is very much a prototype to evaluate how perceptual rules can be applied to critiquing web pages. First, our analysis of animation is limited to animated .gifs; we do not analyse DHTML, or the content of the animation itself. Second, we do not extract any information from images : many sites render text into bitmaps, or use images to divide up the page; our current rules ignore these distinctions. Third, we are unable to process the content of the page in any way. Content will have a strong impact upon the search and scan phases.

Future work will attempt to improve the critiquing rules, and to provide a more useful end user display of the critiquing information. We are also planning a number of eye tracking studies to attempt to qualify the tool's predictions. The value of the tool is that it forces us to be explicit with our visual hierarchy model, and thus allows us to generate test materials which contain clear experimental questions.

10. References

1. Ameritech Web Page User Interface and Design Guidelines. http://www.ameritech.com/ corporate/ testtown/ standard/web_guidelines/principles.html
2. Arnheim, R. Art and Visual Perception. Faber & Faber, 1968.
3. Bernstein, M. Judging Web sites : Usability or Criticism ? http://www.eastgate.com/HypertextNow/archives/ Merit.html
4. Bertin, J. Semiology of graphics. Madison, University of Wisconsin, 1983.
5. Brandt, H. The Psychology of Seeing. New York : The Philosophical library, 1954
6. Lewis, C. & Walker, P. Typographic Influences on reading. Journal of Psychology, 80,241-257,1989
7. Web Graphics – Great tips from CNET designers. http://www.builder.com/Graphics
8. Fischer G., Lemke, A. & Morch, A.Using Critics to Empower Users. ACM CHI'90, 1990 p.337-347
9. Fleming, J. In Defense of Web Graphics : Graphic designers offer more than just flashy graphics. http://webreview.com/97/07/25/feature/index4.html
10. Glynn. S., Britton, B. & Tillman, M. Typographic cues in text : management of the readers attention. In Technology of Text. Ed Jonassen, D. Educational Technology Publishing, 1985.
11. Hartley, J. Designing Instructional Text. London : Kogan Page, 1978
12. Hillstrom, A.P. & Yantis, S. Visual motion and attentional capture. Perception & Psychophysics, 55(4), (1994), 399-411.
13. Hochberg, J & Brooks, V. The Perception of Motion Pictures. In Handbook of Perception and Human Performance 10, 1978
14. Lynch, J. & Horton, S. Yale Centre for Advanced Media WWW Style Manual. http://info.med.yale.edu/ caim/manual/pages/editorial_style.html
15. McConkie, G. & Zola, D. Visual Attention During Eye fixations while reading. In Attention and Performance XII, 1982, Ed Colheart, M. LEA.
16. Meads, J. Usability is not Graphic Design. http://devedge.netscape.com/viewsource/medads_usb.htm
17. Nielsen, J. (1997) Alertbox. http://www.useit.com/ alertbox/
18. Spool, J. Web site Usability, User Interface Engineering 1997
19. Theios, J. & Amrhein, P.C. Theoretical analysis of the cognitive processing of lexical and pictorial stimuli. Psychological Review, 1989, v96, n1, 5-24.
20. Triesman, A. Features and Objects : Fourteenth Bartlett memorial lecture. Quarterly Journal of Experimental Psychology, 1988, 40A (2), 201-237.
21. Tufte, E. Visual Explanations. Graphics Press, 1997
22. Wertheimer, M. Principles of Perceptual Organization. Van Norstrand, 1958.
24. Yarbus, A.L. Eye Movements and Vision. Plenum Press, 1967.
25. Stone, D. & Glock, M.D. How do young adults read directions with and without pictures ? Journal of Educational Psychology, 1981, v73, n3, 419-426.

ANTS: An Automatic Navigability Testing Tool for Hypermedia

Martín González Rodríguez

University of Oviedo, Computing Science Department, Campus de Llamaquique, c/Calvo Sotelo s/n 33007 Oviedo, Asturies, Spain
martin@lsi.uniovi.es

Abstract. Multiple navigational graphs can be obtained as the result of the *design stage* of a hypermedia-based artifact. The only way to know which one adapts better to the user navigational metaphor is by mean of usability testing. This technique is expensive in terms of the number of human resources needed to perform it, and it isn't able to record spontaneous user behavior. The use of automatic testing tools is an interesting and cheap alternative that avoids the problems commented. We tested our own automatic navigability testing system (ANTS) conducting an experiment to determine where users expect to find the navigational bar of a web site.

1 The Hypermedia Development Process

Hypertext documents can be cheaply introduced in educational environments (such as high schools and universities) where their use has been highly increased in the last years. In the mentioned educational environment, hypertext is a powerful and flexible source of information that is employed for both reference and knowledge transmission. But this wonderful teaching tool only seems to work when the information provided by its nodes is well-structured [1].

1.1 The Design Stage

During the design stage of a hypermedia product, the knowledge to be transmitted is structured into small didactic units, following a divide and conquer strategy. Every didactical unit will represent a conceptual node in the resulting hypermedia system.

This is a recursive process that will provide the full list of nodes of the hypermedia artifact as result. Every node will represent the smallest knowledge unit possible and will be considered as an autonomous source of information [1].

The resulting nodes are linked each other by hyperlinks, creating a directed graph structure generally called *navigation model*, using the terminology of some hypermedia design methods such as the Object Oriented Hypermedia Design Method (OOHDM) [2]. The importance of this structure becomes obvious. It will determine how the user moves around the nodes and –even more important– how he or she retrieves knowledge from them and from the whole hypermedia product.

Usually, designers finish this task with multiple resulting graphs depending on the different approaches used to explain the knowledge to be transmitted [3]. The complexity level increases even more if we consider that the resulting graphs may depend not only of the knowledge to be transmitted but also of the kind of user who will receive the information [4]. The nature of certain kind of hypermedia products such as hypermedia kiosks or web sites, implies the necessity of designing them to comply with the expectation of more than one kind of user [5].

In some cases goals are so complex that they can not be satisfied by a single navigational graph, so more than one is required. In this case, some kind of cognitive analysis must be performed on the input given by users in order to promote them to another navigational graph [3]. Some hypermedia design methods such as OOHDM allows the design of different graphs from a unique knowledge-base [6], This goal is reached by the design of different navigational graphs depending on the different kind of final user.

Even when a simple graph can be used to satisfy the knowledge necessities of more than one kind of user, the contents of every single node can be designed with different approaches depending on the target user. Different designs for the same node are generally related with the language and cognitive factors related with universal access to the interface for people who have a physical disability that requires additional access methods. People in this group of users mainly have difficulty with computer input devices such as the mouse or keyboard so a proper user interface must be provided to the final view of this kind of nodes [7].

1.2 The Testing Stage

Once the *design stage* has finished, it is time to convert the navigational graphs into a fully working educational tool. As the *developing stage* is the most expensive stage, it is necessary to assure the quality of the navigational graphs before translating them to code. Unfortunately, during the *design stage* there is not a clearly way of knowing whether the behavior of the final user will match what it was expected.

The best way to measure how useful a navigational graph will be to the target audience is by exposing it to the scrutiny of users. This exposure can be done by prototyping. Under this approach, the developing of preliminary versions of the navigational graph is required to verify its workability [7]. Once the prototype is ready, it can be verified by usability testing, watching and listening carefully to users as they work with the prototype when they are encouraged to perform certain tasks.

The main goal to be reached during the *testing stage* is to get as much information as possible about how the final user moves around the set of different navigational graphs proposed. This information should be contrasted with what designers expected, in order to measure the quality of the design. The information required consists usually of the following items:

- The list of the most visited nodes.
- When these nodes are visited.
- Time of user arrival/departure to/from a node.
- How long user remains in a single node before moving to another one (how long user takes to obtain the information he or she was looking for)

- Which are the most popular destinations (links) from a single node.
- The set of visited nodes during a single user session (including its order).

Usability testing is a quite useful for revealing hidden user behavior, and for discovering internal user-generated metaphors when dealing with the user interface of some machines [8]. However its use to perform validations on navigational graphs has some disadvantages which can make it a slow and expensive process.

1. Classic usability testing requires permanent observation of use behavior.
2. As navigation thorough the graph is not a simple task, long time of observation will be required.
3. Users who participate in the experiment know that they are being observed. This situation may add external factors to the testing such as nervousness, confusion, timidity and son on, which could influence user behavior when navigating through the hypermedia artifact.
4. U are dedicating an important part of their free time to usability testing, *so it must show a clear purpose* or users could think that they are working for nothing. Knowledge about the experiment can influence navigability, because user can know or at least guess, what is expected from them, adapting their own internal navigational metaphors to the navigational model of the prototype provided.
5. It is quite difficult to discover new kind of –not already identified– users, as participants selected for testing have to match the same demographic background and experience level as typical users in target audience.

2 ANTS: An Automatic Navigability Testing System

If designers want to avoid subjective influence during usability testing, they should never bring volunteers to the laboratory. The ideal condition to validate prototypes will be to test them under the same conditions that the final product will be used, that is, testing it in the user-computing environment. Under this ideal situation, users feel free to explore the navigational graphs provided, so external factors will not be added to the results obtained. Obviously, experimentation using this technique needs a completely new approach and additional tools to support usability testing in situations not under observer's control.

In order to reach this goal, we have developed an automatic navigability-testing tool, which we have called ANTS, an *Automatic Navigability Testing System.* The aim of this tool is to observe users while they navigate through any kind of hypermedia artifacts, registering their navigability behavior on a database for a post hoc analysis.

As the current implementation of ANTS was coded using Java technology, it can run in almost every computing platform, including Macintosh, Unix or Windows. Java is also supported by a healthy collection of Internet browsers (such as Microsoft Explorer or Netscape Communicator), so ANTS can be used for testing navigational graphs of both, platform dependent hypermedia applications and web sites on Internet.

Another quite important advantage of using Java for the implementation of this kind of systems, is the great versatility of its communication libraries and the variety of communication frameworks provided, such as sockets, RMI or CORBA. Also, the servlets technology included with the Java 1.2 release might allow ANTS to test user navigability through nodes dynamically created in the domain of adaptive hypermedia.

2.1 The Anthill Metaphor

The design of ANTS is based on the client-server paradigm, following a metaphor based on the life of a community of ants. In this metaphor, the ants (very small agents) go out the anthill (a central server) looking for food (the information) in every picnic available (a single user navigability session). Once the ant gets its food, it comes back to the anthill and stores it carefully in one of the anthill's warehouses.

When testing, the ants that serve as agents must be *included in every node of every navigational graph*. This task can be performed automatically by some Hypermedia developing tools based on Java (such as the *European Project JEDI*, [9]). Once the ants have been included, the testing version of the product is ready to be distributed among the volunteers who participate in the usability test.

Once the user has arrived to a single node during a navigation session, the ant inside the node is downloaded from the anthill (the server). When the ant arrives to the user machine, it establishes a connection with the server, which is used to send the data collected. In the current version of this system, the ant sends a complete identification of the node visited, along with the specific instant of time of arrival.. Our ants also report other events, such as for example, the time when the user abandons a single node. This task is performed even when the user moves to a different application, a common practice detected in multitask environments. If the security manager of the Java Virtual Machine allows it, the ant might collects information about the user too [10].

Future extensions of the ant agent class would allow the creation of even more elaborated reports. They could include the set of components selected by users, the list of the window locations clicked by them or the collection of components that are visible or hidden during scroll tasks. The kind of information provided by the little ants will depend on the information required by designers in order to improve the quality of their products.

2.2 Configuring an Ant

The information received by the anthill (the server) is compiled and organized depending on the navigational graph that is being tested. The multi-threaded nature of the server's design allows the concurrent testing of more than one navigational graph. In fact, there are no limits to the number of multimedia projects that can be tested concurrently by ANTS.

In order to know where to store the information received from an ant, this little agent must notify the server about the project that it is monitoring. To perform this task, an identification code must be assigned by designers to every navigational graph under testing. The parameters needed to setup a right configuration for an ant agent include that identification code and also another identification code for the node the ant is monitoring. Both codes must be unique and can be easily assigned by a hypermedia development tool.

The piece of html code below shows how easy an ant agent can be configured for testing a web site. Parameter SITE indicates the code assigned to the navigational graph (in this case a web site called *EDIWeb*) while parameter ID shows the code assigned to the node (the web page *EDIEval/c-intro.html* inside the *EDIWeb* site), which gives a clearly indication of the node visited by the user. Other parameters are implementation dependent and indicate the socket connection port and the host where the server is running. In the current implementation of ANTS, the agents establish communication with their server using sockets technology. Future implementations could use RMI technology (Remote Method Invocation) in order to avoid firewalls.

```
<applet
 code="uniovi.cognition.lure.Ant10APP.class"
 codebase = "../../ServiWeb/BinJava"
 width=10
 height=10>
  <param name="HOST" value="polar.uniovi.es">
  <param name="PORT" value="1932">
  <param name="SITE" value="EDIWeb">
  <param name="ID" value="EDIEval/c-intro.html">
</applet>
```

Java code below shows the equivalent ant configuration for the node's constructor of a desktop-based hypermedia application. Identification for the node and its navigational graph must be provided as part of the constructor's parameters.

```
/**
a constructor for the node

@param theGraphID the graph identification
@param theNodeID an identification for the node
*/

public node (String theGraphID, String theNodeID)
{
 // setup for the ant agent
 ant = new Ant (polar.uniovi.es, 1932,
               theGraphID, theNodeID);

 // Other actions to be performed by the constructor
          ...
}
```

2.3 Testing Navigability Using ANTS

Once the designers have finished the prototype to be tested, it can be distributed among the volunteers, as it would be done with the beta version of the final product.

Because users don't know that they are being observed, users will work with the product, as they would do under normal circumstances. Using this approach, navigation through the hypertext system will not be altered by the external factors mentioned before such, as nervousness or confusion. Only when the experiment finishes, volunteers will be informed about the technique used.

Notice that volunteers are informed, from the just beginning of the experiment, that they are participating in a usability testing. The only fact they ignore is the observation technique used by researchers. This is a common practice in merchandising, where researchers observe customer behaviour through hidden video cameras [11].

This approach not only eradicates irrelevant noise from the experimentation process but makes it also cheaper a more efficient too. By mean of automatic testing tools, the data collected flows freely from the source to the server storage system, where it can be analyzed off-line. Testers are liberated from the boring task of capturing data, so they can focus their efforts in analyzing the results obtained, in order to improve the navigation of their hypermedia designs. As there is no need to assign human resources for conducting user observation, the whole process of usability testing is cheaper. This way, many more volunteers can be observed using limited human resources.

The following report was obtained using ANTS when testing user behavior for the navigational graph of a web site. User identification corresponds to the IP Address (159.55.11.111) and the host name of the machine (pinon.uniovi.es) used by the user to navigate to the web site. The arrival was at 17:50:45 Hrs. (server local time) from a computer located inside the scope of the ECT time zone. User movement along the web site was also registered. Time expended in every single node and in the whole site is also computed from this data.

```
DATE: January 16Th 1999 (Saturday)
TIME: 17H50' GMT+00:00

IP ADDRESS: 195.55.11.111 (pinon.uniovi.es)
TIME ZONE: ECT (-2)


LOGS: (All dates are local to server)

17:50:45 -> Log in.
17:50:46 -> User arrives to site.
17:51:08 -> User moved to <Computing/InXena>.
17:52:01 -> User abandons site.
17:52:12 -> User moved to <Agenda>.
17:53:23 -> User leaves site definitively.
17:53:23 -> Log out.

User was here about 00:02:35 seconds.
```

When compiling data about every navigational session in a site, important information can be obtained, such as which are the most visited nodes, which are the links more suitable to be chosen by the average user, and so on. With all this information, testers are able to contrast the average time spent by user in each node, with the expected values calculated during the *design stage*. This information is quite useful in order to know whether the design of the navigational graph is realistic or not.

4 The Best Location for a Navigational Bar

To measure the usefulness of an automatic usability testing tool, we made use of ANTS to perform some research about user behavior when navigating through real hypermedia sites, especially when choosing certain kind of links commonly found in many web sites.

When the World Wide Web became a profitable business and a massive corporate presence was a reality in the net, many graphic designers moved to the new medium bringing their technical knowledge. As their techniques were designed for the printed medium, they adapted them to the new electronic one.

The headlines included in the cover of a magazine are the most important section of it as they act as a real advert to promote its content [12]. In printed publications, which use the Roman writing system, headlines are commonly located at the left hand of the cover, because this side is considered by designers to be the most suitable to catch customer's attention. It is supposed to be because reader expects to find the beginning of a sentence at the left-hand of the page, so it is the zone that has more probability to be explored first.

When cover headlines were ported to the web, they done it grouped together in a bigger visual object (usually a frame), which acts as a navigational bar for the site. Although navigational frames can be found in any side of a web site, left-handed locations are still the most popular among graphic designers.

The experiment we conducted tries to determine just how much important –in terms of human attention– represents a horizontal navigational bar location. The question to ask is which is the most suitable position for a navigational bar. Shall designers place it left-handed or right-handed?

5 The Experiment

The web site designed for this experiment is quite simple. It consists of an entry node provided with a central information panel and two lateral navigation bars (frames) which both are identical. One of them is left-hand located and the other one is right-hand located. The simplest interface possible was designed in order to avoid irrelevant noise to user, so both navigational bars were provided with only one link.

As both frames are identical (in color and shape) and both have the same content (a single link), users who arrive to this node face the problem of choosing between two identical links; as no more links (choices) are provided. Under this situation, user must decide between two identical options.

Although a user may choose more than one link during a navigational session, only the first link selected was considered. Notice that the action of selecting a link depends directly on human cognition and implies ergonomics considerations too. Choosing a link is not a cost-free action in terms of cognition. It is clear than when users choose a link, they are considering it as the fastest and cheapest way of getting the information they are looking for.

The information used as the *lure* for this experiment was the result of the first exam we did this course in one of our second level computing subjects at the university. The central information panel provides information about the evaluation itself while the two lateral navigation bars allow students to reach the evaluation results. All the information we provide to the students is given by mean of web pages, so the working of hypertext documents is well known by all participants in the experiment.

Visual design for the main node can be seen in figure 1. The interface design obliges users to read at least one of the links (left-handed or right-handed) in order to reach the desired evaluation results. Both navigational bars were designed using a low colour contrast. Blue text stands against a purple background. Our intention was to oblige users to explore carefully those areas.

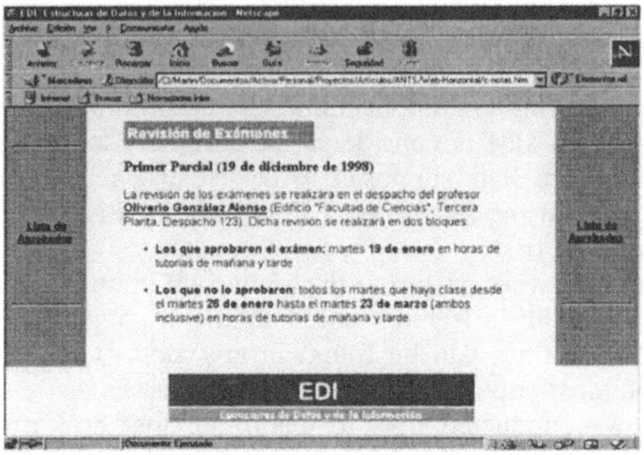

Fig. 1. Screenshot of the experimental site proposed. The central panel provides general information about the evaluation process and anything more. No mention about how to obtain the evaluation result was provided by this panel. Both lateral panels include a link to the evaluation result.

The information that we extracted from the reports generated by ANTS was the following:

- Which link did users choose first (left-handed or the right-handed)?
- How long took users to make such decision (measured in seconds)? We called this parameter **Reaction Time** (RT).

The main goal of these questions is to detect user preference for one of the links, depending on the link selected first, as it is reflects the most important preference for users. Although some users alternated between both navigational bars during a single session, only the first one selected was considered.

The secondary goal tries to identify any observation pattern related with the link selected, depending on the RT parameter. Depending on the amount of time spent by users before they really made the decision, it should be possible to detect user observation strategies, such as analytic observation vs. Naive, look vs. bet, etc. [13]. Users who spend long time before choosing a link might follow an analytic observation strategy while users who quickly select a link, might follow a naive observation strategy. When measuring RT we are trying to detect any possible relationship between the link selected and the observation strategy followed.

6 The Results

The number of user sessions that were reported by ANTS was 353. Some of these observations (11) were considered outside the scope of the experiment, as students in these observations were unable to obtain the information they were looking for. Although they correctly arrived to the web site, they didn't use any of the navigational bars provided, leaving the site after a short period of time.

The final number of valid observations was 342. Conducting such a high number of observations would have been impossible using the classic usability testing approach. Only the automatic nature of the process made it possible. The results – once the data collected was processed– are compiled in table 1.

Table 1. Results of the experiment once data collected was processed. Left-hand location was selected more than right-hand location, although the difference is not significant. *Reaction Time* for both locations coincides (global average = 23.94 seconds)

GLOBLAL RESULTS

Universe: 342 valid sessions.	**Left hand choices:** 179 (52.5%).
Global Average for the Reaction Time parameter: 23.94 seconds.	**Right hand choices:** 160 (47.5%).

LEFT HAND LOCATION	**RIGHT HAND LOCATION**
Chosen: 179 times. (52.5%)	**Chosen:** 160 times. (47.5%)
Average for the Reaction Time parameter: 23.83 seconds.	**Average for the Reaction Time parameter:** 24.08 seconds.

The results obtained clearly show us that although graphic designers weren't wrong when they affirmed that left-hand location is the preferred one by readers, the difference between the number of choices for both locations is lower than expected. Although important, this isn't a decisive difference. The result does not indicate where a navigational bar should be included considering only the horizontal direction, as both locations are suitable.

The secondary goal of our analysis wasn't reached because the user reaction time average for both locations seems to be the same (23.94 seconds), so it was impossible to recognize any kind of user observation pattern. We can observe however that the horizontal location of the navigational bar doesn't seem to have any influence over the reaction time average, as both coincide. The result seems to agree with the main goal findings.

Results from the post-hoc analysis indicate that the horizontal location for a navigational bar doesn't affect user performance in a decisive way when navigating through a hypertext device. This finding might conduct to deeper studies about different cognitive factors that affect human behavior when using hypermedia. As the horizontal frame location has very little influence on user behavior, the appearance of both, left-handed and right-handed frames can be modified in order to test the grade of influence that different visual cues such as color, size, shape, etc. could have. Of course, a research of the effect that vertical locations have is also pending. This research would allow the construction of hypertext devices adapted to the behavior of every user.

The accurate, reliable and quickly collected information provided by automatic usability testing tools allow this kind of researches, monitoring real user behavior in the fastest and cheapest possible way.

Acknowledgements

Thanks are especially due to all our students of Data Structures and Algorithms at the EUITIO (University of Oviedo) who participated in the experiment commented along these pages. I wish to thank also Agueda Vidau Navarro, Juan Manuel Cueva Lovelle and all my mates of the Laboratory of Object Oriented Technologies for the encouragement given to the InXena program, the real core of the ANTS-based technologies.

References

1. Nielsen, Jakob: Hypertext and Hypermedia. Academic Press, Cambridge. (1993) ISBN 0-12-5118410-7
2. Schwabe, Daniel, Rossi, Gustavo: Abstraction, Composition and Lay-Out Definition Mechanism in OOHDM. Proceedings of the ACM Workshop on Effective Abstractions in Multimedia. San Francisco, California (1995) http://www.cs.tufts.edu/~isabel/schwabe/
3. González Rodríguez, Martin: A Hypermedia Development Process for Jedi-Leia. Cuadernos de Investigación Ingeniería Informática (2). Editorial Servitec, Oviedo (1999)
4. Olsina, Luis Antonio: Cognitive criteria in the development of Hypermedia Applications Conferences at EUITIO, University of Oviedo (1998) http://www15.uniovi.es
5. Olsina, Luis Antonio: Process Model in the Hypermedia Development (1997) Conferences at EUITIO, University of Oviedo http://www15.uniovi.es
6. Schwabe, Daniel: Summary of OOHDM (1995) http://www.cs.tufts.edu/ ~isabel/schwabe/
7. Apple Computer Inc: Macintosh Human Interface Guidelines. Adison-Wesley Publishing Company (1992) ISBN 0-201-62216-562216
8. Shulz, Erin, Van Alphen, Maarten, Rasnake, William: Discovering user-generated metaphors through usability Testing. Proceedings of the Second International Conference on Cognitive Technology. Aizu, Japan (1997)
9. Transtools: JEDI: Java Enabled Database over Internet. ESPRIT Project (EP24231) (1998) http://www.transtools.com/jedi
10. Weber, Joseph: Special Edition Using Java 1.1; Third Edition (1997) ISBN 0-7897-1094-3
11. Masson, J. E., Wellhoff, A.: El Merchandising: rentabilidad y gestión del punto de venta. Deusto, Madrid (1990) ISBN 8423405117
12. Gordon, Druce: Designing Covers, Mac Format, Future Publishing, Bath. January 1994
13. Ittelson, William H.: Visual Space Perception. Springer Publishing Company, Inc. New York (1960)
14. Newell, Allen: Unified Theories of Cognition. Hardward University Press (1990) ISBN 0-674-92101-1

Educational Applications of WWW-Based Asynchronous Video

prof. dr. Betty Collis and drs. Oscar Peters

Faculty of Educational Science and Technology, University of Twente, Postbus 217, 7500 AE Enschede, The Netherlands
{Collis, Peters}@edte.utwente.nl

Abstract. In this paper we briefly inventory some of the traditional educational applications of video, and indicate how the integration of asynchronous video within WWW environments makes those applications more efficient and flexible. Second, we indicate a variety of ways in which the integration of asynchronous video and WWW environments introduces new forms of learning possibilities not available to either medium (video or WWW environments) in isolation. Third, we illustrate these new forms of learning possibilities via the example of a course recently (March-May 1999) completed at the University of Twente.

WWW-Based Environments and Asynchronous Video

WWW-based learning environments allow the integration of hyperlinked information systems, databases, interactive learning resources, communication tools, publication tools and tools to support collaborative and individualised learning (for a discussion, see Collis, 1999). Each of these types of activities can be supported in a variety of modalities, including text, images, animations, audio and video. Important technological innovations are occurring to enhance the power, efficiency and security of WWW-based learning environments. Although asynchronous video accessible via WWW environments has been available for several years, an important development in these respects is that of streaming video, a technique which allows a audio/video signal to begin to display on a receiving computer as soon as received by the computer, rather than having to wait for the complete audio/video file to arrive as an entity over a data network. Being able to access video and audio *on demand* (as opposed to the two-way video and audio communication streams that occur in conferencing situations), in whatever segments that are wished and whenever desired, for appropriate learning goals, offers two levels of educational opportunities: (a) to capitalise on the traditional benefits of video for learning situations, by making the video directly available to the learner or instructor without having to first obtain a videotape from a distributor (a process that can take considerable time) and then in turn make the videotape available to the intended users (a process that can involve the need for users to come to a centre to view the video, or require extensive duplication of the videotapes and the consequent distribution procedures; and (b) to bring new dimensions of use to video materials through their integration with the tools and resources available in WWW environments.

In this paper, we focus on these two aspects. First we inventory some of the traditional educational applications of video, and indicate how the integration of asynchronous video within WWW environments makes those applications more efficient and flexible. Second, we indicate a variety of ways in which the integration of asynchronous video and WWW environments introduces new forms of learning possibilities not available to either medium (video or WWW environments) in isolation. Third, we illustrate these new forms of learning possibilities via the example of a course recently (March-May 1999) completed at the University of Twente. Throughout this paper, when we use the term asynchronous video, we mean video segments that are digitally stored and available on demand via a WWW server, or via the integration of WWW server and locally stored (i.e., CD-ROM) segments. When called from a server, we are assuming streaming video, for its current superiority in terms of loading and waiting times. Also, we assume audio and video, not video (images) alone but for convenience will only use the term *asynchronous video*.

Making Traditional Uses of Video More Efficient and Flexible

Research relating to the impact of audio-visual stimuli on learning has a long history. Verhagen (1994), for example, identifies ten categories of cognitive and instructional impact: content-related use of photographic pictures or moving video, depicting the invisible or the non-accessible, logistic use, cognitive help (visualizations as tools for thinking), modeling of psychomotor skills, video feedback, providing observation materials, psychologically realistic simulation, video to present gifted teachers, video design for emotional involvement. Bell (1997) notes the particular value of rich visual contexts, the depiction of spatial organisation, the depiction of change, dynamic illustration, the depiction of social interaction, and dramatic effect.

Video sequences however, have limitations. The linear format and single-direction temporal format are not always best for a particular learning situation. A video sequence that is digitally available can bring new flexibility to the use of the video, for both instructor and students. The digital equivalent of fast-forwarding of the video to a desired location is more efficient than the analog alternative. The ability to use segments of the linear video sequence, as desired and in a variety of orders (i.e., as *hypermedia* or *interactive video*), has long been demonstrated as having educational benefits (see for instance McNeil & Nelson, 1991).

From a usage perspective, however, the benefits of hypermedia or interactive video as well as of linear video, have always been limited by issues relating to costs, distribution, and display. The duplication and distribution of video products via videotape is a relatively slow and expensive process, especially as the number of users and the range of their physical locations increases. Presentation of a video sequence during a lesson or study period requires a video player and monitor. Video segments are increasingly becoming available on CD-ROMs as well as analog videotapes, but this process still brings the same difficulties in distribution and access as with videotapes if the CD-ROMs have to be physically sent or made available to users. Interactive video products, on optical disks or in CD-I format, required users to have an appropriate player as well as the physical disk. Institutions which wished to use the technology with large numbers of students were faced with supplying adequate numbers of players and disks. Different and rapidly changing formats for optical and CD-I disk technology made such investments undesirable. And in addition, the costs of making any sort of video production, linear or interactive, were high and generally required professional development teams and long time lines.

From the perspectives of efficiency and flexibility, the capability now becoming increasingly available of compressing and streaming video and making the video available via an ordinary WWW browser (with appropriate viewers) is a major step forward in overcoming these usage problems. Assuming the video segments are available and copyright issues are appropriately handled (the same problems that confront video use in videotape or CD-ROM form), the segments can be accessed via a WWW browser using streaming technology from wherever the user has adequate network access, and whenever the user wishes. The issue of adequate network access remains, but is rapidly loosing its prohibitive nature given the on-going and rapid changes in video compression and streaming technologies, the rapid growth of highspeed connectivity to educational institutions, and the improvements in connectivity in general that are occurring via highspeed modems, ISDN connectivity in the home or office, and network developments in general. A vast amount of video material is now available, via WWW sites, on demand, to users in any location. Such access is unprecedented. In general, it will increasingly be the case that any of the benefits of linear analog video products and interactive video products (either of the hypermedia resource type or the instructionally organised type) can be available to any user via his or her WWW browser. (Of course, costs related to this access, as determined by those who hold the copyright to the products, are another issue). The implications for more efficient use of video, in a wider variety of viewing locations, instructional contexts, and times of viewing, are obvious.

Bringing New Forms of Learning

Not so obvious are the new forms of learning resources and activities that are now emerging because of the integration of asynchronous video and WWW environments. In Table 1 we indicate five of these new forms and the possibilities that come from the combination of video and WWW functionalities. Following Table 1, some examples of each of these forms will be further discussed.

Capturing & Re-using a Presentation

There are many examples now of how a classroom or lecture-hall presentation can be captured as it is delivered (usually digitally), stored as digital video on a video server, and then made available for re-view or re-use via a WWW site. The intended users include: students and non-students who could not be present at the actual presentation and students who were present but wish to review portions of the presentation. The presentation may be made available in linear form (with a controller to slide forward or backward within the video sequence), but most usually is also synchronised with slides or presented along with an index relating to different portions in the video sequence, so that the user can jump immediately to the portion desired (this is the new meaning of interactive video in these situations). Bidarra and Peters (1999) present 20 such examples of captured presentations from university lectures, each labeled in terms of institution, technology for the video capture and access, synchronisation with PowerPoint-type slides, availability of indexing (by text, by thumbnails of video fragments, etc), and way in which the lecturer is presented (i.e., "top-left corner, options for audio only"). Techniques for the capture and re-view/re-use of presentations are being developed and practiced at a variety of institutions, including the University of Mannheim and the University of Freiburg in Germany, the University of Minnesota and Old Dominion University in the USA, and the University of Twente in The Netherlands. The presentations being captured do not have to be lectures; student presentations also can be captured and re-viewed and re-used (see the illustration from the University of Twente, described below).

Giving Access and Depth to Real Events

There are many examples of WWW sites that focus on particular real events, as they are happening or extended in time before or after they happen, in which video segments play a major role. One example is the site of *America's Health Network* (http://ahn.com/liveevents/default.asp), aimed primarily at health professionals or medical students, but also for the layman with a particular medical interest. At regularly scheduled intervals, via real-time video streaming, users can watch an operation as it is occurring and hear the comments being made by the medical team as they carry out the operation. Following this, the operation segments in edited form are available as asychronous streaming video segments via the WWW site, as well as other video segments including interviews with the patients and their doctors, discussions among medical specialists, and interviews. As another example, the site *Share the Journey,* (http://www.sofweb.vic.edu.au/claypoles/) developed by the Department of Education in Victoria, Australia, is designed to serve as a year-long learning resource for students in the province to help them learn about Antarctica. As a focal point for the learning activities, and the WWW site, two Australians are spending a year in Antarctica and regularing transmitting video segments of their daily activities. These are posted on the WWW site, and serve as the stimuli for a variety of learning activities.

Supporting a Learning Process

When the focus of a learning activity is a process, rather than the learning of pre-defined content, WWW sites integrated with video segments can play a major role in support. An example is the site *Biological Timing Online Science Experiment* (http://www.cbt.virginia.edu/Olh/exp.html) from the University of Virginia. This site is designed to help students in the process of carrying out scientific experiments by showing them (via video fragments) many examples of aspects of this process, including aspects relating to the reasons for carrying out a process and aspects relating to the setting up and conducting of experiments.

Table 1. New forms of learning resources and activities, related to video aspects and WWW functionalities

	Video aspects	WWW aspects:		
Learning activities:		*Support communication*	*Link to other information*	*Re-use in other contexts*
Capturing & re-using a communication event (such as a lecture or presentation)	Can be locally captured during a presentation	Add forms to send questions to the presenter; collect frequently asked questions	Add links to course material, to external resources (students/users also can add the links)	Portions of the material can be ULMs (see below) for use in other settings
Giving access and depth to real events	Specialised capture of original material	Add forms to send questions and e-mail to experts; participate in discussion groups	Add links to external and up-to-date information (students/users also can add links)	Re-use in courses, for professional development, for personal learning
Supporting a learning process	Small tutorial sequences, documentary type sequences, interviews with specialists, etc., can be available	Add forms for contacts with others involved in the process, with experts, with resources, persons; Add tools to support collaborative learning if process involves a group	Add links to examples, to support materials; Products resulting from the process also can be entered as objects of study in the database	Re-use products made previously as examples or models for those starting out on a process

Developing and accessing a library of cases or units of learning material (ULMs)	Cases or ULMs including video segments can be captured in a variety of ways, such as action with commentary (Goodyear & Steeples, 1999)	Add forms for e-mail contacts	Store in a database; provide links on the ULMs to relevant supporting materials and/or to other items in the database	Re-use in courses, for self-study, for professional development, for personal learning
Constructing and sharing one's own resources (ULMs)	Video capture and handling is now available to the layman	Add forms for e-mail contacts	Link products made to a WWW site, so that become accessible and useful to others	If added to a database, re-use by others

Developing and Accessing a Library of Cases or Units of Learning Material (ULMs)

The site *Learn & Live* (http://www.glef.org/learnlive/toolkit/clearview.html) is an example of how a collection of video segments, with voice overlay, can serve as cases, or units of learning materials, related to a particular theme or context. In the Learn & Live context, the focus is on how 4th- and 5th-grade students conduct a research project when they have the opportunity to work collaboratively with university scientists. In each of the cases linked to the site, a video segment showing the children carrying out various learning activities, is available, with voice-over comments by either the teacher or the scientists. The intention of the site is that others (teachers, teachers-in-training, scientists, and those who design such special collaborative projects) can see what actually occurs in the classroom during such an interaction. Each segment has a general title, for example, "How can parents become involved?", "When students act as researchers, what are they actually doing?", and "How can student work be evaluated". The video segments can then be re-used individually for many different contexts, beyond those of the particular project from which the videos were obtained.

As another perspective on the use of video for cases, Goodyear and Steeples (1999) focus on continuing professional development and illustrate how video can be used to capture "rich examples of working practices and tacit knowledge, and for sharing and subjecting these artefacts to scrutiny, debate and refinement within a community" (p. 16). They discuss the "making of sharable representations of practice as 'raw' videoclips and videoclips of action with commentary" (p. 19) and the subsequent use of these videoclips, via a WWW site, as a tool for the learning community (see http://www.lancs.ac.uk/users/edres/research/sharp/index.htm).

Constructing and Sharing One's Own Video & WWW Resources

From a constructivist perspective in which learning by doing is emphasised, the possibilities for learners to create their own video segments and the surrounding WWW environments through which those segments are available, can be an example of a new type of collaborative learning activity. Simons (1998) describes constructivistic learning environments as environments where students are being challenged to learn actively together, with a clear focus on the functionality of learning and the learning content. Within such environments the learning is situated in a concrete context where the authenticity of that context is as high as possible. By doing so students will be more likely to learn stimulated by their own intrinsic motivation and they will be expected to steer and control their learning as independently as possible. The teacher is more a coach and guide than a transmitter of information. In the next section, an illustration is given of how this sort of environment has been realised in the course *Tele-Learning* at the University of Twente.

Illustration: The course Tele-Learning at the University of Twente

The course *Tele-Learning* in the Faculty of Educational Science and Technology (see http://education2.edte.utwente.nl/98193524.nsf/framesform?readform) at the University of Twente in The Netherlands is a senior-level elective course whose objectives include the following:

- To use appropriate terminology when discussing tele-learning applications and to understand the relationship of various communication technologies to various forms of tele-learning;
- To be competent in the use of the WWW as a tool for the personal organisation of learning and study materials and as a publication medium; in the use of the course WWW site and of BSCW, the course shared-workspace;
- To experience and reflect upon a variety of tele-learning activities, including different forms of communication, different forms of collaborative learning, and different forms of creative expression, all of which make use of communication technologies, and in particular, video, integrated as part of a WWW environment;
- To become well informed about the possibilities for using asynchronous video in WWW environments;
- To have an informed opinion about the future of various tele-learning applications in different educational contexts.

A major way in which the learning takes place in this course is through the students working together in groups on a project for real context and audience. In the 1999 cycle of the course, the audience was instructors in our own faculty and the context was to help them become aware of opportunities in their own classes (all of which make use of a WWW-based course-support system, called *TeleTOP*, http://teletop.edte.utwente.nl) in which video integrated with their WWW sites could bring added value to their courses. Each of the four groups of students had to develop a performance-support site for the instructors, in which a different form of video use was illustrated, and described and defended from an educational perspective. The forms chosen by the groups included video-illustrated case studies and video as part of WWW-based tutorials for various learning processes. Thus the students themselves participated in a learning experience as indicated in the fifth row of Table 1 (constructing their own uses of video), but with a focus on showing examples of the third and fourth rows in the table (supporting a process, and examples from practice). One of the sites made by the students is described below.

A Video-illustrated Case as Part of WWW-based Tutorials

An example of a performance-support site made by a group of students for instructors is shown in Figure 1. This group of students choose to develop a video-illustrated case study as part of WWW-based tutorial. They developed a WWW-based tutorial with video that combines the benefits of video, tutorial and the WWW. The tutorial mode of instruction guides the learner throughout the material, the video adds visualisation and the WWW environment allows more flexibility in time, place and pace of learning. The site has the following generic structure that all the 4 groups used: a) the instructional example - the example of a tutorial with video integrated; b) educational issues - an essay on issues surrounding video in a WWW-based tutorial; c) design issues - discusses guidelines for using video in a WWW-based tutorial; e) technical procedure - steps to be taken when making video for the WWW; f) external examples - other examples of WWW-based tutorials with video; and g) group members – the Tele-learning students that worked on the project. The topic of the performance-support site shown in Figure 1 is 'Shooting a good video!' The students want instructors to learn in this lesson about the characteristics of video, as well as, how to take them into account when creating good educational videos for the WWW. The sequence of the lesson starts with the first option, called "Common problems". Here instructors can find out what students usually don't like about educational videos. The second option is a case study where instructors are prompted to think about how to shoot a good video for the WWW, followed by a presentation where the instructors have the chance to study the lesson materials and a quiz to test themselves. The lesson ends with resources for further learning and a forum where instructors can share their ideas about making video for the WWW.

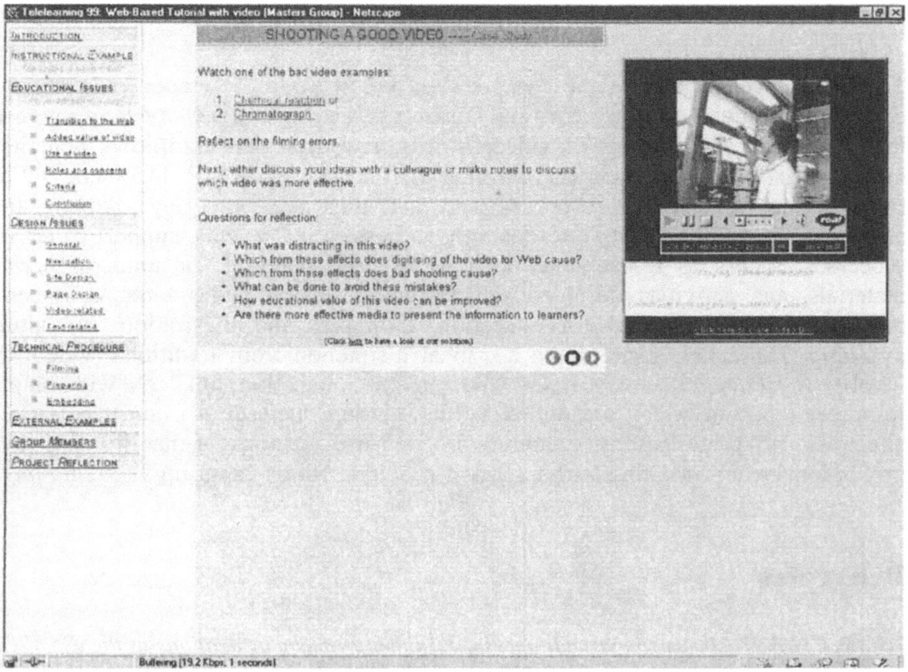

Fig. 1. An example of a performance-support site made by a group of students (Hall, Nehm, Alayyar, Golovko, & Efimova (1999).

In addition to designing and producing their own WWW-sites integrated with video as examples for instructors, the students in the Tele-Learning course also made use of video in many other ways within the course. Video integrated within educational WWW sites was the content of the course as well as a medium for the content of the course; thus the students used the course WWW environment as a framework in which to place their links to examples of external WWW sites making good educational use of video (in all of the categories in Table 1), their evaluative and reflective comments about the use of video in WWW sites for learning purposes, and for the study of captured presentations of the students in the previous cycle of the course. These presentations captured the students during the final class session of the 1998 cycle, and made these comments available as asynchronous video synchronised with presentation slides made by the students, related to different aspects of the course. The students in the 1999 cycle of the course could thus see and hear their peers in the 1998 cycle comment on their own work (the work also was available to the students in the 1999 cycle as learning resources, another example of re-use of video segments). During the last session of the 1999 cycle, this same process of capturing on video the presentations and reflections of the students and making these immediately available for re-view and re-use was continued.

Conclusion

Technical developments in the compression and streaming of video over networks commonly available to instructors and students is leading to a new cycle of interest in the educational applications of video. In this new cycle, the traditional benefits of video are given a wider audience, through their access via WWW browsers, but also more forms of learning resources and activities are emerging. Among these categories, those of captured presentations, access to real events, support of learning processes, access to re-usable collections of case materials or units of learning materials, and activities involved self-expression that includes video are seen as having particular potential for education. Examples and illustrations are already available. These new forms have a critical distinction from traditional video: they involve, in an integrated way, links to human communication, links to a wide range of resources (such of which are added by the learners themselves), and the re-use of examples or presentations captured in real-life settings, generally not by a professional team operating with a script and actors, but by capturing the *real thing*.

References

Bell, B. L. (1997). *Instructional multimedia: Preliminary recommendations in the use of video and alternative media.* [WWW document] URL http://www.tc.columbia.edu/~academic/edtech/video/recommen.htm (Date accessed: 31 January 1999).

Bidarra, J., & Peters, O. (1999). Audio-visual presentations. Faculty of Educational Science and Technology, University of Twente. [WWW document] URL http://televideo.edte.utwente.nl:81/videobase/videolec.htm (Date accessed: 21 May 1999)

Collis, B. (1999). Applications of computer communications in education: An overview. *IEEE Communications, 37,* (3), 82-86.

Goodyear, P., & Steeples, C. (1999). Creating sharable representations of practice. *Alt-J* (Advanced Learning Technologies Journal), *6,* (3), 16-23.

Hall, M., Nehm, S., Alayyar, G., Golovko, A., & Efimova, L. (1999). *Telelearning '99 Web-Based Tutorial with video (The Masters Group).* [WWW document] URL http://televideo.edte.utwente.nl:81/telelearning98/master2/launch.htm (Date accessed: 31 May 1999).

McNeil, B.J., & Nelson, K.R. (1991). Meta-analysis of interactive video instruction: A 10 year review of achievement effects. *Journal of Computer Based Instruction, 18,* (1), 1-6.

Simons, P.R.J. (1998). De rol van ICT in het onderwijs: een constructivistische visie [The rol of ICT in education: a constructivist perspective]. *COS, 10,* (6), 4-10.

Verhagen, P.W. (1994). Functions and Design of Video components in Multi-Media applications: a Review. In: Schoenmaker, J., & Stanchev, I. (Eds.) *Principles and tools for instructional visualisation.* Enschede: Faculty of Educational Science and Technology, Anderson Consulting – ECC.

EcoVasco, an Ecological Multimedia Adventure

Pedro Faria Lopes, Maria Vasconcelos Moreira, Miguel Lapa Duarte

ADETTI/ISCTE, Av. das Forças Armadas, 1600 Lisboa, Portugal
{Pedro.Lopes, Maria.Moreira, Miguel.Duarte}@iscte.pt

Abstract. The development of a multimedia computer game for young people is a complex task. It should take into consideration technical and human factors, applied to the development team and to the target audience. Topics like development platform, background and experience of the developing team, outsource material to be integrated, are important elements to consider. Also to consider are topics such as the end platform, content and technical quality expectations of the target audience. The challenge is harder when the target audience varies widely in age, implying different computer game interests. The paper describes the approaches we followed to achieve the original objectives.

1 Introduction

In 1998, a cooperation protocol was established between ADETTI/ISCTE and the Municipality of Lisbon (Câmara Municipal de Lisboa – CML) to develop an educational multimedia computer game, named "Eco Vasco & Co. – Uma Aventura Ecológica". The general aim of the game, to be freely distributed to Lisbon public schools, is to contribute towards the ecological awareness of young people.

According to the project's specification [1], the target audience intended for the game are pupils from 5th to 9th grade, which, in Portugal, corresponds to an age group from 10 to 16 years old. An indirect audience was also specified, consisting of the family and the social community of each youngster, their teachers and schools' staff. The game, based on a successful TV video campaign "Lisboa Agradece" ("Lisbon Thanks You"), had to be appealing and educational. It should integrate aspects such as the use of previous and newly acquired ecology concepts, the acquisition of social and individual skills and the stimulation of quick reasoning and fast action.

The first step consisted in assembling a nuclear team that would be able to cope with the different technical subjects involved. Multimedia and programming skills being only a supporting base of development, adding to the team a person experienced with youth behaviour and psychology was an important decision. Other skills, original music composition and character animation, were planned to be commissioned to professionals with whom we already had worked in previous projects.

One of the first topics that caught our attention was the wide span of age defined as the direct target audience. A first background analysis of the target audiences' profile(s) showed that at least two distinct stages of psychological, emotional and intellectual development occur between 10 and 16 years of age [2]. The issue raised was, therefore, how to appeal, in identical terms, to such different audience.

The first steps were to get information about the type of games available and to see if any approach similar to what we needed had already been developed. In the next section we summarise our findings on this topic.

1.1 Games' Analysis

We analysed some of the games on the market that seemed to have the general acceptance of our target group [3, 4, 5] which enabled us to draw some observations on the types of games, acceptability and age targets, not always coincident with the authors or distributors' vision:

- Games based on animation cartoons: originally for younger children aged 4 to 12, based in cartoon characters, often a well know one, using the same graphical paradigm: a static or scrolling scenario with an overlay of cartoon animation with low demanding motion needs since only a fraction of the screen is manipulated;
- Graphical adventure: based on graphics with some action or motion, with 3D scenarios or originally 2D drawn material, targeted to older teenagers or adults; these are strong thematic games with an enigma to solve or a strategy to develop;
- Fast action games: 3D fast and realistic graphics, based on 3D polygonal scenarios rendered with highly optimized algorithms using extensive image maps for realism; based on fight, pursuit or sport; players usually invest in new graphic boards, sound cards or extra hardware to improve the playing experience.

Trying to look to the games with some objectivity, some comments would arise:

- An interesting game does not mean a really *top notch fancy* graphics interface
- Not all games advertised as *fabulous*, *exciting* or *poetic*, are really interesting
- Some of the games get strong initial interest based on sound and graphics effects
- Some of the games allow the player to choose different difficulty levels

2 First Steps

Based on our previous experience developing Virtual Reality environments [6], an analysis was made on how attractive it would be to have the game based on navigation and exploration of virtual 3D worlds. This approach was soon dismissed mainly due to speed performance and level of realism available in the development kit: the virtual worlds were slow and not intuitive to navigate, and the rendering, done in real time, was only constant or Gouraud shading [7]. Speed could be improved if new and faster computers were used but public schools are, generally, not equipped with the latest models available on the market.

A decision was taken to develop three different levels, beginner, intermediate and advanced, which would enable the different players to select a difficulty level appropriate to their skills. It was also considered that the identification with the game itself, and with the situations presented, plays an important role in motivating players. Therefore it was decided to include as many customisable aspects as possible to make the game more specific to each age group and school environment.

To link the game to the already existing TV campaign "Lisboa Agradece", we decided to integrate the video clips [8, 9, 10, 11]. The clips were digitised from analogue video tape, processed and integrated as AVI digital video clips. This was done in a conventional way, applying digital video integration rules [12]. The digital video clips are 320*240, at 10 fps, inserted in a 640*480 image size scenario. As the original video was done using clay stop motion animation [13], the 10 fps limitation, due to the CD-ROM access bandwidth, does not affect the digital video clips' motion perception which is very similar to the original tape.

We considered important to have the best possible motion perception: "cartoon like" motion is acceptable to children, and for this 10 to 15 fps is more than enough, but we also have to attract older players, used to very high frame rates, to whom a jerky motion appearance is less acceptable. With clay animation, distinction between the original video and the digital version was hard to notice, even at 10 fps, because the characters' motions are not done with continuous video shooting. This would not be the case if the footage contained, for instance, natural human motion which, in the video jargon, is referred to as "real image video footage" [14].

When the clay animation digital video clips were shown to a test group the acceptance level was high. An interesting reaction was: "Why can't the video be full screen?" The obvious technical answer was "because of bandwidth problems" and blowing up the original 320*240 image to 640*480 was not an acceptable option: image compression artefacts would be visible. However, it is not the audience's problem if we have technical limitations to respond to; to them, things should be transparent and natural, otherwise the product can be considered not well designed. This lead to the search of better digital video multimedia integration.

3 Looking for Video in Multimedia

Although our primary goal is a CD-ROM based application, we looked for digital video integration in multimedia both in the Web and in CD-ROM distribution. In the Web it is not uncommon to find institutional important sites with stamp sized images with slow frame rate and poor contents, both on image quality and video framing, with files that take quite some time to load and look amateur in contents when finally played, showing a complete absence of the very minimum video capture and editing rules [15]. Better technical approaches, like video streaming, are used as another possibility of distributing professional video contents without taking into consideration the specific limitations of the media. Clearly, all in all, we got the strong impression that video on the Web is in its infancy: it is used more as a gadget than as a working tool. When looking to CD-ROMs we found three different approaches:

- Games: digital video in games is generally done with very high quality standards regarding content and using non disclosed proprietary solutions; for "full frame", or almost 640*480 video window size, a mixed coding scheme can be detected: apparently more than 15 fps are used – motion looks good, and only half of the horizontal image lines seem to be used, evenly distributed over the image surface, maintaining the full image look, but reducing the amount of information needed;
- Multimedia encyclopaedias: here video is integrated as AVI short clips, Indeo or Cinepak compressed, with 10 or 12 fps and 240*180 image size; image quality and

motion reproduction is acceptable for the type of document it pretends to be, a repository of information packed on a CD: the more compressed it is, the more information can be delivered; high quality on image and motion is not mandatory;

- Marketing: in this category we found MPEG-1 coded video to market multimedia services in video coding [16] and in movies advertising – a cinema magazine distributing a CD-ROM with movie trailers [17]; all video clips showed a very good image quality with motion playing at 25 fps; the videos could be played at the original image size, 352*288, blown up to full screen or zoomed to any intermediate image size; zooming up shows slight scalability problems, more noticeable in bigger image size; motion reproduction perfection was striking.

One of the games incorporating video that we analysed fits in a category of its own: *Eve* [18]. This game "breathes" design and artistic care in every, single and apparently non important detail. Technically it includes some conventional approaches to real image integration over a designed scenario, filming an actor over a blue screen and doing chroma keying or alpha channel processing for multi-plane layering, with the typical problems of detail and definition on the actor's body/image limits and some, acceptable, motion limitations with translation panning and self walking motion mixture. Another part shows an interior where the player can chose among several numbered panels: a video clip will play in the background wall. In the distant wall we see a person's face talking. And the motion seems flawless, causing a very good impression. There are several reasons for this, and it can be inferred that great design care was applied into overcoming the technical limitations:

- When taken apart from the scenario, the clip's image lacks detail, as an ordinary AVI clip would look: the integration in that scenario makes the difference;
- Slow action, as it is the case, in a small image, is less problematic at a lower frame rate: when looking carefully one can detect that a low frame rate is being used;
- All video clips consist of image framing specifically to show only the face of the person talking: we don't see full body or half body framing, only the face is shown; that particular framing and video capture was done for that particular design;
- Each video is short in duration: time contention was applied because, with such a small image, with so little to see, it wouldn't capture attention for long.

There is a wide diversity of digital video approaches when it comes to multimedia: in coding and content terms, in integration with other media. In the next section we analyze the importance of good quality motion perception as a step towards our selection of better digital video integration in multimedia, applied to the EcoVasco game.

3.1 Quality of Motion Reproduction

In the early stages of television development, analog video was standardized at 50 half frames per second, not 25 frames per second (European TV standard). This was done to minimize bandwidth in broadcasting the TV signal and to ensure good quality motion coding. In television terms, we are used to very good motion reproduction.

The higher limit at which singular events can be distinguished from each other by the human eye is 10 Hz, 10 fps if we talk about video or cinema. The frame rate of 16 fps was established by Louis Lumière in the beginning of moving pictures [19] as to minimise film cost enabling motion reconstruction at an image rate already better than the visual limit in perception: the image rate "is a balance between two contradictory needs, one being of technical order (the more the images per second the less flickering occurs) another of economical nature (the less images per second the cheaper the film production costs)" [19].

In cartoons the viewer is not expecting the same type of motion as in real image footage. However, even in animation, there are cases where the lack of 25 fps produces undesired effects: for example the Road Runner cartoons, 3D realistic fast computer animations, or in poetic subtle animation – like in Digital Pinscreen animation [20, 21]. In Figures 1 and 2 we present an example of a fast 3D realistic motion sequence from the video *CPI'90* [22], a cork popping out of a champagne bottle, and the consequences of moving from 25 to 10 fps. Figure 1 shows the complete original images of the sequence, while Figure 2 shows the same time span when converted to 10 fps.

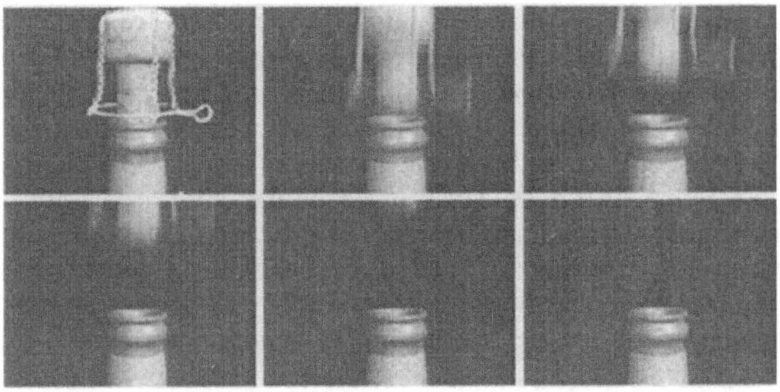

Fig. 1. Original motion sequence in *CPI'90* [22] at 25 fps.

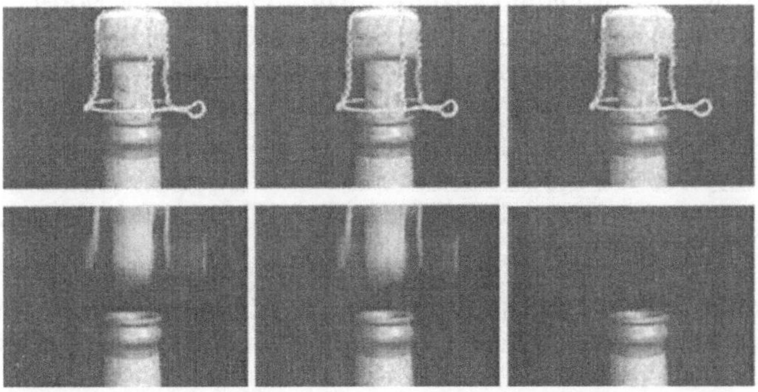

Fig. 2. Motion reproduction when coding at 10 frames per second.

Visual tests showed that the motion at 10 fps was perceived as having less quality. Applying the same tests to natural motion, like human walking, the results at frame rates other than 25 fps looked artificial and fragmented.

Based on the collected information, a strategy was developed to catch the interest from our targeted audience. This will be presented in the next Section.

4 Strategy for the Game Development

In order to appeal to a broader audience we developed the idea of extending the use of video to include real image footage as part of the game action: each player can play with the "live" presence of his/her colleague or even be inside the game.

This could be done with background and foreground manipulation with real image integration over a fixed scenario, filming a player over a blue screen and doing chroma keying or alpha channel processing for multi-plane layering, as existing games do. However there are problems when synchronising between the player's action and the background. This is a good approach to be done once but it is much more expensive and time consuming than conceptualising a game structure where video clips are an important element and short full motion video actions are integrated.

Let's think of a wastebasket in a scene. Clicking on it makes the video action to start and a student/actor enters the scene and uses the basket. This approach also enables an affordable, easily updateable full motion video action for different players to enter the scene: it can be done with a 10 or a 16 year old participant. It can be customisable for any player integration. It can also be thought as an opportunity to involve all aspects of school activity, with students, teachers and auxiliary employees to take part in the "eco actions". It is updateable on a school environment basis.

With an open architecture approach we can develop the game without forcing a rigid link between the game and the video clips, enabling an update of the video clips independent of game. When rerunning the game the new video clips will play.

In computer games a "battle" for the highest frame rate and image quality is permanently running [23]. The popularity of computer games drove games' developers and hardware manufacturers to provide better and not so expensive graphic cards, already integrated in the PC configuration. Any video oriented solution has to cope with that, and, as far as we could analyse, quality video means MPEG. Although we are able to code on MPEG-1 and MPEG-2, only MPEG-1 will be used because it is already main stream and easily playable on a software basis. This is not yet the case with MPEG-2. Games made graphic boards more accessible, it is expected that DVD video distribution will lower the prices of MPEG-2 solutions.

4.1 Development Platform

The video section of ADETTI's laboratory, the development platform for this project, uses three Personal Computers linked in a 100 MHz network, two Pentium II 450 and one Pentium 166 machine:

- Pentium II 450 MHz, 128 MB RAM, a 18 GB U2SCSI disk, a DVD drive, a hardware MPEG-2 player: dedicated to analogue/digital video acquisition, output and non-linear editing with a miroVIDEO DC30 and DV300 boards;
- Pentium II 450 MHz, 128 MB RAM, a 18 GB U2SCSI disk: dedicated to MPEG-1 acquisition with MovieMaker, a real-time MPEG-1 encoding board [24];
- Pentium 166 MHz, 32 MB RAM, a 8 GB UWSCI disk, a 2G JAZ drive, a CD-RW and a Nikon CoolScan III (film and slide high resolution scanner): dedicated to other forms of IO and backup.

All machines have sound cards, microphones and speakers and the two PII have OpenGL based boards (ASUS V3400TNT/TV) enabling real-time analogue video output. This enables one machine to run an interactive demonstration that the MPEG machine can code in real-time into a MPEG-1 file for distribution or editing.

As video equipment we have a Canon XL1 miniDV Digital Video camera with IEEE 1394 to link to the DV300 board, a Sony 3 CCD Hi8 video camera and a Sony EVO Hi8 single frame video recorder. Several video monitors and VHS, stereo or mono, recorders are available. As software platform we use MacroMedia Director and Mpeg Xtra® [25]. As the MPEG software coder we can use MainActor V2.05 from MainConcept [26]. Other software packages include the common software applications found in multimedia environments (painting, animation, morphing, etc.).

4.2 Current State of Development and Results

The game, in its current state of development, is based on different screens representing the areas where the action takes place. These screens can be either drawings, digital photos or a still frame from the beginning of a video clip.

There are three main regions that the player can explore: the house, the school and the streets. The house includes: two bedrooms, a corridor, the bathroom, the dining room, the kitchen and a hall. The school includes: a classroom, a corridor, a cafeteria and a playground. The starting screen shows the school, on the left, and the house, on the right. There is also a "hidden" alley between the house and the school. Navigation is not always evident, there are hidden paths.

To conceptualise the scenario we built a positioning map and a navigation chart. Using A4 page sized printouts of all the different screens we built a storyboard on a 3 by 2 meters size panel, where the printouts were placed in accordance with the positioning map and the navigation chart. This storyboard enables a global vision of the game and a better planning for game actions inclusion and distribution over the different screens. The positioning map, the navigation chart and the storyboard are development tools and, as such, the player does not have access to them. The player has to navigate to acquire the perception of the space being explored and this is considered part of the game.

Along the navigation, the player is able to learn about ecological behaviour, to solve puzzles and perform tasks, some of them with time constraints and/or a score counting mechanism. For instance, in the rear street screen, not well educated neighbours throw "monsters" (refrigerators, washing machines, dish washers, ...) to the street. The player, clicking the left mouse button over the falling monsters, has to grab and put them in a collecting truck.

For specific actions, video sequences can be used. For this, a set is chosen complying to the storyboard structure. Camera positioning and action planning have to take into consideration the "in" and "out" points of the actor/player. The best results are achieved when the actor enters the set from one side and leaves from the other, keeping the action motion natural. When filming outdoors, relative positions between camera, set and sun has also to be taken into consideration: shadows cast by trees or the moving actor should be seen and thought of as another element in the scene. If the same action is to be shot in the same set with some time lapse, using another actor, the sun's orientation should be taken into consideration since, for the same hour of the day, the sun can be in such a relative position to the camera as to make it impossible to shoot. "External" elements, such as passing pedestrians, cars and other moving objects, should be avoided: action continuity must be preserved. Between shots clothing continuity should be also preserved, either shooting all scenes the same day, or using some reference clothes. These details may seem excessive. In fact they are quite simple and they are part of the basic elements of video composition: as it is the case in writing a text, video has its own composition rules.

Finding the right degree of natural behaviour in the planned action can be a challenge, especially when younger actors are participating. With an older actor, three to four takes can be enough since perception for what is needed is sharper than with younger actors. With these a greater degree of explanation and practice is necessary. The first takes will tend to be a succession of well started actions followed by sudden stops, in the middle of the set, looking to the camera and asking for instructions [27]. Repetition is the key for success and, after each repetition, an explanation should follow analysing what was good and less good, what should be changed and why. Even if the same action is made again and again over 10 minutes of continuos filming to correctly record a 6 second scene, the whole experience is perceived by the young actor as a game in itself.

Fig. 3. *Papeleira* sequence: on the left played by Susana, on the right played by Sofia.

Figure 3 shows two sequences in the same natural set, Praça do Império garden in Lisbon, one with Susana aged 10 and the other with Sofia aged 16, who show up when the player clicks the container (*papeleira*). The two sequences were shot with a 3 month interval. On the second sequence only visual clues were used to reposition the camera and frame the scene. It was easy and almost straightforward. The main issue to consider was to visually place the container in the same relative position so that any clicking on the container would be effective in both clips. The standard procedure, after filming, is to digitize the sequences.

The following are values taken from MPEG coding the sequences *susana* and *sofia* using a software approach in two different machines. This is to show that MPEG software coding is a feasible solution. For the test, a common case departing video clip was built, coding the sequence with Adobe Premiere to 640*480 resolution, 25 fps, with no compression. This way we ensured that the two machines would departure from exactly the same video clip and only software would be analysed.

The two machines used were a Pentium II 450 MHz machine with 128 MB 100 MHz SDRAM and a Pentium 166 MHz machine with 32 MB EDO RAM. As it should be expected, times with the PII machine are better:

Output files: 352 x 288	susana.mpg (828KB)	sofia.mpg (1.10MB)
Pentium II 450 MHz:	1' 56"	2' 33"
Pentium 166 MHz:	5' 12"	8' 30"

From our experience an AVI coding is less problematic than an MPEG coding with a software approach: the software MPEG coder takes more CPU time and is more sensitive to less quality original video. In some cases the digital video acquisition has to be enhanced in contrast and/or brightness before passing it to the MPEG coder while the Cinepak or Indeo codecs are less demanding. But the extra time MPEG takes to code pays off in much better image quality and full motion quality. After playing the same sequence coded with the different codecs (Indeo or Cinepak), one has no doubt on the MPEG quality and coding time value: it is more than worthwhile to wait 8.5 minutes, on a Pentium 166 MHz, to get the sequence MPEG coded because the final digital video is of such superior quality.

5 Conclusions

Developing a computer multimedia game for such a broad age span of students, from 10 to 16 years old, has been a great challenge. Results with the concept we developed of integrating live action where the students become part of the game, the real actors in the scenes, has shown to be feasible and appealing: students participate in a positive way. Not only will they be able to learn while playing the game, they can also learn participating in the making of the video clips for the game. The details necessary to master in good video composition for integration into the game are worthwhile when seeing the actions played inside the game. The MPEG approach is an essential part for the motion and image quality needed to stand in similar terms to the eye catching 3D fast computer games older students like so much.

With the adopted open architecture where, without changing the game nucleus, the video clips can be updated at any time, we make it possible for a high level of customisation with players of all ages participating in the game's video clips. We can also envisage that this could be done using not too much expensive video capture boards which, adding to MPEG software coding, would enable interested schools to adapt and update, on a regular basis, the video clips. This would maintain and expand the interest of the game as a learning tool for the new students that each year arrive to school. Using public accessible places, like gardens and city streets, facilitates the updating process.

Acknowledgements

We would like to acknowledge the support of Câmara Municipal de Lisboa. A special thank you is due to Mirada Audiovisuais for sharing industrial knowledge on professional video applications. To Nicolau Lima Antunes, Cristiana Serejo, Susana Lopes, Sofia Pinto, Miguel Santos Silva, Pedro Moreira, Ricardo Moita, for participation, suggestions and comments. To Miguel Dias for the support. Last, but not least, to Rosário Deodato and Fátima Estevens for their patience.

References

1. "ECO VASCO & Companhia (uma aventura ecológica)", Departamento de Higiene Urbana e Resíduos Sólidos, Divisão de Sensibilização e Educação Sanitária, CML, 1997.
2. Rice , F.P., Child and Adolescent Development, Prentice Hall, September 1996.
3. PC Format, magazine issues from March to June 1998, Future Publishing, 1998.
4. PC Game, Future Publishing, 1999 (Available on July, 1999 at http://www.pcgame.com).
5. Games Domain website 1999 (Available on July, 1999 at http://www.gamesdomain.com).
6. Virtual Reality project, ANMP 1997 Congress, idea by OA, Oficina de Arquitectura, developed by ADETTI – M. Dias, P.F. Lopes, V. Preto, J. Drey, J.S. Paiva, Porto, 1997.
7. V. Preto, A. Santana, Virtual Reality & computer games, Internal report, ISCTE, 1998.
8. *O Monstro Tirano*, video, clay animation, Estratégia Publicidade, CML, 1997.
9. *O Pátio das Limpezas*, video, clay animation, Estratégia Publicidade, CML, 1997.
10. *O Vidrão da Estrela*, video, clay animation, Estratégia Publicidade, CML, 1997.
11. *O Contentor de Perdição*, video, clay animation, Estratégia Publicidade, CML, 1997.
12. J. Williams, A. Lock, C. Burnett, "Digital Video for Multimedia: Considerations for Capture, Use and Delivery", Multimedia Resources Unit, University of Bristol, 1996 (Available on May, 1999 at http://www.man.ac.uk/MVC/SIMA/digital_video/title.html).
13. P.F. Lopes, *SARA: Um Sistema de Animação por Computador*, MSc thesis, IST, Nov. 1988.
14. H. Martins, Industrial video applications, private communication, Lisbon, 1998.
15. R. J. Compesi, R. E. Sherriffs, *Small Format Television Production*, 2nd Edition, 1990.
16. *ThinkPad MPEG Sampler*, CD-ROM, Interactive Media, IBM, 1995.
17. CinéLive Magazine et CD-ROM, CinéLive, April issue, 1999.
18. P. Gabriel, *Eve*, game, Real World, 1996.
19. V. Pinel, *Louis Lumière: Inventeur et Cinéaste*, Éditions Nathan, Paris, 1994.
20. P.F. Lopes, M.R. Gomes, "A Computer Model For Pinscreen Simulation: A New Animation Paradigm", *Computer Graphics Forum*, 11(1), March 1992, pp. 31-42.
21. P.F. Lopes, *Tela de Alfinetes Digital: Um Novo Paradigma de Animação por Computador*, PhD thesis, IST, January 1996.
22. P.F. Lopes, *CPI 90*, video, 3D computer animation, 1' 40", Official opening of the 6th Portuguese Congress of Informatics, INESC, July 1990 (Auditório 1, Fund. C. Gulbenkian).
23. T. Pabst, "tom's hardware guide", Web site, http://www4.tomshardware.com/, May 1999.
24. MPEG MovieMaker, Real-time high quality MPEG-1 encoding board, Optibase, 1998.
25. Mpeg Xtra® 3.1 for MacroMedia Director® 5, 6, 6.5, 7 on Windows® 95, 98 and NT , Tabuleiro da Baiana 1999 (http://www.tbaiana.com/frmpegx.htm).
26. MainActor V2.05, software MPEG coder, MainConcept, GbR Moenig/Zabel, 1998.
27. P.F. Lopes, *EcoVasco, uma aventura ecológica*, video demonstration, ISCTE, 1999.

Involving the Audience in Distributed, Interactive Entertainment Systems

Nikitas M. Sgouros[1]

[1] Department of Informatics, University of Piraeus, Karaoli & Dimitriou 80, 185 34, Piraeus, Greece
sgouros@unipi.gr

Abstract. One of the main criteria for judging the effectiveness of Web-based, interactive entertainment forms such as interactive stories or games is their ability to involve large numbers of participants during their performance. This paper describes a novel, distributed interaction framework for audience involvement in interactive entertainment systems. This framework allows multiple users on the Web to participate in the performance of the event either as players or spectators. The method supports a centralized communication scheme in which a server module is responsible for relaying all the messages generated by the participants. In addition, the server monitors the game/story action along with the audience response and sends messages of its own in an effort to emphasize the dramatic nature of the performance and stimulate audience participation. This method has been applied in the creation of MISSION, a multi-player game on the Web.

1 Introduction

One of the main criteria for judging the effectiveness of interactive entertainment forms such as interactive stories or multi-player games, is their ability to have an effect on a group of people, to focus their attention and to stimulate their participation. Currently, the majority of these systems try to satisfy this criterion by allowing multiple users to join an ongoing story or game performance as one of the actors or players in it. We refer to this type of user participation as *direct* interaction. Although interesting, the provision of a unique, direct mode of user interaction with such systems limits their appeal as it excludes users that prefer to follow more *ritualistic* forms of interaction during performance. By ritualistic we refer to types of interaction similar to the ones found in quite popular events such as football matches, theater plays or musical concerts. In these cases the performance of the event motivates the expression of shared understandings and emotions by a group of people (the spectators or the audience) that, in turn, influences the performance of the event. In contrast with direct interaction, which is often utilitarian in aim since it serves the goal of the player in the story or game, ritualistic interaction is often celebratory and decorative, seeking to unify the participants and to mobilize sentiment and action during performance.

This research provides a novel, distributed interaction framework that supports both direct and ritualistic forms of expression and facilitates their interplay in interactive entertainment systems such as stories or games. In particular, this framework allows multiple users to participate in the performance of the event either as *players* or *spectators*. A player takes the place of one of the characters of the story or game and decides on its current behavior. A spectator, on the other hand, is able to freely observe and comment on the game/story action and to express his/her emotions during the performance by sending messages to the rest of the participants. Messages may include text, or a variety of multimedia effects (e.g. audio clips, image effects etc.) that affect the presentation of the event at each participant site. The framework supports a centralized communication scheme in which a server module is responsible for relaying all the messages generated by the participants. In addition, the server monitors the game/story action along with the audience response and sends messages of its own in an effort to emphasize the dramatic nature of the performance and stimulate audience participation. This method has been applied in the creation of MISSION, a multi-player game on the Web that enables two players to participate in a 3-D arcade game, while a group of spectators observes the game action and provides feedback during the performance. The game has been deployed on the Web and user feedback is solicited.

Among the possible uses for this research are the development of novel, interactive entertainment systems similar in form and appeal to more traditional forms involving public performance (e.g. sporting events, festivals etc) and the enhancement of existing computer games or interactive story systems with capabilities for audience participation.

The rest of this paper is organized as follows. Section 2 describes in detail the distributed interaction architecture. Section 3 discusses the implementation of this interaction framework on a multi-player game on the Web, while section 4 presents related work. Finally section 5 provides conclusions and an indication of future work.

2 Architecture

Figure 1 depicts the system architecture. Each participant (user or spectator) is connected to a central server module that is responsible for passing around information related to the game/story action or the audience reactions. The system assigns a unique id to each participant site. The server accepts two types of messages from each site; *action* and *reaction* messages. Action messages are produced by the players and describe the actions of the characters they control during the performance. The server automatically relays all these messages to the rest of the participants. For example, action messages may include information on the motion of each character in story space. The server assumes that all processing related to the presentation of player actions is handled locally at each participating site. Consequently, action messages can be short and only contain directions for updating the presentation locally at each site, thus conserving valuable network bandwidth. For example, messages describing player motions in story space describe only the direction of each motion step. Each participating site uses this information to update locally the presentation.

There are two types of reaction messages. Those sent from the audience members to the participants (*A→P*) and those send from the server to the participants (*S→P*). The rest of this section describes these messages in more detail.

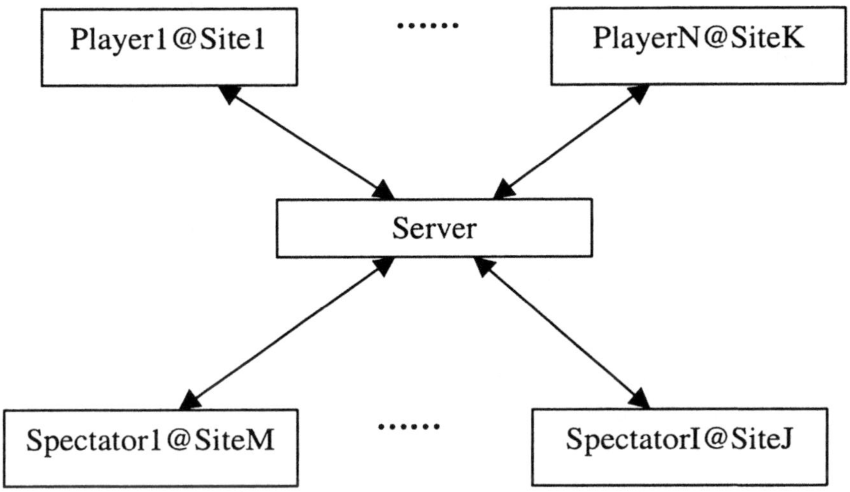

Fig. 1. Distributed Interaction Architecture. All messages in the system are relayed through the server

2.1 A→P Messages

An A→P message originates from an audience member (e.g. *X*) and it can have as recipient a subset of the players and the audience. In particular, X can specify the group *P* of players that will receive his/her message (e.g. *M*). In this case, M will be also sent automatically to all the spectators that observe the behavior of any of the players in P at sending time. Consequently, spectators will receive only relevant reaction messages concerning the players they are currently watching. A→P messages may include text, or a variety of multimedia effects (e.g. audio clips, image effects etc.) depending on their goal and on the affect state they want to induce on the players and on the rest of the spectators.

Table 1 describes the types of A→P messages currently available. These messages can have either standard forms and goals (rows 1-5) expressing the approval or disapproval of current player actions or their results or warning a player on possible danger. In addition, they can be composed on the fly by the spectators (row 6). In the first case, a spectator can choose from one of several standard forms of expression for his/her message. For example, if a spectator wants to congratulate a player on his/her actions s/he can send a standard message in either one of the forms (text clip, audio clip or image effect) described in row 1. The server assumes that all processing related to the presentation of A→P messages is handled locally at each participating site. Consequently, these messages can be short and only contain directions for updating the presentation locally at each site, thus conserving valuable network bandwidth. On the other hand, free-form messages can be arbitrarily long. Consequently, they can have significant bandwidth requirements for their transmission in real-time, especially if they involve audio or image effects. This is why the system currently supports the composition of free-form messages only in text form (see row 6).

Table 1: Types of A→P messages.

#	Goal	Text Clip	Audio Clip	Image Effect
1	Congratulate on the results of player actions	Bravo!	Applause	Trophy
2	Reject the results of player actions	Awful!	-	-
3	Encourage current player actions	Go on!	Rhythmic Drum Sound	-
4	Discourage current player actions	Stop!	Braking sound	Stop sign
5	Warn of possible danger	Watch out!	-	-
6	Other	User-supplied Message Text	-	-

2.2 S→P Messages

S→P messages originate from the server. Their goal is to emphasize the dramatic nature of the performance and to stimulate audience participation. More specifically, the server module plays an active role during the performance and monitors the behavior of the players and the audience in order to:

1. Detect audience preferences.

2. Emphasize the dramatic nature of the performance.
3. Express collective reactions from the audience.

The rest of this section analyzes each task in more detail.

Detect audience preferences. The server keeps track of the spectators that appear to support each player. In particular, the server tracks the A→P messages sent to each player and classifies spectators that encourage or congratulate a player consistently (i.e., more than a number of consecutive times) as this player's *fans*. Similarly, the server classifies spectators that consistently oppose a player's actions as this player's *opposers*.

Emphasize the dramatic nature of the performance. The server affects the performance at each spectator site using two kinds of multimedia effects: *suspense* and *atmospheric*. Suspense effects seek to capture audience interest in the story. Atmospheric effects aim to communicate the mood of the events and the nature of the relationships between the players in the performance. The server assumes that the particular implementations of both types of effects are provided by the story or game developer and they are stored locally at each spectator site. The server can automatically trigger the execution of these effects at appropriate points during the performance. In particular, the server constantly monitors the game or story action, marking points where:

1. Players have their physical or emotional state changed. For example, winning or loosing are two such points in a game performance. Changes in the state of a player can affect the emotional state of its fans or opposers as well. Consequently, whenever the server detects such changes it triggers a series of atmospheric effects at the sites of this player's fans and opposers. For example, each time a player wins in MISSION the server triggers the execution of a joyful audio clip at every fan site for this player and the execution of a sad audio clip at every opposer site.
2. Conflict between players reaches a climax. For example, in numerous video games the conflict between two players reaches a climax during their violent confrontation. Climactic points have significant suspense potential for spectators since they result in changes in the physical or emotional state of the players. Consequently, whenever the server detects such points it triggers a series of suspense effects at the sites of all the spectators that observe the actions of the players involved. For example, whenever a player in MISSION misses its target by little the system executes a suspense audio clip at each player or spectator site involved in the incident.

Express collective reactions. One of the main goals of ritualistic forms of interaction is to express and reinforce sentiments of unity, common beliefs and values between the participants. Consequently, an interaction framework that seeks to support audience involvement in interactive performances should emphasize collective reactions from the participants. In our case, the framework seeks to achieve this goal through the *amplification* of group reactions during performance. More specifically, the framework assumes that similar A→P messages sent very close in time from different spectators reflect common collective reactions from the audience. Consequently, the presentation of these messages should be emphasized. For this reason, the server maintains a short history of the recent A→P messages it receives. This history is implemented as a FIFO queue in which each message has a strength counter associated with it. Whenever a message matches the content but not the sender of any of the previous messages in the queue, its strength counter is incremented and appended to the message relayed by the server to the participants. The emphasis with which each message is presented at each participant site is proportional to its strength counter. Emphasis can be achieved locally through the manipulation of presentation parameters such as the screen space allocated for the display of each message, the intensity of the audio clip played, or the number of messages displayed on the screen.

3 An Example

The interaction framework has been applied in the creation of MISSION, a simple, multi-player game on the Web. The game enables two players to confront each other in a 3-D space battle. A group of spectators can observe the game action on the Web and react during the performance. The system is available on the Web at:

http://thalis.cs.unipi.gr/~sgouros/Demos/MultiUser/index.html

Apart from the 3-D game space MISSION allows each player to see or hear the A→P messages sent to him/her by the spectators. On the other hand, each spectator can freely navigate in 3-D space so that s/he can view the game action from any view. Spectators are invisible to the players. A spectator can send A→P messages to either a certain player by placing the player inside a player selector area in the screen, or to all of the players that are visible from his/her current position. A spectator receives and views all the A→P messages and all the suspense effects concerning the players s/he watches. In addition, a spectator receives all the S→P messages sent by the server to the players s/he supports or opposes.

Figure 2 shows a typical screenshot from the game. This shot depicts one of the player spaceships and two A→P messages. As the figure shows, text or image messages flash at random positions on the player's or spectator's screen. The small circle to the right side of the figure is used in the case of players as a targeting device during battle and in the case of spectators as a player selector area for sending messages to any player inside this area.

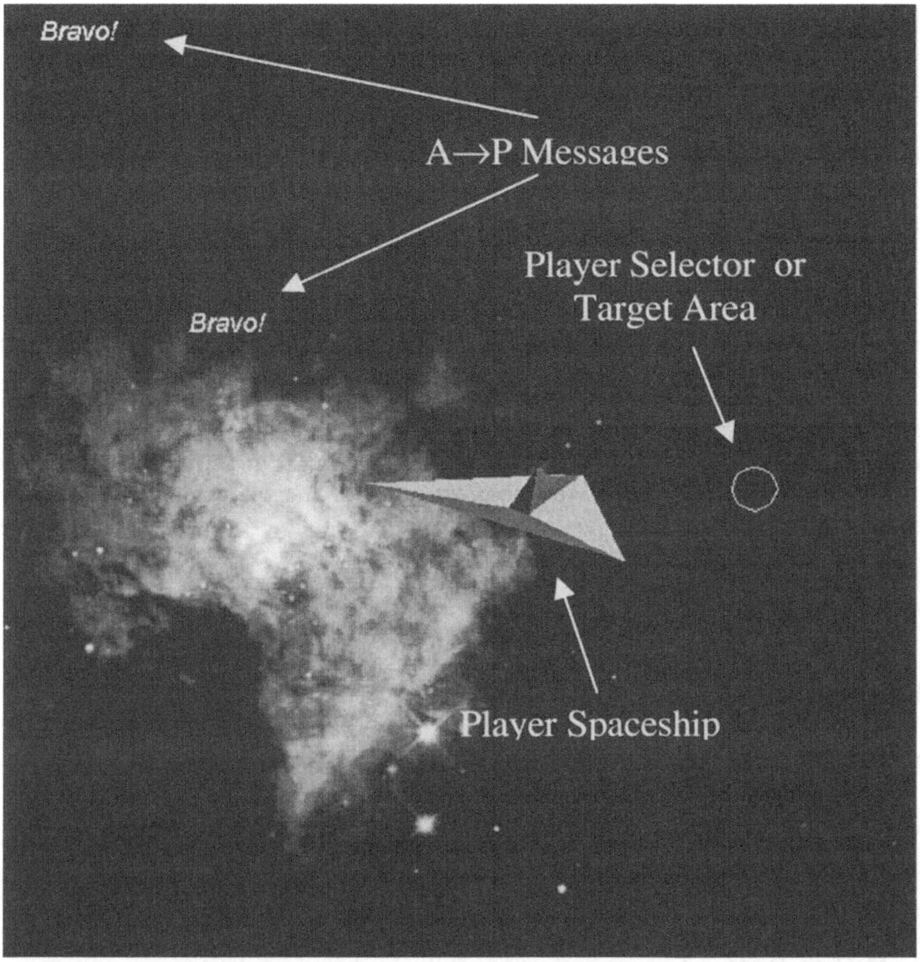

Fig. 2. Screenshot from MISSION

4 Related Work

Recently, there has been considerable research interest in the development of interactive entertainment systems, especially interactive narratives [1, 2]. Most of these systems assume a direct form of interaction with the system. This work complements this research focusing on multi-user systems that offer the chance for audience involvement during the performance.

Furthermore, there has been a tremendous amount of work on story dramatization techniques for the performing arts, on the investigation of the relation between the performance and the audience and on the psychology of the crowd (e.g. [3, 4, 5]). Our research seeks to use the results of this work in the creation of multimedia user interfaces for the expression of group behavior and for the creation of novel entertainment forms that combine direct and ritualistic forms of interaction.

5 Conclusions & Future Work

This paper describes a distributed interaction framework that supports audience involvement in interactive entertainment systems. This research can be used for the development of novel interactive entertainment forms that allow audience participation or for the enhancement of existing multimedia applications such as interactive narratives or games.

Future work in this area will seek to extend the means of expression of the audience in interactive entertainment systems by experimenting with direct audio and video connections between the performance participants. Furthermore, it will further investigate alternative methods for automatically linking the content of a performance with appropriate multimedia dramatization techniques such as more complex suspense or atmospheric effects.

References

1. Sgouros, N. M., Dynamic generation, management and resolution of interactive plots, *Artificial Intelligence*, 107, Elsevier, 1999, pp: 29-62.
2. Waters, R. C. 1995. The 1995 AAAI Spring Symposia Reports; Interactive Story Systems: Plot and Character, *AI Magazine*, 16(3): 8-9.
3. Pfister, M., *The Theory and Analysis of Drama,* Cambridge University Press, 1988.
4. McQuail, D., *Mass Communication Theory*, Sage Publications, 1994.
5. Hogg, M. A., and Vaughan, G. M., *Social Psychology: An Introduction,* London: Prentice Hall, 1995.

Multi-Media Access and Presentation in a Theatre Information Environment

Anton Nijholt

Parlevink Research Group
Centre of Telematics and Information Technology
PO Box 217, 7500 AE Enschede, the Netherlands
anijholt@cs.utwente.nl

Abstract. This paper discusses a virtual world for presenting multimedia information and for natural interactions with the environment to get access to this information. Apart from mouse and keyboard input, interactions take place using speech and language. It is shown how this virtual environment can be considered as an interest community and it is shown what further research and development is required to obtain an environment where visitors can retrieve information about artists, authors and performances, can discuss performances with others and can be provided with information and contacts in accordance with their preferences.
Keywords: Virtual Reality, Multi-modal Access, Multimedia Presentation, Speech and Language Interactions, Agent Technology

1 Introduction

World Wide Web allows interactions and transactions through WebPages using speech and language, either by inanimate or live agents, image interpretation and generation, and, of course the more traditional ways of presenting explicitly pre-defined information by allowing users access to text, tables, figures, pictures, audio, animation and video. In a task- or domain-restricted way of interaction current technology allows the recognition and interpretation of rather natural speech and language in dialogues. However, rather than the current twodimensional web-pages, the interesting parts of the Web will become three-dimensional, allowing the building of virtual worlds inhabited by interacting user and task agents and with which the user can interact using different types of modalities, including speech and language interpretation and generation. Agents can work on behalf of users, hence, human computer interaction will make use of 'indirect management', rather than interacting through direct manipulation of data by users. In this paper we discuss a virtual world for representing information and natural interactions about performances in an existing theatre. Apart from mouse and keyboard input interactions take place using speech and language. It is shown how this virtual environment can be considered as an interest community and it is shown what further research and development is required to obtain an environment where visitors can retrieve information about artists, authors and performances, can discuss performances with others and can be provided with information and contacts in accordance with their preferences.

2 Information Spaces for Interest Communities

Web-based digital cities have been around for some years. Like many computer games they have evolved from text environments to 2-dimensional graphical and 3D virtual environments with sounds, animation and video. Visitors, or maybe we should call them residents, of these cities visit libraries, museums, pubs, squares, etc., where they can get information, chat with others, etc. In these environments people get the feeling of being together, they are listening to each other and, in general, they take responsibility for the environment and their and others' behavior in such environments.

Today there are examples of virtual spaces that are visited and inhabited by people sharing common interests. With virtual spaces or environments we want to refer to computer accessible environments where users (visitors, passers-by) can enter 3D environments, browse (visual representations of) information and can communicate with objects or agents (maybe other visitors in the same environment). These spaces can for example, represent offices, shared workspaces, shops, class rooms, companies or cities. However, it is also possible to design virtual spaces that are devoted to certain themes and are tuned to users (visitors) interested in that theme or to users (visitors) that not necessarily share common (professional or educational) interests, but share some common conditions (driving a car, being in hospital for some period, have the same therapy, belonging to the same political party, etc.).

As an example we mention a virtual world developed at a cancer research institute in Seattle. This world enables people struggling with cancer to obtain information and interact with others facing similar challenges. Patients, families and friends can enter the three-dimensional world (a rendering of the actual outpatient lobby), get information at a reception desk, visit a virtual gift shop, etc. Participants can engage in public chat discussions or invitation-only meetings. A library can be visited, its resources can be used and participants can enter an auditorium to view presentations.

3 A Virtual Theatre Community: A Case Study in Progress

3.1 Introduction

We present research on visualization and interaction in a realistic model of an existing theatre. This existing 'Muziekcentrum' offers its visitors information about performances by means of a yearly brochure. In addition, it is possible to get information at an information desk in the theatre (during office hours), to get information by phone (by talking to a human or by using IVR). The database of the theater holds the information that is available at the beginning of the 'theatre season'. Our aim is to make this information more accessible by using multi-modal accessible multi-media web pages. A more general aim is to do research in the area of web-based services, in particular interactions in virtual environments using speech and language.

Our virtual theatre has been built according to design drawings of the architects of the building. Visitors can enter the theatre and walk around. Information about today's performances is available on a screen that is automatically updated. Visitors may go to the information desk in the theatre, see previews and start a dialogue with an agent called 'Karen' (cf. Figure 1). One aim that we currently explore is the embedding of this particular environment in a virtual cultural arena where people can ask, retrieve and explore information about theatre and music performances in general. Agents, like Karen, will help the users with these tasks.

Fig. 1. Agent Karen

3.2 Providing Modalities

When a user has the possibility to change easily from one modality to an other, or can use combinations of modalities when interacting with an information system, then it is also more easy to deal with shortcomings of some particular modality. Multi-modality has two directions. That is, the system should be able to present multi-media information and it should allow the user to use different input modalities in order to communicate with the system. Not all communication devices that are currently available for information access, exploration of information and for transaction allow more than one modality for input or output. This is especially true if we look at world wide web interfaces. Research done on information access and transaction in the context of modalities (and especially the sequential and simultaneous combination of modalities), that is, a multi-modality approach for WWW, can be embedded in the attempts to develop standards for access to the web and presentation on the web. For example, standards are being developed for speech access (voice browsing), 3D visualization (virtual reality modeling languages) and the combination of access and visualization (MPEG standards). When we look at multi-modal human-computer interaction it is clear that hardly any research has been done to distinguish discourse and dialogue phenomena, let alone to model them, for multi-modal tasks. The same holds for approaches to funnel information conveyed via multiple modalities into and out of a single underlying representation of meaning to be communicated (the cross-media information fusion problem). Similarly, on the output side, there is the information-to-media allocation problem.

Our second observation, certainly not independent from the observation above on modalities for access, exploration and presentation, deals with the actors in a system that has to deal with presenting information, reasoning about information, communicating between actors in the system and realizing transactions (e.g. through negotiation) between actors in the system. In addition to a multi-modality approach, there is a need for a multi-agent approach, where agents can take roles ranging from presenting windows on a screen, reasoning about information that might be interesting for a particular user, and being recognizable (and probably visible) as being able to perform certain tasks.

3.3 Providing Visual Context

We decided to visualize the environment in which people can get information about theatre performances, can make reservations and can talk to theatre employees and other visitors. VRML, agent technology, text-to-speech synthesis, talking faces, speech recognition, etc., became issues after taking this decision. They will be discussed in the next sections. Visualization allows users to refer to a visible context and it allows the system to disambiguate user's utterances by making use of this context. Moreover, it allows the system to influence the interaction behavior of the user in such a way that more efficient and natural dialogues with the system become possible.

It has become clear from several studies (cf. Friedman [2]) that people engage in social behavior toward machines. It is also well known that users respond differently to different 'computer personalities'. It is possible to influence the user's willingness to continue working even if the system's performance is not perfect. They can be made to enjoy the interaction, they can be made to perform better, etc., all depending on the way the interface and the interaction strategy have been designed. It makes a difference to interact with a talking face display or with a text display. In experiments it has been shown that people display different behavior when interacting with a talking face than they do with a text-display interface. This behavior is also influenced by the facial appearance and the expressions that are shown. People tend to present themselves in a more positive light to a talking face display and they are more attentive when a task is presented by a talking face.

¿From these observations we have concluded that apart from visualization in general, introducing talking faces and animated characters can help to make interaction more natural and to make shortcomings of the interaction technology, in particular speech and language, more acceptable to users. For that reason we are developing virtual faces and animated characters in our 3D-design environment. The faces consist of various three-dimensional coordinates, connected through faces. These faces are shaded to visualize a three-dimensional virtual face. The 3D data is converted to VRML-data that can be used for real-time viewing of the virtual face. A picture of a real human face can be mapped onto a virtual face. We are researching various kinds of faces to determine which can be best used for our application. Some are rather realistic and some are more in a cartoon-style. Karen's face is the interface between the users of the virtual theatre and the theatre information system. A dialogue window is shown when users approach the information-desk while they are navigating in the virtual theatre.

Karen's face is capable of visualizing the speech synchronously to the speech output. This involves lip-movements according to a couple of visemes. The face visualizes facial expressions according to user's input or the system's output. For pronouncing the utterance templates we use the Fluent Dutch Text-to-Speech system which runs on top of the MBROLA diphone synthesizer.

4 Agents, Interactions and Retrieval

4.1 A Navigation Agent

Navigation input through keyboard and mouse allows the user to move and to rotate, to jump from one location to an other, to interact with objects and to trigger them. In addition, a navigation agent has been developed that allows the user to explore the environment and to interact with objects in this environment by means of speech commands. Obviously, we do not want completely separated modalities. It should be left to the user to choose between the interacting means or to use both, sequentially or simultaneously. A smooth integration of the pointing devices and speech in a virtual environment requires means to resolve deictic references that occur in the interaction, and the navigation agent should be able to reason (in a modest way) about the geometry of the world in which it moves. We slowly extend and improve the interaction and navigation intelligence of our present navigation agent. At this moment we are exploring the possibility of speech recognition for several clients on a central server and the advantages of making the navigation agent visible for the user. One of our conclusions is that current web technology hardly allows smooth integration of speech recognition and browsing a virtual world.

4.2 An Information and Transaction Agent

As mentioned before, a second agent called Karen allows a natural language dialogue with the system about performances, artists, dates, prices, etc. Karen wants to sell tickets. She is fed from a database that contains information about performances in some of our local theatres. Developing intelligence for Karen, in this particular environment, is a main aim of our project. Presently the input to

Karen is keyboard-driven natural language and the output in our for the general audience WWW accessible virtual world is screen and menu based (Lie et al.[3]). In a prototype system we allow Karen to use a combination of speech synthesis and information presentation on the screen. Based on the user utterance, the context and the database, the system has to decide on a response action, consisting of database manipulation and dialogue acts. As mentioned earlier, in our experimental system Karen's spoken dialogue contribution is presented by visual speech, that is, a 'talking face' on the screen, embedded in the virtual world, mouths the questions and part of the responses. If necessary, information is given in a window on the screen and the user can click items to get more information. The virtual face that has been designed allows animation of lip and face movements and animation of some simple face expressions. For speech-image synchronization 3D images of visemes are called when corresponding phonemes are spoken. Since our application is web-based, it requires the solution of technical problems dealing with sending and compressing sound files, commands and synchronizing sounds and animations.

The theatre database which can be accessed by Karen (through the system's dialogue manager) contains information about performances. When is a particular performance, who are the performers, are there tickets available, how much do they cost, etc. A seat map allows the user to choose an available chair and to have a view of the stage from this particular chair. In order to decide on performances some previews (digitalized videos) are available that can be viewed on a monitor on Karen's information desk. Reviews of performances available in the theatre data base can be read aloud (using text-to-speech synthesis) by Karen.

4.3 Multimedia Retrieval

Presently we investigate how to store, index and retrieve theatre-related multimedia objects (text, pictures, audio, video) in such a way that a visitor of our virtual theatre environment can address Karen in such a way that she is not only able to inform the user about artists, performances, dates and available seats, but also knows how to provide the user with pictures, audio and video fragments (previews) of performances. In general, if a visitor asks about a particular performance, it is not difficult to present the associated multi-media information. However, if the visitor's questions are about or address associated information rather than explicitly making references to a particular performance, then our theatre agents have to start reasoning with the information that is available in the database and information that is available in a semantic network in which general knowledge about the domain has been stored. As an example, suppose someone asks: "Well, I know she received an Oscar last week. Are there any movies with her showing this week?" At this moment we think that it is reasonable to expect from our system that it starts searching WWW with a question that has as keywords: 'Oscar', 'actress', and maybe 'movie'. The intelligent theatre search engine should deliver the name of the actress and this should be sufficient to search the database for movies showing this week (or maybe later this month) with this particular actress in one of the roles.

A semantic network with the main concepts and their relationships in the world of theatre (opera, musicals, plays, music, cabaret, etc.) and theatre actors (directors, performers, technicians, reviewers, etc.) has to be designed in order to connect information available on WWW and information available in local databases through a process of reasoning. Textual information is important, since it is widely available. Newspapers, magazines and WWW pages contain reviews about performances, movies and performers. However, there is no need to confine ourselves to textual information. Presently, our research group is involved in some national and European projects on indexing and retrieval of multi-media information, including text, lay-out, pictures and captions, video subtitles, transcripts of spoken movie dialogues and spoken language. These projects are

1. Pop-Eye: This project aims at automatic indexing of subtitles of subtitles movies and television programmes and retrieving corresponding visual or soundtrack material.
2. Olive: The aim of this project is to develop a system which automatically produces indexes from the sound track of a programme and retrieving corresponding visual or soundtrack material.

Integrating research on multimedia indexing and retrieval and natural language (spoken) dialogue systems embedded in environments where users can 'say what they see' (ranging from handheld devices to immersive virtual reality environments) is our main aim in the near future. Since we think it is fruitful to consider WWW as an extension of our theatre databases we need an intelligent domain agent that knows how to filter and present the results of a WWW information search to a naive user looking for some information that may help in having a nice evening.

4.4 Future Agents: Conversation, Retrieval and Filtering

As may have become clear from the previous sections, our approach to designing a virtual environment for an interest community is bottom-up. We started with two agents and in order to introduce others a Java implemented agent platform has been designed. Using this platform other agents have been introduced, e.g., an information board showing upcoming events. Users can ask questions to the board and get answers. The board passes the questions to the other agents, in this case questions about performances are passed to the Karen agent.

At this moment the agents do not employ a model of a user or of user groups. In general, when we talk about interface agents we mean software agents with a user model, that is, a user model programmed in the agent by the user, provided as a knowledge base by a knowledge engineer or obtained and maintained by a learning procedure from the user and customized according to his preferences and habits and to the history of interaction with the system. In this way we have agents that make personalized suggestions (e.g. about articles, performances, etc.) based on social filtering (look at others who seem to have similar preferences) or content filtering (detect patterns, e.g. keywords) of the items that turn out to be of interest to the user. These agents can be passive that wait until they are put into action or they sense changes, take initiative and perform actions, e.g. to inform the user without being asked about new information. One of our concerns in the near future will be the introduction of a conversational agent (which has some general knowledge about well known artists and some well known performances). In this way we have obtained three kinds of dialogues (information & transaction dialogues, command-like dialogues and conversational dialogues). A slight sharing of knowledge (in particular, preferences of the user) between agents will become possible. In a next step this knowledge of preferences should be exploited, not only in the interactions with the user, but also in designing an agent that retrieves information that matches with the users profile. Visualization of the domains accessible to users may help to guide the interpretation of questions and requests for retrieval (we give a different interpretation to a question about artists when we are in an opera building then when we are in a music hall).

5 The Role of Presence

'Presence', as defined by Lombard and Ditton [4], is the perceptual illusion of nonmediation, that is, 'a person fails to perceive or acknowledge the existence of a medium in his/her communication environment and responds as he/she would if the medium were not there.'

Causes and effects of presence have been studied in experiments, but the number of parameters involved, e.g., task and user characteristics, makes systematic research difficult. ¿From the previous sections it may have become clear that rather naturally emerging topics of our interest are closely related to the issue of presence. The environment that is offered and the locations that can be visited look familiar, the functions of several objects and what to do with them is clear from their appearance and the multimodality approach allows a variety of user input and the production of different sensory outputs. The agents in the environment are assumed to be friendly and cooperative and the embedding of talking faces and moving avatars in the environment will increase the tendency to treat agents as social actors, rather than as software modules. However, increasing the user's feeling of presence has not been an explicit goal. Rather we have looked at possibilities to increase a user's commitment to the system (like we would in similar systems, e.g., for electronic commerce) with the aim to obtain co-operative behavior. One obvious reason which makes us loose a user is when use of clumsy technology (like speech and language technology) is not sufficiently backed up by context (including other modalities) which seduces the user to a certain interaction behavior and which helps to disambiguate the users utterances.

Needless to say that for many tasks and activities one may not expect that presence will necessarily enhance performance. On the contrary, presence can be noise which distracts a user from performing a task and which throws away the advantages of individual access from a home PC to, e.g., an information service.

There is no need for a virtual waiting queue or the sound of a leaving plane when all we want to know is when the next flight to Amsterdam leaves.

It is clear that in our world mediated entities (our agents in the virtual world) play the role of social actors, they increase the feeling of presence and they help to increase the user's commitment to the system. A more technical reason to have agents as social actors is that they can influence the interaction behavior of the users in such a way that it stays in a certain domain of task and/or domain knowledge, hiding shortcomings of imperfect interaction technology, in particular speech and language technology. With other words, in order to increase the quality of the web-based information and transaction services we are offering, it seems to be useful to exploit the possibility to increase the role of social actors in our environment. As already mentioned in Bates [1] (in the context of agents performing in virtual worlds), rather than build smart but narrow agents we can build agents with rather broad though perhaps more shallow capabilities. That is, for several applications we may be able to use agents that are not intelligent, as long as they are not clearly stupid or unreal. That is,

"An agent that keeps quiet may appear wise, while an agent that oversteps its abilities will probably destroy the suspension of disbelief. Thus, we propose to take advantage of the "Eliza effect", in which people see subtlety, understanding, and emotion in an agent as long as the agent does not actively destroy the illusion."

It should be clear from previous sections that in our environment we decided to explore the possibility to increase the user's feeling of presence in order to increase his or hers commitment to the system. We certainly do not want to advocate such an approach in general. In our application we think this is a useful approach. We don't think this should necessarily be the general approach to the design of computer interfaces for multimedia retrieval.

6 Theatre-related Purposes of the Virtual Environment

In the previous sections we concentrated on:

- the public, that is, men, women, children who want attend a certain performance or who want to know about performances in general, in a certain city or region, and at a certain date or in a certain period; the public has expectations about the information that is provided, it knows, for example, that different newspapers have different opinions about performances, hence, it is necessary to be careful in pushing the visitor to attend a certain performance
- the theatres, that is, the organizations that want to sell tickets, want positive reviews for the performances they hire, want to give correct and relevant information to the public, and have to offer contracts to the managers of artists and theatre companies in such a way that they are not loss-making

However, now that we have a virtual theatre where people can look around and get information on performances, wouldn't it be nice to apply this virtual reality environment to other theater-related purposes? Why not look more closely at possibilities that can be offered to:

- the professionals such as stage directors, choreographers, stage crew, sound and light people, etc.
- the performers, hence, the actors, the musicians, the dancers, the artists, authors and poets who present their work and prefer more or other interaction with each other or/and the audience
- the public in its role of audience attending a performance; not necessarily a passive audience just enjoying a performance, but also a web-audience that can (real-time) influence the running of things during a performance or can even more explicitly take part in a performance by taking the role of an actor

We will not elaborate the possibility to use our environment for scenographic simulations. Rather we would like to add the possibility to look at our environment as a stage on which we can have on-line performances or pre-recorded performances on request. It has been mentioned before, that the computer screen can be looked at as a stage and it has been argued that the theater metaphor can help in understanding human-computer interaction. The metaphor needs to be explored further, especially with regard to interface agents and the 'artistic' agents that have been introduced in CMU's Oz project and the Virtual Theatre project of Stanford University. This requires further investigations in agent theory, but also in the possibilities to use WWW and the computer (not only its screen, but also data gloves, head-mounted devices, special clothing, etc.) to stage performances with real and virtual actors and (real) audience.

Why not have live theatre performances over the web? In the traditional theatre, performers and audience are physically together. There is a focus of attention of the audience in things happening on stage and performers are aware of the audience's attention. Rather than to have one special physical space where performers and audience gather, performers can be geographically dispersed and so can the audience. Moreover, there is no need to maintain the distinction between audience and performers. The environment should allow an (web) audience that can (real-time) influence the running of things during a performance or can even take part in a performance by taking the role of an actor. This requires special attention for the presence issue, both for actors and audience (see Reeve [5]).

References

1. Bates, J.: Virtual Reality, Art, and Entertainment. Presence Teleoperators and Virtual Environments 1 **1** (Winter 1992) 133–138.
2. Friedman, B. (ed.): Human Values and the Design of Computer Technology. CSLI Publications, Cambridge University Press, (1997)
3. Lie, D., J. Hulstijn, A. Nijholt, R. op den Akker: A Transformational Approach to NL Understanding in Dialogue Systems. Proceedings NLP and Industrial Applications Moncton, New Brunswick, August 1998, 163–168
4. Lombard, M. & T. Ditton: At the heart of it all: The concept of presence. Journal of Mediated Communication 3, Nr.2, September 1997
5. Reeve, C.: Presence in Virtual Theatre. BT Presence Workshop, BT Labs, 10–11 June 1998

Representing contemporary architecture using hypermedia «Eight Italian architectures in the postwar period»

Marco Gaiani, Corrado Loschi, Marco Luitprandi– University of Ferrara
Stefano Zagnoni – University of Udine Michele Zannoni – IUAV

The Mac and Windows hybrid CD-ROM *«Eight Italian architectures in the postwar period»* took its cue from a fortuitous event: in 1995, the Solomon R. Guggenheim Museum donated 8 scale models developed for the Architecture section of the exhibition «The Italian Metamorphosis 1943-1968», held in New York in 1993, to the MusArc - Museo Nazionale dell'architettura located in Ferrara's ancient Rossetti Mansion. The donation of the models appeared the ideal subject matter to shape a virtual environment that, while supplying an appropriate framework for the donation, could fully partake in the overall cultural project around which MusArc is being structured. Prepared with the involvement of some 20 experts, the hypertext is the first large effort in Europe to represent and analyze contemporary architecture using digital methods and is intended to be more than a scientifically research document. It aims to be readily understood by the non-expert user, eliminating the difference between works for popular dissemination, historical reviews and critical analyses that are a constant feature of hardcopy publishing. It is mainly conceived with two aims: to be an accompaniment to material on display in the Museum and to be available to the public. That is why the technical solution adopted was a multiplatform CD-ROM.
The CD-ROM holds 8 Quick Time VR «objects», 32 minute Quick Time 320 x 240 films, generated entirely from virtual digital animated models and edited in compositing; over 250 photographs; more than 120 drawings; animated cards and over 100 text cards. Models and computer graphics animation were developed and computed on eight Silicon Graphics 02 R5000 and R10000, RAM 256 Mb workstations, using Alias/Wavefront Studio 8.5 and Composer 4.0, Bentley Microstation SE. A total of 45000 PAL 720x576 pixels frames was calculated.

The architectures represented by the scale models cover a very distinct period of contemporary Italian architecture, which began immediately after the Second World War and ended at the beginning of the 70's. The historical-critical project was shaped taking into account two simple considerations:
- From a general point of view, such a period had already been amply studied. The body of literature and criticism agrees that, as early as the first post-war years, the yet frail and not deeply rooted tradition of 'modernity' meets a process of fragmentation that finally goes astray into 'autobiographism'. The result was a plethora of different approaches, «heresies» and retrenchments. Nonetheless these years were marked by a profound civic and social commitment which animated debate in all quarters.
- On the other hand, it can be said that in most cases we have a very scant documentation easily available for an in-depth understanding of the single

architecture. This prompted a research program that, starting from the «random sampling» represented by these eight works, aims at investigating and reviving the self standing existence - in space and time - of individual architectural items, providing, at the same time, the tools with which to conduct further investigations. This, however, does not mean forsaking the draft of a wider plot of correlations. In fact, each work can be taken as a separate perspective from which to scan the physical and cultural framework into which it took shape and belongs.
But have a look at each work and at some of the special features characterizing them.
- The Memorial to the Fosse Ardeatine massacre (by Nello Aprile, Cino Calcaprina, Aldo Cardelli, Mario Fiorentino, Giuseppe Perugini, Rome 1944-52) and the Monument to the victims of the German concentration camps (by the BBPR group, Milan, 1945-55) are both considered cornerstones of post-war architecture in Italy. They also mirror the dialectic that offset the two most important hubs in post-war Italy: Rome and Milan. In fact the young architects who gravitated around Rome had made a clear break with the past, that culminated in the founding of the Association for Organic Architecture. On the other hand, Enrico Peressutti, designer of the Milan Monument as part of the BBPR group, returned explicitly to the rationalist avant-garde of the thirties.
- The Lago Nero Hotel and Ski complex (by Carlo Mollino, Sauze d'Oulx - Torino 1946-47) is an appreciated example of design excellence in the immediate post-war period: totally personal, yet consistent with the artistic avant-garde of the time. Mollino embraced many elements of traditional Alpine architecture but at the same time produced a wholly original and modern piece of architecture.
- The Provincial Headquarters of ENPAS in Bologna (by Saverio Muratori, 1952-56) is an emblematic example of a theoretical and methodological approach which developed out of radical criticism of the principles underlying contemporary avant-garde architecture.
- The Apartment Block in Via Marco Polo (by Mario Ridolfi and Wolfgang Frankl, Rome 1952-56) is an example of the meticulous, somewhat cerebral design technique typical of Mario Ridolfi and of an architectural thought and practice that was very important during the post-war reconstruction years.
- The Loro & Parisini Office Block (by Luigi Caccia Dominioni, Milan 1951-57) is a very successful exercise in extending and renovating a former factory building. A bridge-type horizontal volume - housing management and technical functions - was added to the side of the existing factory building that faced the street.
- The Olivetti Factory (by Marco Zanuso, Merlo - Argentina 1955-61) brings us inside the social and industrial conceptions promoted by Adriano Olivetti. It is also an insight into the approach typical of Italian industrial designers of that time: Zanuso starts with a core element - a hollow circular beam -, which is repeated to generate a highly flexible spatial continuum.
- The Monte Amiata Housing Complex at Galleratese district (by Carlo Aymonino & Partners, Aldo Rossi, Milan 1967-72) is one of the best known and emblematic examples of the architecture produced towards the end of the period that started with the Liberation. Here the Utopian concept of providing new life styles reaches its zenith in a work, which deliberately and somewhat pretentiously, disregards the surrounding context.

The language of architecture has developed over the centuries and relies on a series of specific codes. Transmitting this language is no easy matter in a digital environment.

A key concern when developing this hypertext was to tailor communication to content and animation and kinetic graphics have been expressly employed as a key element of the whole project. Movement affords dynamism and 3-D; it extracts and delineates spatial representation, disrupting the traditional interface between user and medium, just well as the two-dimensional concept of the «page». Care has been taken to present familiar graphic objects which by means of the «buttons» will give access to the various sections. The hypertext is structured as follows:

A - Main menu. It is conceived as a metaphor of the exhibition space where donated *maquettes* are displayed resting on a plinth of weighty volumes. In the background - like the information panels at an exhibition hall - are the appendices providing a synopsis page and introduction to the research project. The main menu constitutes the basic user guide to access, throughout the *maquettes*, the individual architectural works.

B - The individual architectural works. The eight works are presented in the same manner to enable multiple cross-referencing and each of them is divided into:

B.1 – Cover. The front page presents a concise overview of the work. The express aim was to use clear, yet flowing prose providing the user with an understanding of the project as a whole. This has been achieved using the following:

- Voice narrative, in contrast to the rest of the CD-ROM which is silent or with just background noises or, in the case of the "author videos", with a musical sound track.
- Video animation. It is important to occupy the eye of the user while the text is being read to keep the user's attention focused. Although immobile, architecture is not inert; to get across this «immobile transformation», a very slow animated sequence was devised starting from a particularly representative image of the work.

b. 2 - The Sections. Each project is divided into two sections and both the sections are subdivided into further information cards. The two sections clearly indicate the intention of providing two levels of user investigation in order to try and answer the recurring question in educational field of whether the users acquire knowledge better in a structured environment or when they can freely explore the subject material for themselves:

- The Work section, where a walk-through guided visit provides a structured learning environment that gives an interpretative synthesis of historical research results. Here the cards are not rigidly pre-defined to take into account the specificity of each architecture.
- The Documentation section, which provides all the original research documents.

Here document access is unstructured and interactive as regards further reading possibilities, zoom on images and drawings, and retention of bookmarks to allow comparison of different material either on the same or other works. This section is subdivided into the following cards: data identification, historical essay, drawings, photographs, biography of designers, bibliography on the work and archival sources. At last, both the sections have the "author video". Eight architect designers were asked to provide a 4 minutes script for a computergraphics movie presenting a particular work as they see it. Here the building becomes art in movement, fragmented and then recomposed with the intent of unveiling its elementary language by removing it from its real context and developing an interpretative virtual model.

ETNIAS: Multimedia Performance Involving Music, Dance and Images

JÔNATAS MANZOLLI

Interdisciplinary Nucleus for Studies on Sound Communication
University of Campinas - SP, BRAZIL
Jonatas@Nics.Unicamp.br

Abstract. ETNIAS is a multimedia performance describing a metaphoric travel through a set of sound-images. Based on the concept of soundscapes, this paper elucidates how a compositional process was developed to create this artwork.

1 Introduction

Popular culture issues such as creation of myths and legends inspired this work. The author created an allegory stating that *rivers are mixed to people's life, and both have similarities for bringing mixtures and complexity to life*. Sonic materials were derived from three basic sources: a) environmental water sounds such as river runs, waterfalls and sea waves, b) sounds from Brazilian instruments like *berimbau, atabaque, afoxê and caxixi,* and c) samples from people's voice while performing Brazilian dance such as *Congada, Folia de Reis and Bumba-Meu-Boi.* Computer graphics applied to images portraying people faces, river landscapes and drawings from Brazilian myths and legends generated counterpart images. The visual result was a set of two-dimensional panels projected into three large screens located at the stage set.

Fig. 1. Follows a gallery of ETNIAS images

A brief report of the applied methodology starting up on the artistic statement followed by comments derived from the author's aesthetic viewpoint describing the creative process is presented below.

2 People and Rivers Allegory

ETNIAS' artistic statement: People are like strong rivers moving lots of water, rain and transformations. Rivers are like people bringing many colours and faces filled with beliefs, dances and music. People and rivers are ethnic - they are mixtures crowding the earth. First a Breath from the Earth, which brings to birth myths, legends, moonshine, backlands, forests and the people who live there. Suddenly, Colonies of Fire stripped the green tapestry to turn it into steel and ashes. Then came fear, and purification came in a rite of passage with profound songs and melancholy dances. After everything, back to the riverheads, for the river mouth had become cloudy. On returning the waters of the river has become crystalline and ready for new rains and new transformations. Dance taken possession of the peoples' souls and their steps continue to recreate life.

2.1 1.2 From Images to Soundscapes

The compositional process begun constructing an image database with photos of rivers and people of all over the world. The World Wide Web was a source of people's visual expressions and river landscapes and these were used as the work's scenery. Similar manipulation of images was used on author's previous works in which a dancer interacted to her self-generated images [1] and to the lamascope [2].

A study on the structural synthesis of multimedia contents in time and space is presented in [3]. Their Counterpoint Movies related several sound transformations to image constructs. ETNIAS integrates also music to images and dance in a multimedia montage manner. Nevertheless, it combines image textures to sonic environments produced with digitally manipulated sound samples. These environments are called *soundscapes* for the author's goal is to create a symbolic travel through myths and rites. Wishart [4] mentioned: *by articulating the relationship between the sound-images we could develop not only sonic structures ... but also a whole area of metaphorical discourse.*

Therefore ETNIAS makes integrated portraits connecting images to sounds. These images are presented on the text's left side where it is possible to apprehend the process applied.

2.2 1.3 From Soundscapes to Symbols

ETNIAS soundtrack merged several sound sources in the same way images were interlaced. The concept of soundscape can be enlarged [4]: using sound-images in the virtual space of the loudspeakers, we can create a world somewhere in between the concreteness of the opera staging and the world of musical relationships.

The sonic method extended the process applied at the visual domain. Sound samples were superimposed and merged to construct sound-images. This concept is connected to the Granular Synthesis technique applied to soundscape composition [5].

Using Computer Music techniques the author tied diverse samples of Brazilian instruments and people's voice to sounds of river runs, waterfalls and sea waves. As a movie montage process, digital audio samples were concatenated to create complex panoply of sound textures.

2.3 1.4 From Symbols to Dance

A choreography was created by Christiane Matallo for five dancers interacted to three large screens. Such as AtoContAto (Manzolli et all, 1998) dancers act along sonic and visual structures produced by images and shadows projected in their bodies. Body motion was supported by the composed soundscapes and dancers developed movement and gestures in line with images and sonic profiles. Visual structures were re-built during the performance by the dancers' shadows and their space-time interaction.

The images were mixed and multiplied in the screen, arisen a public share of dramatic components. Observers were able to appreciate and apprehend the relationship between the performers' actions and the corresponding soundscape symbolic contents.

3 Conclusion

ETNIAS was presented to an estimated audience of ten thousand people that watched dancers to be transformed into imaginary figures. Three screens of 20 m^2 controlled by three 300 MHz machines supported the stage set plus a digital soundtrack and a live mixed choir. The 10-sections soundtrack recorded on a CD resembles a sonic symbol of Brazilian myths and rites.

Multimedia performances based on soundscapes enlarge the space of possible interaction among music, images and dance. The artist is not tied to synchronization of the soundtrack with images and body motion, but to sound-space architectures; nevertheless he needs effective symbolic contents to communicate his play to the audience. For the performers, it opens the concept of dance along music proposing a broader view. *Using concrete [sound] metaphors (rather than text) we are not 'telling a story' in the usual sense, but unfolding structures and relationships in time* [4].

ETNIAS communicated sound-images metaphors proposing to the audience an immersion on soundscapes profiles bringing new views and panoramas to their own imagination.

4 References

[1] Manzolli, J., A Moroni and C. Matallo. "AtoContAto: new media performance for video and interactive tap shoes music." Art Demos Proceedings of The 6th ACM International Multimedia Conference, Bristol, pg 31, 1998.

[2] Fels S., J. Manzolli, A Moroni, C. Matallo and K. Mase. "Me, Myself and I: Being an Imagician The Fusion of AtoContAto and the Iamascope." The Leonardo Electronic Abstracts, January 1999.

[3] Suzuki, R. and S. Inoue. "Dance Canonica: an Experiment on a Counterpoint Movie." Art Demos Proceedings of The 6th ACM International Multimedia Conference, Bristol, pg 37, 1998.

[4] Wishart, T. Sound Symbols and Landscapes. In The Language of Electroacoustic Music, ed. Simon Emmerson, Macmillan Press, pg. 41-60, 1986.

[5] Truax, B. "Composing with real-time granular sound. " Perspectives of New Music 28(2):120-134, 1990.

SpringerEurographics

Michael Gervautz,
Axel Hildebrand,
Dieter Schmalstieg (eds.)

Virtual Environments '99

Proceedings of the Eurographics
Workshop in Vienna, Austria,
May 31–June 1, 1999

1999. X, 191 pages. 78 figures.
Softcover DM 85,–, öS 595,–
ISBN 3-211-83347-1. Eurographics

The special focus of this volume lies on augmented reality.

Problems like real-time rendering, tracking, registration and occlusion of real and virtual objects, shading and lighting interaction and interaction techniques in augmented environments are addressed.

The papers collected in this book also address levels of detail, distributed environments, systems and applications and interaction techniques.

Dani Lischinski,
Ward Larson (eds.)

Rendering Techniques '99

Proceedings of the Eurographics
Workshop in Granada, Spain,
June 21–23, 1999

1999. XI, 382 pages. 212 partly coloured figures.
Softcover DM 118,–, öS 826,–
ISBN 3-211-83382-X. Eurographics

The papers in this volume present newresearch activities in the "classical" rendering workshop topics:
radiosity and Monte Carlo global illumination algorithms and illumination models, alongside papers on near-interactive ray tracing, hardware-assisted rendering algorithms, techniques for acquisition and modeling from images, image-based rendering, novel shadow algorithms, and inverse lighting and design.

All prices are recommended retail prices

SpringerWienNewYork

Sachsenplatz 4–6, P.O.Box 89, A-1201 Wien, Fax +43-1-330 24 26, e-mail: books@springer.at, **Internet: http://www.springer.at**
New York, NY 10010, 175 Fifth Avenue • D-14197 Berlin, Heidelberger Platz 3 • Tokyo 113, 3–13, Hongo 3-chome, Bunkyo-ku

SpringerEurographics

Bruno Arnaldi,
Gérard Hégron (eds.)

Computer Animation and Simulation '98

Proceedings of the Eurographics Workshop in Lisbon, Portugal, August 31–September 1, 1998

1999. VII, 126 pages. 82 figures.
Softcover DM 85,–, öS 595,–
ISBN 3-211-83257-2. Eurographics

Contents

- J.-D. Gascuel et al.: Simulating Landslides for Natural Disaster Prevention
- G. Besuievsky, X. Pueyo: A Dynamic Light Sources Algorithm for Radiosity Environments
- G. Moreau, S. Donikian: From Psychological and Real-Time Interaction Requirements to Behavioural Simulation
- N. Pazat, J.-L. Nougaret: Identification of Motion Models for Living Beings
- F. Faure: Interactive Solid Animation Using Linearized Displacement Constraints
- M. Kallmann, D. Thalmann: Modeling Objects for Interaction Tasks
- M. Teichmann, S. Teller: Assisted Articulation of Closed Polygonal Models
- S. Brandel, D. Bechmann, Y. Bertrand: STIGMA: a 4-dimensional Modeller for Animation

Eduard Gröller,
Helwig Löffelmann,
William Ribarsky (eds.)

Data Visualization '99

Proceedings of the Joint EUROGRAPHICS – IEEE TCCG Symposium on Visualization in Vienna, Austria, May 26–28, 1999

1999. XII, 340 pages. 230 figures.
Softcover DM 118,–, öS 826,–
ISBN 3-211-83344-7. Eurographics

In the past decade visualization established its importance both in scientific research and in real-world applications.

In this book 21 research papers and 9 case studies report on the latest results in volume and flow visualization and information visualization. Thus it is a valuable source of information not only for researchers but also for practitioners developing or using visualization applications.

All prices are recommended retail prices

SpringerWienNewYork

Sachsenplatz 4–6, P.O.Box 89, A-1201 Wien, Fax +43-1-330 24 26, e-mail: books@springer.at, **Internet: http://www.springer.at**
New York, NY 10010, 175 Fifth Avenue • D-14197 Berlin, Heidelberger Platz 3 • Tokyo 113, 3-13, Hongo 3-chome, Bunkyo-ku

SpringerEurographics

Nadia Magnenat-Thalmann,
Daniel Thalmann (eds.)

Computer Animation and Simulation '99

Proceedings of the Eurographics Workshop in Milano, Italy, September 7–8, 1999

1999. X, 230 pages. 148 partly coloured figures.
Softcover DM 89,–, öS 625,–
ISBN 3-211-83392-7. Eurographics

The 20 research papers in this volume demonstrate novel models and concepts in animation and graphics simulation. Special emphasis is given on innovative approaches to Modelling Human Motion, Models of Collision Detection and Perception, Facial Animation and Communication, Specific Animation Models, Realistic Rendering for Animation, and Behavioral Animation.

David J. Duke,
Angel Puerta (eds.)

Design, Specification and Verification of Interactive Systems '99

Proceedings of the Eurographics Workshop in Braga, Portugal, June 2–4, 1999

1999. IX, 280 pages. 89 figures.
Softcover DM 118,–, öS 826,–
ISBN 3-211-83405-2. Eurographics

The collection of papers in this volume covers specification methods and their use in design, model-based tool support, task and dialogue models, distributed collaboration, and models for virtual reality input.
Strong emphasis is laid on formal representations and modelling techniques and their use in understanding interaction and informing the design of artefacts.

All prices are recommended retail prices

SpringerWienNewYork

Sachsenplatz 4–6, P.O.Box 89, A-1201 Wien, Fax +43-1-330 24 26, e-mail: books@springer.at, **Internet: http://www.springer.at**
New York, NY 10010, 175 Fifth Avenue • D-14197 Berlin, Heidelberger Platz 3 • Tokyo 113, 3–13, Hongo 3-chome, Bunkyo-ku

Springer-Verlag
and the Environment

We at Springer-Verlag firmly believe that an international science publisher has a special obligation to the environment, and our corporate policies consistently reflect this conviction.

We also expect our business partners – printers, paper mills, packaging manufacturers, etc. – to commit themselves to using environmentally friendly materials and production processes.

The paper in this book is made from no-chlorine pulp and is acid free, in conformance with international standards for paper permanency.

GPSR Compliance

The European Union's (EU) General Product Safety Regulation (GPSR) is a set of rules that requires consumer products to be safe and our obligations to ensure this.

If you have any concerns about our products, you can contact us on ProductSafety@springernature.com

In case Publisher is established outside the EU, the EU authorized representative is:

Springer Nature Customer Service Center GmbH
Europaplatz 3
69115 Heidelberg, Germany

Batch number: 10584556

Printed by Printforce, the Netherlands